KW-128-557

PASTORAL LITURGY

A Symposium

ST. DEINIOL'S
HAWARDEN
LIBRARY

Contributors

Patrick Byrne
J. C. Buckley
Frances Collins
J. D. Crichton
Philip Gleeson OP
Martin Hall
Clifford Howell SJ
A. J. McCallen
Edward Matthews
Brian Newns
Patrick Reyntiens
Mark Searle OFM
Christopher J. Walsh
Austin Winkley
Harold Winstone

Pastoral Liturgy

A Symposium

✳

EDITED BY
HAROLD WINSTONE

COLLINS

Collins Liturgical Publications
187 Piccadilly, London w.1.

English translations of the Order of Mass and the Rites
for Holy Week from the Roman Missal, and the
interim Rite of Anointing and Pastoral Care of the Sick,
the Rite of Blessing of Oils, the Rite of Funerals and
the Rite of Penance from the Roman Ritual, copyright
© 1969, 1970, 1971, 1973, 1974.
International Committee on English in the Liturgy Inc.
All rights reserved.
Much of chapter 2 first appeared in *Life and Worship*.

Nihil obstat: R. J. Cuming DD, censor
Imprimatur: David Norris
Westminster 21 April 1975
The Nihil obstat and Imprimatur are a declaration that a
book or pamphlet is considered to be free from doctrinal or
moral error. It is not implied that those who have granted
the *Nihil obstat* and *Imprimatur* agree with the contents,
opinions or statements expressed.

First Published 1975
© 1975 William Collins Sons and Co Ltd

ISBN 0 00 599527 2

Set in Monotype Baskerville
Made and printed in Great Britain by
William Collins Sons & Co Ltd, Glasgow

Contents

Contents

Abbreviations

Church   The Constitution on the Church, Vatican II
CL   The Constitution on the Liturgy, Vatican II
CMW   The Church in the Modern World, decree of
           Vatican II
D   Directory for Masses with Children
GI   General Instruction on the Roman Missal
RA   Rite of Anointing and Pastoral Care of the Sick
RP   Rite of Penance

Part One

SOME ASPECTS OF CELEBRATION

1. The Meaning of Celebration

Harold Winstone

The world has become a very earnest place. Economics and the state have taken control and now every man must have his place in the system and do a useful work in and for the system, or else be kept at the expense of the system – provided he falls into one of its recognized categories of cases deserving assistance. Alternatively he becomes a drop-out, fated to live by his wits or to haunt the doss-houses of our cities and find what consolation he can in alcohol and drugs.

These pressures are upon us from our earliest years: the struggle for life, the struggle for acceptance among one's peers, the struggle for one's individuality and independence, the struggle for economic security, for sheer survival, for a home and sufficient means on which to raise a family; the struggle against illness and economic ruin and disgrace and the onset of death.

A man who refuses to be dominated by these harsh realities, who buries himself in books and cultivates the aesthetic rather than the commercial arts, is labelled an escapist, a wishful thinker, or the inhabitant of a world of fantasy. Everything has to be justified by pragmatic standards. No one is allowed to go to the moon 'for the hell of it'. It must be done in order to gain military advantage or medical knowledge or technological skill. A world which can see no sense in sport and the arts and sex and Christmas unless they be well and truly commercialized has become an earnest place indeed. Holidays are no longer festivals. They are times for earnest relaxation so that the human frame and the human spirit may be able to withstand the pressures of continued work. They are times of pleasure-seeking in exotic and, of course, commercialized resorts, as though pleasure were a reluctant goddess who shunned the homes of ordinary mortals and reserved her favours for those who could afford the pilgrimage to her costly shrines.

But even while outwardly conforming to this view of life,

the spirit of man is restless, for there is more in man than even the cleverest advertisers have discovered. He is the inhabitant of two worlds. One is indeed the material world of sense and sound and touch – a demanding world which will annihilate him if he refuses to accede to its demands. The other is a world which he dreams of but can never fully understand. It is a world of poetic truth, somehow liberated from the categories of common sense, a world of mystery and wonder, of purest fantasy. It is no figment of his imagination for he experiences it as real, and nothing in the material world has real meaning except in reference to it. The two worlds interpenetrate so completely that they seem almost to be two facets of the same world – or the one has become incarnate in the other.

Indeed, it is in man that these two worlds make contact. In and through him every reality of the material world becomes a symbol, an expression, of some deeper reality which transcends the limitations of time and space and obeys other laws than those of material causality. In the material world water is the fusion – if that is the right word – of two atoms of hydrogen with one of oxygen. It is needed to sustain every kind of life on earth and must be harnessed for irrigation purposes and for hydro-electric power. It forms a barrier between continents and collects in streams and lakes and rivers. It is used for cleansing and cooking, for heating and cooling, for every kind of water-sport, and provides a livelihood for sailors and fishermen and officials of the Metropolitan Water Board. But to the spirit of man it is more than all this. It is laughter and purity and immortality. It is the womb of life and the cleansing of the spirit. It is the blessing of the Almighty and protection from evil.

In the material world wine is the juice of grapes grown in the vineyards of sundrenched lands. It is treated, no doubt, with certain additives, bottled, matured and exported, and drunk by those who can afford to drink it. But to the spirit of man wine is more than this. It is 'dance and provençal song and sunburnt mirth'. It is love and friendship and self-sacrifice. It is blood – the blood of Christ.

If man is to retain his sanity in his enforced subjection to material bondage in a world where he is constantly made to work the treadmill of life, it is imperative that from time to time he be allowed to give full expression to that other side of his being which transcends the purely pragmatic and the harsh dictates of cold logic. He must be allowed to do things not because they are rational, but because in a certain sense they are irrational; they are fantastic; they proclaim a logic which transcends the logic of the material world and makes a mockery of it. He must become the devotee of a God whose foolishness is wiser than man and who 'laughs men to scorn' (Ps 2). In a word, he must learn once again to celebrate.

In ordinary usage the word celebration has lost much of its original connotation. From being a carefree liberation of the spirit of man and a public proclamation of those values which he shares in common with his brothers and sisters but which find such scant outlet in his workaday life, it has become almost a duty, an irksome necessity. We celebrate birthdays and weddings and retirements, but we hardly know *how* to celebrate them. Too often we resort to a false gaiety induced by alcohol because, immersed as we are in material things, we lack the ability to rise out of our mundane selves and to join with each other in giving expression to the poetic, the fantastic side of our nature. We have lost the key to that inner life which liberates the spirit and suffuses it with pure joy. We have lost our faith.

Where can we find it again if not in the Church? It is Christ, the 'Lord of the dance', who holds the secret of true celebration and who has given his Church such ample cause for celebration. Mary of Nazareth celebrated the good news of the incarnation when she cried out in the Spirit 'My soul magnifies the Lord, and my spirit rejoices in God my Saviour'. How she must have danced and sung in the house of Elizabeth. St Paul, judging from his letters, must have been the perfect celebrant and the perfect liturgist. Completely captivated by his inner vision of God, singing and making melody in his heart, he seems always to have been on the verge of ecstasy: 'To him who is able to do so much more than we can ever ask for, or even think of, by means of the power working in us: to God be the glory in the church and in Christ Jesus, for all time, for ever and ever!' (Eph 3:20–21).

In order to celebrate we come together joyfully as a people. We proclaim our faith and share a common meal. But nothing that we do in our liturgy is of this world. It is all out of this world. We use water and ashes and palm-branches and oil and bread and wine; but not as ordinary mortals use these things. Even our meal is no ordinary meal. The bread that we break is a communion in the body of Christ. The cup that we bless is a communion in the blood of Christ until he comes again. Liturgy is music and song and drama and dance and all things fantastical. It has to be, for in no other way can we express the joy that is in us through Christ Jesus our Lord.

It is only when we try to rationalize liturgy, to make everything we do answerable to a purpose, when every word has to make sense and every reading carry a lesson and every gesture be significant, when we prune away and cut out those things for which we can find no obvious reason, that joy recedes and celebration becomes mere ritualism and Mass attendance an obligation.

In this book we will be exploring ways and means of making Christian celebration a reality in our parish churches and schools and homes. Sometimes the wood may seem to be obscured by the trees and we may get lost in a jungle of directives and decrees. Never mind; *quod scripsi, scripsi.* It is impossible to devise a liturgy which will answer the needs of all ages and all cultures. The principle of pastoral adaptation is well established and has been written-in to all the Roman decrees on liturgy.

> 'Let us then celebrate our feast
> not with the old leaven,
> but with the new, unleavened bread
> of sincerity and truth' (1 Cor 5:8).

2. The Holy Spirit in Eucharistic Celebration

J. D. Crichton

When we speak of Christian celebration, by which we mean the creation of an atmosphere of joy through the use of song, light, colour and movement, are we speaking of a merely natural thing, of a complexus of devices for the production of a psychological effect? The means are good and the aim is good and unless worship is to be turned into something that is ineffably boring, they must be constituent parts of it. But is this all that is to be said? Or to put the matter another way, does the liturgy, and the Roman liturgy in particular, suggest that the Holy Spirit is present in the process of celebration? Everyone knows that the celebration is done by people who have been baptized by water and the Holy Spirit, that there are prayers for the intervention of the Holy Spirit at one time or another and that certain sacraments like confirmation and holy order give special emphasis to the communication of the Holy Spirit. At the level of sacramental theology we know that the Holy Spirit is active in the giving of grace, a point that is deliberately emphasized in the new Orders for the Anointing of the Sick and for the Reconciliation of the Sinner. But the question remains: is the Holy Spirit present in the act of celebration? Are the people who celebrate moved by the Holy Spirit or not?

A brief look at the New Testament suggests an affirmative answer. There is no need to make a prolonged examination of the Acts of the Apostles: it is agreed that it is at once the Book of the Church and the Book of the Holy Spirit. The primitive Church was keenly conscious of the presence of the Holy Spirit in its assemblies. If we move to St Paul we find in phrases scattered here and there a similar awareness. The liturgical community that can be glimpsed in 1 Corinthians 14 was certainly a community conscious of the (often visible) working of the Holy Spirit and its celebrations were not without their excitement. In Colossians 3:17 he speaks of the community singing psalms, hymns and 'inspired songs' and in 1 Corinthians 12:3 we are told that without the Spirit we cannot say 'Jesus is Lord' (*kyrios*), which may well have been a liturgical expression. 'Rejoicing in the Spirit' whether within or outside the liturgical assembly seems to have been a characteristic of the primitive Christian communities.

Is this discernible in our worship today? It was a charge for long levelled against the old Roman liturgy that it lacked emphasis on the Holy Spirit, and in fact only two texts concerning the *action* of the Spirit *in the eucharistic assembly* have been discovered.[1] One was a preface for the consecration of the church; the other an offertory prayer for the same occasion. In the latter the Church asked for the descent of the Holy Spirit on the altar, for the sanctification of the people's offerings that lay on it and for the cleansing of their hearts in holy communion. Of course there were other parts of the liturgy where the Holy Spirit was given prominence, as for instance in the sacraments of confirmation, holy order and baptism, especially if the latter was restored to its proper context in the Easter Vigil. There the rite of the plunging of the Paschal Candle into the water with its invocation that the Holy Spirit should come upon the water and permeate it emphasizes the presence of the Spirit. There was also the celebration of Pentecost when, however, the Holy Spirit was, at least in popular esteem, rather detached from the Trinity; and there was the feast of Holy Trinity when some of the texts and the discourses given on this occasion seemed to suggest that it was a theological rather than a liturgical exercise. But none of this had any reference to the Spirit's action in the liturgical celebration.

With the coming of the revised liturgy the situation has been immeasurably improved and the implications of this situation are the theme of this chapter. The first and most obvious improvement is the insertion of the invocations (*epicleses*) of the

[1] See A. Verheul, *Introduction to the Liturgy* (Eng. trans. 1968), p. 68. The prayer is found in the Gregorian Sacramentary, no. 196 (ed. Lietzmann) and in the Gelasian there is another, asking that the offerings laid on the altar 'may be permeated with the dew of the Holy Spirit' (ed. Mohlberg, no. 694). Both therefore are Roman and not Gallican.

Holy Spirit in the three new eucharistic prayers, and let it be said that they are not merely verbal additions. They are meant to make explicit the *action* of the Holy Spirit in the eucharistic celebration which is performed by the whole assembly. As will be evident from what follows, this chapter is not however restricted to a consideration of these prayers, much less is it concerned with the old theological dispute about the consecratory role of the Holy Spirit in the eucharist nor yet with the historical question whether or not there was once an epiclesis of the Holy Spirit in the Roman Canon.

Before approaching the subject from a rather different point of view it may be interesting to ask whether the new Missal has anything to say of the worshipping community as the community of the Spirit. A rapid examination of the texts does not reveal a great deal. In the prayers suggested for the Church (formula 1, B) we read in the collect that God brings together '*in the Spirit*' a people that is his own. In another prayer for the local church (formula 1, E) the text states that God has brought together a people '*in the Holy Spirit*'. This latter has a certain interest, for it sees the local church as the sacrament-sign of the Church spread throughout the world, a Church that is one, holy, catholic and apostolic. The implication is that the local assembly is brought together by the power of the Holy Spirit and acts or celebrates by that same power. Again, in a prayer for the laity (formula 12) the Church asks that those who are called to live in the world may be filled with the Holy Spirit, though this seems to refer more particularly to their vocation in the earthly city. All told, not a very rich harvest. Evidently, then, a somewhat different approach is called for.

THE CHURCH, THE SPIRIT-FILLED BODY OF CHRIST

If we are to reach satisfactory conclusions in the matter, it is necessary to consider first the nature of the Church and secondly to re-examine our notions on the mystery of Christ.

1. The eucharist is the supreme sacrament-sign of the Church, at once manifesting its true nature and making it present in the here and now (CL 2, 41, 42). But this Church is the Spirit-filled body of Jesus Christ which in its liturgy, in its missionary outgoing and in its care for the material condition of mankind, is manifesting the Spirit and making him present among men.

Abbot Vonier liked to say, by a somewhat strained use of the word, that the Church was the 'incarnation' of the Holy Spirit.[2]

2. The link between the Church thus conceived and the liturgy as such is to be found in the paschal mystery of which the eucharist is the celebration. That mystery as we know consists of the passion, death, resurrection and ascension of Christ. But perhaps we do not reflect often enough on what was its issue. One way of approaching the matter is through a consideration of the account of the passion according to St John. There in 19:30 he uses the curious expression: 'he gave over' or 'handed over' (not 'up') the spirit (*paredōken to pneuma*). The synoptists say simply 'he breathed his last' or something similar. St John is often puzzling or rather conveys *two* meanings rather than one and it is not fantastic to see in this expression the giving of the Spirit to the Church. This view moreover is confirmed by the well-known passage that follows, stating that from his pierced side flowed blood and water. For St John himself this seems to have been a 'sign' of the giving of the life of the Spirit,[3] an interpretation confirmed by the witness of the Fathers who from the second century onwards have seen the flowing of the blood and water as the sign of baptism and the eucharist by which the Spirit is given. To this witness we may add the phrase from the Verona Sacramentary, cited in the Constitution on the Liturgy(5), that from the side of Christ as he slept the sleep of death on the cross there came forth the wonderful sacrament of the Church. And the Church that came forth was the Spirit-filled body of Christ which is constituted, as medieval writers liked to say,[4] by the sacraments of baptism and the eucharist. Spirit, Church and sacraments here all come together.

When, then, we speak of the eucharist as the sacrament of the paschal mystery we must realize that the mystery includes not only the saving acts of Christ but also the sending of the Holy Spirit which is their consequence. Nor was this a once-for-all event. The Church lives by the Spirit, he is constantly coming to it and it follows that in every eucharistic celebration there is

[2] See his *Spirit and the Bride*.
[3] See J. B. Westcott, *The Gospel of St John* (1898), *in loc.*, and for the patristic evidence, *ibid*. Additional Note, pp. 284–6.
[4] Cf Y. Congar, *The Mystery of the Church* (Eng. trans. 1960), p. 67.

a sending of the Spirit and, if our hearts are open, a receiving of the Spirit. Indeed not only is there a receiving of the Spirit but the praise and thanksgiving that constitute our worship is a response in the Spirit to the Father.

To sum up: since the eucharist is pre-eminently the sacrament of the paschal mystery and since the Holy Spirit must be included in that mystery, it follows that the Holy Spirit is present in the eucharist, prompting our praise and thanksgiving and coming down on us so that our very offering and reception of communion are made effective by his work.

Where then is the Holy Spirit active in the eucharist? It may be that his action is not always explicit in the rite but, as I hope to show, if we understand the different parts of the Mass aright, we shall find that he is present and active throughout it. It is convenient to put the whole matter under the following heads: the assembly, the prayers (collects), the chants, psalms and responses, the readings, the eucharistic action proper.

The assembly

It is now a commonplace of liturgical writing that the people are called to worship so that they may form the local community, that is, the people of God here and now. In the words of the General Instruction on the Order of Mass (7) they are to form a *communion*. For St Paul the Christian people are the temple of the Holy Spirit and the Spirit of God is living among them (1 Cor 3:16). In Ephesians 2:20 we read that Christians are being built up into a spiritual house and this word, I think, is not to be interpreted in the weak sense as if it meant a spiritual as opposed to a material or earthly house. He uses the expression 'en pneumati', 'in (the) spirit', and this is usually seen as a reference to the Holy Spirit. The most explicit teaching is given in 1 Peter 2:19: Christians are living stones built up into an *oikos pneumatikos*, a spiritual house, in which they are to offer *pneumatikas thusias*, spiritual sacrifices, which probably refer to the eucharist but also to the offering of the worshippers' lives.[5] But again this does not mean merely a people who are spiritually-minded offering sacrifices that are nothing more than interior 'intentions'. The house of the Holy Spirit and the sacrifices correspond to each other. We are reminded of the

[5] See E. G. Selwyn, *The First Letter of St Peter* (1946), *in loc.*

worship of the New Testament which Jesus said would be a worship in spirit and truth (John 4:23, where some would spell spirit with a capital 'S'). The whole context of the Peter passage is liturgical. It is here that he says Christians are a royal priesthood, he refers to baptism (verse 2) and almost certainly to the eucharist (verse 3, cf psalm 33). We note too that the people are approaching Christ, the Living Stone, to offer their spiritual sacrifices.

When, then, the Christian people come to worship they are led by the Holy Spirit.

The assembly, a charismatic community

One of the central teachings of the Constitution on the Liturgy is that the liturgical assembly is a functional community. Different members and groups of members have different 'ministries' to perform for the perfection of the whole celebration.[6] Although this statement pre-dates the Constitution on the Church, it may be regarded as the liturgical expression of that document in which the Council teaches that the Church is a charismatic community, each member of which receives the gifts of the Holy Spirit for the building up of the body of Christ.[7] The New Testament is emphatic that these gifts differ. Without prejudice to the question whether those recorded in 1 Cor 14, and indeed elsewhere are to be expected to emerge in worship, as they did in Corinth, there are others which may be fairly called 'ministries' like those mentioned in Romans 12:6-8. They are to be used 'according to the grace given', and include 'administration',[8] teaching, exhortation, but also simple 'services' like contributing (to the community), helping and acts of mercy. It is these gifts that may be regarded as necessary for the normal running of the community that come into play here. As has been indicated above, there is a wide variety of ministries performed by different members of the community: the president, readers, singers, instrumentalists, servers, ushers, collectors and so on. In principle all the ministries these people perform are exercises of the gifts of the Holy Spirit which in fact help to construct the sign of the local Church

[6] CL 26, 30, 41–2 and cf 29 Latin: *'ministerio liturgico'*, *'ministerium'*.
[7] Constitution on the Church 12.
[8] Thus JB and Knox, for once agreeing in translating the Greek word *diakonia*.

which thus becomes the sacrament of the universal Church and indeed a manifestation of the Spirit.[9]

There is here an interpenetration of the natural and the supernatural. The gifts belong to human persons and enhance their natural talents, but they need cultivating and in that very cultivation and their eventual exercise in worship (as well as outside it) the Holy Spirit is active. In practice people need to realize this and to direct or dedicate their gifts to the praise and worship of God. This would seem to be particularly important for the role of the president who has to 'preach', 'exhort' and 'prophesy', and for those who read and sing, for they are conveying God's word in a special way. If there is this realization on the part of the ministers, the Holy Spirit will animate them and through them lift up the whole community in praise and thanksgiving to the Father.

The prayers
The obvious place to go here is the famous conclusion of the collects which goes back to the fifth century. Unfortunately there is a difference of opinion about its interpretation among the experts. Jungmann sees in the phrase '*in unitate Sancti Spiritus*' (in the unity of the Holy Spirit) a reference to the unity of the Church of which the Holy Spirit is the bond. If this were so, it would be easy to maintain that when we are praying the collects we, as the local people of God, are praying in the Spirit. Botte contests Jungmann's view and sees the phrase as referring to the unity of the three persons in the Godhead, and it must be said that he is almost certainly right. This great phrase does however remind us of the trinitarian pattern of all Christian prayer: to the Father, through the Son, in the Holy Spirit.[10] We need however to look at the matter rather differently. The classical pattern of the collect is to address God the Father (*Deus, Dominus*).[11] This is the ancient rule of public prayer, going back at least to the time of Origen.[12]

[9] See J. D. Crichton, *Christian Celebration*, vol. I, *The Mass* (1971), p. 34.
[10] For B. Botte see *La Maison-Dieu*, no. 23 (1950), pp. 49–53. For Jungmann see *The Place of Christ in Liturgical Prayer* (Eng. trans. 1965), p. 204 where in footnote 2 he seems to concede Botte's point but maintains his own view in the text.
[11] Only very rarely and in late prayers is any other person addressed. Cf *Missale Romanum*, 1970, *Corpus Christi* where the second person is addressed – the only instance I have noticed.
[12] See his *De Oratione*, c. 14 and Jungmann *op. cit.* pp. 156ff.

We address the Father, and as the conclusion of the collects usually makes plain, we pray through the Son, and if the text does not say explicitly 'in the Holy Spirit', he is certainly associated (*in unitate*) with the Father and the Son. Indeed in the early fifth century when the termination of the prayer begins to appear this phrase seems to have been alternated with '*cum Spiritu Sancto*' (with the Holy Spirit).[13] Not to press the phrase too far, we can say that the Christian community is praying through the Son to the Father with both of whom the Holy Spirit is united and living in communion. Nor does it seem too much to say that we are reminded that through our prayer we are entering into that life, that communion, that *koinonia* that is in fact the life of the Godhead.

In the background of all this is to be seen the teaching of St Paul that when we pray, and especially when we pray as the people of God, the Holy Spirit prays within us, inspiring our prayer and even directing it, for he gives utterance to desires of which we are hardly or not at all conscious (Romans 8:26). As the descending line of our worship is in the Holy Spirit – he comes upon us – so is the ascending. It is he who makes it possible for us to go out from ourselves in a worship that is acceptable to God.

The chants and responses

Before considering the readings it will be as well, I think, to take a look at the chants, hymns, acclamations and any other responses the people make during the Mass. For, though the collect is a presidential prayer, these other texts are in the same line. Nor is this inference supposition or mere imagination. St Paul speaks of the people praying and making petition 'in the Spirit' (Eph 5:18), of their singing 'spiritual songs' (*ōdais pneumatikais*) where the adjective 'spiritual' is, I think, to be taken in the strong sense: 'of the Holy Spirit'.[14] As the sacrifice for St Peter is a 'pneumatic' one, so are the songs of Christian worship.[15] All that the worshipping people sing or say is

---

[13] See Botte, *art. cit.*, pp. 50–1 and p. 53.
[14] It is suggested that these were charismatic songs and utterances with the implication that they are not 'liturgical'. But N.T. worship *was* frequently charismatic. See 1 Cor 14.
[15] Cf also 1 Thess 5:18–19; note the juxtaposition: 'In all things give thanks (*eucharisteite*) . . . and quench not the Spirit.'

prompted by the Holy Spirit, and through it they enter into a dialogue with God. This, in my view, is the deeper meaning of that much maligned phrase 'active participation'. It is not just a human activity or a psychological device (which of course has its value): it is a divino-human activity in which the Holy Spirit is present and through which, once again, we enter into communion with God.

The ministry of the word

It is here that the dialogue through Christ and in the Holy Spirit with the Father reaches its climax. The Word of God, which St Paul calls 'the sword of the Spirit' (Eph 6:17), is proclaimed and the people respond in the psalm and in the lesser responses. As we remember from the Constitution (7), Christ is present in the scriptures when they are read in church and we also recall that he began his teaching mission 'in the power of the Spirit'. That same Spirit was upon him as he proclaimed, in words borrowed from Isaiah, the Good News of salvation (Luke 4:14, 17-19). Further, the Spirit that was his he poured out on the Church which thus in turn was able to begin its mission (Acts 2:1-33). The Church acts through the power of the Holy Spirit and if the liturgy is the exercise of the priesthood of Christ, it is also the exercise of the teaching, guiding and enlightening power of the Holy Spirit. It is this twofold action that is to be found in the Mass where God is speaking to his people 'and Christ is still proclaiming his gospel' (CL 33). This is the descending line of worship: God approaches us with his word which is still proclaimed by Christ and in the Holy Spirit.

There is a second aspect of the ministry of the word that is also important. It is not to be thought of as mere instruction in the sense of giving information even *about* the bible, it is not an inefficient kind of catechetical lesson. It is above all an action, and a divine action at that. As the Old and the New Testaments make very clear, God's word is event.[16] Something happens. It is not merely that words, even the words of the bible, are pronounced but that through them God approaches

16 'The Word of God is not only an intelligible message . . . It is a dynamic reality . . .' as the writer in *Dictionary of Biblical Theology* (ed. X. Léon-Dufour) puts it, s.v. 'Word of God', p. 667.

us, enlightening our minds, stimulating our faith which he calls for, and offering us his love through which we are saved. It is a manner of sanctifying us, and wherever there is sanctification there is the Holy Spirit. Just, then, as the Spirit was with Jesus in his earthly preaching, so is he with him in his Church as he proclaims through men the gospel of salvation in the eucharist.

But if we are to receive the word, if it is to become a living and life-giving word, if our faith is in fact to be stimulated and our love enkindled, then we must be open to the action of God. It is this function that the psalm, deliberately responsorial, is devised to perform. We ruminate on the word proclaimed, and the response, so often in the form of a petition, makes it possible for us to understand the word and take it to ourselves. As we have already seen, the Spirit is present in this response too, enabling us to go out from ourselves to the Father through Jesus Christ. Thus is the invitation and the response initiated, thus is the ministry of the word to be thought of as a dialogue with God.

The ministry of the eucharist

The addition of the three new eucharistic prayers to the Roman liturgy has very considerably changed its face and makes a treatment of the subject rather easier. The presence of the Holy Spirit in the eucharistic action is now very clear. But before giving glimpses of the obvious let me point out that the basic pattern of the eucharistic prayer is trinitarian: to the Father, through the Son, in the Holy Spirit. We have only to look at the texts to see that this is so.

The address is to God who is called Father, Lord, almighty, holy and eternal ... The texts go on to speak of the saving deeds done through Jesus Christ our Lord, and the three new eucharistic prayers see those deeds as now being made operative by the intervention of the Holy Spirit. All of them end with the ascription of glory and honour to the Father through the Son and in the Holy Spirit. There is no need to elaborate this point any further, though in practice it is to be hoped that there is a growing realization that this is so. Not only does the Holy Spirit play little enough part in the life of the ordinary Catholic of the Western church, but too often the Catholic seems to be what one can only call *untrinitarian*. Yet the liturgy is there all the time to recall to him that the very mode of salvation and sanctification is trinitarian.

Let us then consider the various parts of the eucharistic prayer:

a. THE PREFACE. Of the prefaces inserted into the Order of Mass, I find only four in which the Holy Spirit can be said to have an operative function in the history of salvation narrative and a fifth (St Joseph) in which there is a mere mention.[17] If this provision is better than that of the old Missal, it is still meagre enough. In addition, however, there is the preface for use on Whit Sunday which sees the giving of the Spirit as the 'completion' of the work of salvation, as the birth of the Church and as the beginning of the Church's mission. It is a good piece of work and presumably may be used on other occasions, though another text (a good one, echoing the Acts of the Apostles) is provided for Votive Masses.

b. THE FIRST EPICLESIS (only in Eucharistic Prayers II, III, IV). The insertion of an epiclesis at this point in the new eucharistic prayers is one of their most striking features. It is found in the Egyptian-Alexandrian tradition and Rome has thought good to take it from there. These epicleses, which do not differ a great deal in wording, and not at all in sense, are clearly petitions or invocations for the coming of the Holy Spirit on the offerings and for their consecration. They are not, I think, to be regarded as 'consecratory'. They are petitions that the elements may be consecrated, though, 'moments of consecration' apart, we should have no hesitation in saying that even in the consecration the Holy Spirit is active, as he is in all the works of Christ done for mankind.

A second feature of these epicleses is of considerable importance from another viewpoint. They all ask that the offerings made by the people shall be sanctified and made the body and blood of Christ. This text, then, takes up the gestures and words of the offertory action, links them with the eucharistic action proper and shows that the offerings made by human

---

[17] They are Sunday VI, VIII, Our Lady I (no mention of the overshadowing by the Holy Spirit in II) and Common VI. I have not examined in detail the other 33 or 34 to be found elsewhere in the Missal.

beings are only 'valuable' in the sight of God if they are caught up and sanctified by the Holy Spirit so that they may be en-folded in the self-offering of Christ. This would seem to be the solution of the 'offertory problem' (we have nothing to give to God) and it may be that this was why the revisers wrote these texts into the new eucharistic prayers.[18]

C. THE SECOND EPICLESIS. Thanks to the Antiochene tra-dition, represented in its best known form in the Byzantine liturgy, we have come to think that this is the classical place for an epiclesis. That there is a high appropriateness in this arrange-ment can be seen from what has been said above about the nature of the Church of which the eucharist is the sacrament-sign. We make our thanksgiving to the Father through the Son who as high priest and head of the body is active in the euchar-istic action, and now through the intercession of the Church the Holy Spirit comes to complete that action. This is expressed by the epiclesis. Is this liturgical expression of the action of the Holy Spirit *essential* to the rite? It is difficult to say. The Roman canon has apparently always been without it, and the epiclesis in the *Apostolic Tradition* of Hippolytus (early third century) *may* not be authentic. The first certain appearance of it is in Jerusalem in the second half of the fourth century. All one can usefully say here is that whether or not the action of the Holy Spirit is expressed, it is always present, and that since liturgy is by nature sacramental what it contains, it ought to express.[19] This has been very effectively done in the three new eucharistic prayers and we need to ask: what is the exact purpose of this second epiclesis?

1. We note that all of them ask that the Holy Spirit shall come upon the *people*, those gathered for worship and taking part in the celebration. It is they who are the objects of the action of the Holy Spirit.

2. The purpose of this action is spelt out more or less fully in the three prayers: 'May the people be brought together in unity by

[18] This point is made with particular clarity in the *second* epiclesis of EP IV: '. . . by your Holy Spirit, gather all who share this bread and wine into the one body of Christ, *a living sacrifice of praise*'. It is the people, now united with Christ, who become the 'living sacrifice'. Cf Rom. 12:1.

[19] Probably the slow development of the doctrine of the Holy Spirit had something to do with the matter which cannot, I think, be said to be closed.

the Holy Spirit'; 'May we who have been fed by the body and blood of Christ be filled with the Holy Spirit and become one body, one spirit in Christ' which echoes 1 Cor 12:13; 'May all who receive from the one bread and cup be gathered into one body by the Holy Spirit and made a living sacrifice in Christ to the praise of your glory' (cf Eph 1:12). Here the people are to become a living sacrifice through the Holy Spirit.

3. This union is to be achieved precisely through the reception of the body and blood of Christ, and this indicates that this epiclesis looks forward to communion rather than back to the consecration. In other words, if we wish to understand holy communion we shall find its meaning in the second epiclesis.

4. Yet another feature may be singled out, found with particular clarity in EP IV though there is a similar statement in EP III less closely connected with the epiclesis. EP IV runs: 'Look upon this sacrifice (*hostiam*) which you gave to your Church, that all who receive . . .' EP III asks that God may look on his Church's offering (*oblationem*) and then goes on to the epiclesis. EP IV, then, clearly associates the Holy Spirit with the act of *offering* (as well as the reception of communion) but does not go as far as the prayer of Hippolytus which asks that the Holy Spirit may come upon 'the offering (*oblationem*) of your holy Church' with the implication that it is the action of the Holy Spirit in the offering (as well as in receiving the elements) that is going to draw the people into unity. The whole passage is worth recalling:

'And we ask you to send your Holy Spirit on the offering of your holy Church. Gathering it together in one, grant to those who partake of your holy mysteries that they may be filled with this Holy Spirit, established in faith, in truth, so that we may praise and glorify you through your servant Jesus Christ, through whom be to you glory and honour with the Holy Spirit in holy church for endless ages. Amen'.[20]

This text sets out admirably the full meaning of the epiclesis: we offer in the Spirit who comes to make us one through holy communion.

[20] *Apostolic Tradition*, ed. B. Botte (Münster, 1963), p. 17. It is disputed whether this passage is original to the *Ap. Trad.* Botte is convinced that it is; Dix that it is not.

The Lord's Prayer

It is St Paul who reveals the implications of calling God our Father: 'When we cry Abba, Father, it is the Spirit himself bearing witness with our spirit that we are children of God' (Rom 8:15, 16 and cf Gal. 4:6). In this context the Lord's Prayer can be seen as a link between the second epiclesis and holy communion. Paul makes clear that in this prayer above all we are praying 'in the Spirit' and we are able to do so with the confidence of those who are children of the Father. Further if we remember that when we pray the Lord's Prayer we are putting ourselves in the posture of Christ, the Son of God, through whom we are children of God, then it is plain that even this prayer is trinitarian: we pray through the Son and in the Spirit, who prompts our prayer, to the Father who is Father of the whole community of believers.

Holy Communion

As we have seen, the meaning of communion is to be found in the epiclesis but it is necessary to consider further what exactly this word 'communion' means. 'Com-union' means exactly what it says: union with others, or more fully, the union of a number of people with each other through and in Christ whom they receive, with the consequence that they must love one another. The General Instruction goes to considerable lengths to establish that communion is a community action in which we manifest our Christian brotherhood and which is to be expressed by the sign of peace, by chants and by the procession. But, as we have indicated above, the deepest insight into holy communion is given by the epiclesis and for that reason there is no need for any specific mention of the Holy Spirit here.

But we may add, where is community, there is the Spirit. Certainly for the writer of Acts the Spirit, *koinonia*[21] and the eucharist (the 'breaking of the bread') all appear in the same perspective. Not to give an exhaustive list, there is the Pentecost event when the coming of the Spirit creates the community whose members are faithful to the teaching of the apostles, to *koinonia* and to the breaking of bread (2:1–42 and cf 4:31). There is the saying of St Paul, echoed in EP III, that in the

[21] Which means 'communion' rather than just 'fellowship'.

one Spirit we are all baptized and all made to drink of the one Spirit (1 Cor 12:12, 13). This last phrase is interpreted by most Catholic commentators as referring to holy communion in which we receive the Spirit.[22] Nor is there need here to refer to 1 Cor 3:16 or to Eph 2:22. It is safe to say that where there is *koinonia*, community and holy communion, there is the Spirit. As he called the assembly together at the beginning of the rite, so here in holy communion he completes the work he began. He makes the *koinonia* one body in Christ, and as it is in him and through Christ that the Church makes the eucharist, so it is in the Spirit and through Christ that the eucharist makes the Church.

The Dismissal

What of the end of the Mass? We have learned to understand that just as we bring our life to the Mass to be offered, so also we must go out from the Mass to live out in the world what we have received. Mass ends and mission begins. Just as the Holy Spirit has made himself present to us over the whole range of the eucharist, so he accompanies us on our mission: 'As they prayed, the house where they were assembled rocked; they were filled with the Holy Spirit and began to proclaim the word of God boldly' (Acts 4:31). While architects and the clergy might be more than somewhat alarmed at the prospect of rocking churches, and the latter perhaps even more alarmed if the laity began to proclaim the word of God boldly, we may take the incident as a sign and an object lesson of what we should want the liturgy to do to us.

---

[22] Cf L. Cerfaux, *La Théologie de l'Eglise suivant St Paul* (1948), pp. 205-10. For a contrary view see J. Ruel, *Paul's Letter to Corinth* (1971), *in loc*. His view (p. 132) is that *potizein* should be translated 'endued' or 'saturated'. He remarks that in baptism we do not drink and in the eucharist the drinking refers to the blood. However, Cerfaux had already pointed to 1 Cor 10:3 'they all ate the same supernatural food and all drank the same supernatural drink' (RSV) which seems to support the view that 1 Cor 12:13 refers to the eucharist, however odd the phrase may seem.

3. A People Prepared to Celebrate

J. C. Buckley

Since the liturgy is the embodiment of the mystery of Christ and the Church it will be seen that 'liturgical formation' must consist of all those elements which make up the awakening of Christians to their vocation as God's people. This consciousness of belonging to the Father through Christ's gift of his Spirit is what the liturgy is intended to convey. The 'condition of their calling as members of a single body' is the death-resurrection pattern of God's plan for the liberation of the human race through the paschal mystery of God's saving work in Christ. This plan is being worked out continually in the Church which, as God's assembled people, gives expression and actualization to what it is meant to be and to become: the covenant sign of God's redeeming love for mankind. Nowhere has this been put more beautifully and concisely than in para. 5 of the Council's Constitution on the Liturgy which says that Christ 'achieved his task principally by the paschal mystery of his blessed passion, resurrection from the dead, and glorious ascension, whereby "dying he destroyed our death, and rising, he restored our life". For it was from the side of Christ as he slept the sleep of death upon the cross that there came forth "the wondrous sacrament of the whole Church".'

The consciousness of being a redeemed and redeeming people, of being called to witness to the 'wonderful works of God', of being adorers of the Father in spirit and in truth, demands an ongoing formation which priest and people must undertake *together* in order to celebrate an authentic liturgy. Preparing the people for the liturgy does not consist solely or even chiefly in giving dogmatic articulation to certain intellectual propositions *about* Christ. Above all, preparing the people means helping them to *be* what they are: the here-and-now co-celebrants of those mysteries which have made them sharers in the divine nature and a communion of life and light for the world. This means, in simple terms, providing them with the means of *knowing* Christ with all the richness of meaning that such knowledge should have. This, in turn, means introducing the people to the fundamental idea of *mystery*. Far from making a divorce between our earthly life and our 'spiritual' life, a sense of mystery in its true Christian meaning will help Christians to see that life and liturgy are not poles apart, but facets of the one mystery which makes their lives centred on Christ who gives meaning and purpose to the whole of creation. The Council has made it clear that the presentation of the faith as the living-out of the mystery of Christ in his Church is the only way in which worship and life with all their permutations can be understood as making a unity. Christ is present in his Church not only, but pre-eminently, in her liturgical actions and that is why all pastoral activity should find its source and goal in the liturgy. This presence of Christ is one which every Christian should aim at being aware of. A mature Christianity must strive to develop the 'knowledge' of the one true God and his Son. In this context one can see the importance of developing a sense of Christ's presence especially in and through the liturgy. The celebration of the paschal mystery is the very purpose of the Church; it is the mystery which makes the Church what it is:

'To accomplish so great a work, Christ is always present in his Church, especially in her liturgical celebrations. He is present in the sacrifice of the Mass, not only in the person of his minister, "the same one now offering, through the ministry of priests, who formerly offered himself on the cross," but especially under the eucharistic species. By his power he is present in the sacraments, so that when a man baptizes it is really Christ himself who baptizes. He is present in his word, since it is he himself who speaks when the holy scriptures are read in the church. He is present, finally, when the Church prays and sings, for he promised: "Where two or three are gathered together for my sake, there am I in the midst of them" (Mt 18:20).

Christ indeed always associates the Church with himself in the truly great work of giving perfect praise to God and making men holy. The Church is his dearly beloved Bride who calls to her Lord, and through him offers worship to the Eternal Father.

Rightly, then, the liturgy is considered as an exercise of the priestly office of Jesus Christ. In the liturgy the sanctification of man is manifested by signs perceptible to the senses, and is effected in a way which is proper to each of these signs: in the liturgy full public worship is performed by the Mystical Body of Jesus Christ, that is, by the Head and his members.

From this it follows that every liturgical celebration, because it is an action of Christ the priest and of his Body the Church, is a sacred action surpassing all others. No other action of the Church can match its claim to efficacy, nor equal the degree of it' (CL 7).

In a very true sense there can be no real preparation for celebrating the liturgy other than the liturgy itself. 'L'appétit vient en mangeant.' That is why, it can be said, all catechesis is for adulthood. The trouble is that we have concentrated so much on catechizing children in preparation for 'receiving' the sacraments that we have neglected the role of the liturgy itself in its task of celebrating the mystery. Of course, a celebration of any kind will demand thought and planning. We take it for granted that weddings and birthday parties have to be prepared. All 'life celebrations' make exacting demands on some of the participants, but these are mainly the physical, material and organizational preliminaries. The essential preparation of mind and heart is one which takes place in the *lives* of those who participate. After all, the wedding reception is a sham if the parties to the marriage have not prepared themselves to form a community of love. Their whole upbringing and family background are the essential preparation for the wedding. Especially is the loving communion of life between their parents the guarantee of a worthy celebration of the son's or daughter's own wedding. The essential spiritual preparation for the celebration of the liturgy is the experience of a 'lived liturgy' – the joyful celebration of the Christian community. Learning to live means learning to love. Celebrating the liturgy means celebrating life and this means celebrating the love of God and neighbour. There will never be a real live celebration which does not demand a personal faith, hope and love. Paradoxically, however, the celebration itself will have a profound effect on the kind of response it evokes, for it is in the nature of the liturgy itself to form the attitudes which it demands.

The formation of the Christian for the liturgy is identical with his formation for life because the liturgy is the highest manifestation of the life of God's people. The life of God's people who live in the world is not different from that which they live in the liturgy – it has different expression. It is essential to realize that preparing the people pastorally for life is of one piece with preparing them for the liturgy. At the same time the liturgy has a great deal to do with preparation for life. If the 'lex orandi', and the 'lex credendi' are convertible so are the 'lex orandi' and the 'lex vivendi'. It can surely be said that the eucharist is primordial in the formation of Christian attitudes to life. It is there that the mind of Christ is not only learnt but acquired. The Christian life is, or should be, a life lived according to that mind. All Christian morality is summed up in the self-giving of Christ in the eucharist – the love-feast which Christ chose as the proof of his loving 'to the end' (John 13:1). It is the law of the new and eternal covenant, proclaimed and responded to in the celebration of the liturgy, which demanded the reforms. The *memorial* (in its full biblical meaning) of him who 'having loved his own who were in the world, showed the depth of his love' and left to his own the means of responding through *living* the new commandment is the source and centre of Christian morality (see Ralph Russell, *The Springs of Morality*, p. 33). It is because of the covenant commitment of the eucharist, the commitment of Christ to the Father and to the brethren and their commitment to him and to each other, that it has always been regarded as the final (on-going) stage of Christian initiation. All morality is in Christ and it is in the eucharist that we are most intensely in communion with him and with one another. It is there that the Church contemplates most deeply the words of life, 'pondering them in her heart'. Such contemplation is necessary for a mature Christian life and, therefore, for a mature celebration of the liturgy. The contemplation – prayerful and guided pondering of the scriptures – is foremost in importance for the preparation of liturgical celebration. Many older priests of a generation uninitiated into group prayer techniques will have seen a true sense of the liturgy developing among young people through their 'gospel enquiries' and the like. The appreciation of a mission arising from their sacramental initiation, the sense of Christ's present care for the world and his continuous, abiding action in their apostolate, this and much else was fed week by week as young working men and women gathered with their priest to read and ponder the scriptures. This pondering led them as by an irresistible impulse to realize that the eucharist is the 'summit and the source' of the Christian life. It is to the glory of the reformed liturgy that the celebration of the word of God has received such profound and merited attention. To many of that same generation the renewal of the Church's worship came as no surprise. The prayer of God's people and the apostolate of the laity together with their contemplation of the scriptures is seen as the expression of a life lived in the paschal mystery of the Church. 'Worship and the apostolate no longer need be treated as separate and unrelated things . . . worship is an integral part of the apostolate and the apostolic commitment will enrich worship' says one of the authors of *The Mass and the People of God* (Oliver Pratt, p. 53). It was a lesson given to many a priest by boys and girls a score of years before the Council.

To prepare for liturgical celebration is, then, a complex matter if it is seen as a matter of prescribed methods. Once, however, the liturgy is seen as the way in which the work of our redemption is accomplished we shall see it less as a means of our apostolic effort and more as the goal towards which all else converges.

The biblical formation of our people, so necessary to their liturgical formation, will take place of necessity and in large part within the celebration itself. Efforts to do this outside the liturgical context, laudable as they are, will have little chance of success apart from schools and the occasional study groups. Hence, the importance of biblical preaching cannot be over-emphasized. We are a biblical people; our symbolism, our history, our culture as Christians and consequently our liturgy are biblical. The need for biblical initiation arises not from any love of archeologism but from the simple facts of the history of God's election and his incarnation. Though the proclamation of the word is by no means confined to the liturgy it is none-theless true that it is in the liturgical assembly that this proclamation reaches the height of intensity and, particularly in the eucharist, reaches its utmost efficacy.

It is, then, of first importance to prepare minds and hearts to listen to the word of God with humble submission to its transforming power. The physical place that the bible has in the church, the enthronement of the Gospel on the altar, the ceremony with which it is carried to the ambo, its ornamentation and everything that speaks of real, unfeigned reverence will help us to understand the value and efficacy of its proclamation. From our attitude to the holy scriptures, engendered and fostered by the liturgical celebration of the word, we come to a realization of ourselves as the people *constituted by that word* with the consequent mission to proclaim it throughout our lives. It is not within the scope of this chapter to develop this notion; it must be left to the section on the parish Mass. It remains to be said, however, that besides a serious effort to make the rites surrounding the proclamation speak for themselves, considerable work remains to be done in the catechetical field in order that the liturgy become truly a *celebration* of the word.

It is of urgent importance for us to realize that the catechesis of adults is of prime importance. As yet the Church of the West has not given sufficient thought to the means of achieving this; and it is certainly true that unless we find structures and other means of catechizing adults in an adult way and thus preparing them for the realization of their role as celebrants of the mysteries the whole of their Christian lives will remain unfulfilled and their worship impoverished. The apostolate which finds its summit in the liturgy and flows from it is the mission of every Christian. The proclamation of God's word to the world cannot be confined to the liturgy. Liturgical proclamation must often be seen as the goal of the proclamation that takes place in the factory, the office, the neighbourhood, the home, the dance hall, the discotheque – wherever men and women have their being. To realize this is to realize the paschal power of God's word which transforms lives and makes them living proclamations of that word of life which speaks the joy, the hope and the love of those who have been reborn into the life of the risen Christ. Whatever helps the Christian to live that life of charity, whatever helps him to be conscious of the needs of his neighbour that he must serve, whatever prompts him to live a life of community out of love for Jesus Christ, is a preparation for an authentic celebration of the liturgy. The apostolate of every Christian is to 'proclaim the eternal life which was with the Father and was made manifest to us' so that the world may have fellowship with the Church – 'and our fellowship is with the Father and with his Son Jesus Christ' (1 John 1:2–3). The paschal character of the apostolate – as of the whole of the Christian life – is summed up in these words: 'We know that we have passed out of death into life, because we love the brethren' (John 3:14).

The introduction of Christians to the worship of the Church will necessarily entail deep insights into the meaning of the Church as mystery, since the Church is never more manifestly herself than when she celebrates the mysteries. As Louis Bouyer remarks (*The Liturgy Revived*, p. 35) '... the meaning of the Church itself is to extend, as it were, the presence, the active presence, of Christ to us'. Such a catechesis must introduce us to and deepen in us an understanding of the biblical and liturgical images and symbols of the Church and its activity. Since the eucharist is the joyful celebration of the Christian community it will be necessary to appreciate the meaning of joy and the meaning of community in order adequately to prepare for such a celebration.

Throughout the life of the Christian the essence of joy and peace will be in the realization of the presence of the living and risen Christ, the appreciation of the fact that Christ is present and acting on and with his people (see CL 6, 7). The joy of finding Christ in the assembly of his people is the very foundation of the liturgy. It is of great importance to persuade our people of the reality of the saving presence of Christ in the assembly. It is not just a kind of frivolity in togetherness but the joy of presence in meeting that we must try to express. As the assembly of God's people we gather to express at its height the Church itself. The assembly is the Church as the event of God's saving power made visible and actualized in the re-enactment of the appearance of the risen Christ to the apostles and 'to all the brethren at once' gathered in one place. From the first years of the Church's history, the assembly is a basic institution of the Christian community (Acts 2:42; 20:7–12); it is taken for granted (James 2:1–4) and must not permit of worldly

divisions. It is particularly in the assembly that we await the
second coming of the Lord (Heb 10:24-25), and Sunday is the
day of the assembly as it is the day of the eucharist, since the
assembly is the ordinary visible sign of the Church as the
pilgrim people of God.

The notions and images of the Church as Body of Christ and
Bride, as a people, as a kingdom, must all be developed in the
consciousness of Christians if they are to appreciate what it
means to be the Lord's assembly. It is then that they experience
the Church as not merely or chiefly a society or institution
(which it is of course) but as an organism living the life of the
risen Christ which vivifies all his members. The assembly must
make these members conscious of their adherence to Christ
and to each other as the branches to the vine. There they will
discover the mystery of the Church as God's espousal of mankind. They become conscious of his design to bring men into
union with himself and with one another through the active
presence of the One who reconciles in himself the world with
his Father. They recognize the Church as the sign of the
priestly, prophetic and royal office of him who is the Church's
husband.

This bridal imagery, so prominent in the bible and beloved of
the Fathers, had been largely forgotten until the liturgical
movement pointed to the Church's own prayer and showed how
fruitful the notion could be. Together with the basic idea of a
covenanting God and a covenanted people, such imagery is
able to prepare the people for their part in the liturgy and
evoke from them the commitment and life-involvement that
authentic celebration calls for and prompts. It may well be
that the decrease in Mass attendance is a consequence of the
realization that the modern reforms in the liturgy point to the
necessity of such commitment and require wholehearted response to the call for obedience to the new covenant law of
self-giving love!

Worship is, in the true sense, the end and goal of all
human endeavour. To praise the creator and give to creation
consciousness of him is the purpose of man's existence. For a
man to become conscious of himself and of his true value is to
become conscious of the creator who gives him existence; to
become conscious of the gift that God makes of *himself* in Christ

is to become a Christian. Every kind of education in true human values is a preparation for the liturgy, for it is there that the Christian finds and expresses God's searching love and his own response. The glory of God and the sanctification of man are two sides of the same coin, and so whatever contributes to man's dignity as a child of God contributes to the Father's glory.

Throughout any book which purports to deal with the liturgy, the idea of a worshipping community will be prominent. Evident as the idea may be, the reality is not nearly so manifest. A recent booklet has put it thus:

> 'The description given above of the eucharist bears little evident resemblance to the Sunday worship of most Christians in this country. The people present hardly envisage them-selves as a particularly coherent community. To many of them it has never even occurred that the Church's function is essentially missionary: that it exists not primarily for the salvation of Christians but for the enlightenment of all men. The Word of God part of the ceremony is often no more than a reading of the texts because they happen to be "in the book", with a sermon. And when it comes to the eucharist itself, the structure of the building is likely to prevent it coming home to the congregation that they are sharing a meal together. Many of the congregation will have rudi-mentary ideas about why it is a meal or what a eucharist is . . .' (Mason, *Christianity in Practice*, p. 13)

What is lacking, in effect, in the lives of most of our Christian people is any experience of community. It is only in relation-ship with others that the human being really discovers himself and in the discovery of himself he discovers God who reveals himself. The spiritual preparation of the people for a living liturgy demands a development of the sense of community. This will entail a wholehearted attempt to bring into being groups much smaller than the parish in order to provide a genuine experience of community and give authentic expression to it.

The principle of liturgical experience should be *a minimis incipe*. The experience of Mass celebrated by neighbours in one of their homes will be of immense value for preparing the participants to take their part in other modes of celebration. Among the most precious of the emphases of Vatican II was its teaching on the 'local church' as the realization, the concretization of the one, holy, Catholic and apostolic Church. In ancient tradition the liturgical assembly and the Church were clearly seen as one and the same reality. Not, of course, that the Church's activity and reality are 'exhausted' by the liturgy but it is in its liturgical action (an event which is necessarily localized) that the Church is most manifestly itself. A genuine experience of community will demand a face-to-face, shoulder-to-shoulder assembly which cannot be easily achieved at a large parish Mass. This is not to deny the value and importance of large gatherings – especially on Sundays and solemnities; but such value and importance will be greatly enhanced by the experience lived in a neighbourhood celebration at which the participants are conscious of one another and have been able to share together true Christian dialogue. For many Christians the opportunities for speaking together about their Christian faith and the experience of being able to live even for an hour at a deeply Christian level of commitment are all too rare. Obviously such small-group celebrations demand an adaptable ritual, and the flexibility of the reformed rites allow much greater scope than had been dreamed of before the Council.

The formation of these small groups will help to open minds and hearts to the true nature of the Church and its worship. 'No mission, no Mass.' The liturgy is essentially outward-looking, missionary. A worship which sees and seeks to serve the world will spring from and help to form a genuine Christian community. One which is *élitiste* or trivializing cannot be genuine for it does not 'manifest the true nature of the Church' which is the servant-Body of the servant-Head. It is a matter of simple experience that those groups of Christians whose outlook is most missionary and apostolic are the groups which appreciate most keenly the centrality of worship in the life of the Christian and the pre-eminence of the manifestation of the servant-Church in the eucharist.

Besides the formation of apostolic groups, groups which are always becoming more and more conscious of the environment in which they live, there must, of course, be the 'formation' of the persons who make up these groups. Each person needs to be brought face to face with the contradiction that exists between his daily life experience and the truth of faith which that daily life is meant to express and incarnate. No preparation for the liturgical celebration of life in Christ can afford to forget this essential element of week-by-week, year-by-year confrontation with the Gospel – or rather, with the person of Jesus whom to know is to have eternal life. The apostolic group should always aim at making the 'review of life' the centre of its meeting: how far has our action, how far has our judgement, how far has our experience been truly that of disciples of Christ? This continual process of the formation of Christian consciousness of the meaning of God's relationship with man, of the dignity to which he has raised his human creatures, of the destiny to which he has called them, is the essential preparation for liturgical celebration and a participation in it which the Council calls 'full, conscious and interior'. The help that the group can give to foster and support this growth in consciousness cannot be replaced by any other activity. But this does not mean, either, that the individual life of prayer and contemplation is any less necessary. The life of the group, the support and inspiration that the individuals can give to each other will depend on the measure of self-dedication through prayer which each is willing to undertake and to share with others. Where the group can help is not always by 'group activity' but by sharing experiences and bringing to bear a shared Christian judgement on those experiences, and thus discovering together the 'faith situation'. For example, an industrial dispute may appear to each member of the group under quite different aspects: to one it may be a means of getting better working conditions, to another a way of consolidating union authority, to a third a blow against capitalist domination and so on. What the group must aim to do is to see what faith in the fatherhood of God, in the brotherhood of Christ, in man's dignity as a sharer in the divine nature has to say about the values inherent in that situation. For the Christian every situation is a faith situation and must be judged accordingly. This brings us back to the necessity of a thorough biblical catechesis for all adult Christians. The whole point about the bible is that it presents human situations as 'faith situations'. The Christian must be led to see contemporary situations in the same light and it is in the liturgy that he expresses and discovers the meaning and unity of the apparently disparate events of history.

A thorough re-education in the meaning of Christian symbols will not stop at an explanation of the meaning of the material elements in those symbols. What we need to discover is the meaning of the situations, of the events which are evoked by the liturgical events of today, events foreshadowed by the history of Israel and brought to fulfilment in Christ. As Jean Daniélou reminds us (*La Maison Dieu*, no. 79, p. 28) the great 'mystagogical catechesis' of the fourth-century Fathers is based entirely on the analogy of the sacraments with the divine wonders of the Old Testament. What the Fathers underline is not just an analogy of signs but an analogy of human situations: St Paul did the same when he spoke of the ancestors of the Jews being 'baptized in the cloud, and in the sea' as a foreshadowing of our baptism. It is not just because water is common to the Flood, to the Red Sea, and to the Jordan, and to the baptismal font that the element is seen to have such importance and value of analogy. Man's sin and the judgement of God, the utter helplessness of mankind, the formation of a people, the deliverance from slavery and death, the many modalities of the saving power of God – these are the situations that need to be understood in order to see that at baptism we are saved from an analogous predicament.

The value of this kind of catechesis is that it presents the liturgy as a saving *event*, a 'mystery' in the true sense of God communicating his life to man in word and in deed. The sacraments are seen for what they are: the acts of Christ, the divine action made present here and now, God entering our history and saving his people. We are thus led to seeing our liturgical celebrations not as 'performances' or just as 'rites' but precisely as *mysteries*. God is not just the saving God of yesterday. He is saving us *now* not only by being eternal but by being contemporary. To belong to the people of God means to belong to that people whose memory is recorded in the book we call the bible. But the wonders of the bible are but the beginning and assurance of the wonders that we partake in through God's continued action in the sacraments. The Old Testament is but a preparation for Christ, it is true, but it is also – like all God's mysterious dealings with his people – an anticipation of the future redeemer. In every liturgical action there are present the three moments of time: past, present and future. In Christ himself was present the accomplishment and embodiment of the history of Israel and also the anticipation of the absolute future to which mankind is called. The sense of eschatology, the meaning of the *already* in tension with the *not-yet*, is a sense which the Christian needs in order to understand that the liturgy is at once means and fulfilment or, in the words of the Council, 'source and summit of the Christian life'. It is this eschatological dimension which allows the liturgy to be what it is meant to be: not a mere nostalgia for the past but a true memorial in its deepest, biblical sense of making available the saving power of God in anticipation of the ultimate triumph. The minds of contemporary Christians need this kind of orientation in order to understand that the new creation is already present in Christ, that the liturgy makes us sharers in that new creation and that the 'already' in Christ is being offered to man in this world of the 'not yet'.

The liturgy needs to be seen by Christians as the expression of their hope. It may well be wondered whether the virtue of hope is not the least understood of all the theological virtues – if not the least practised! Perhaps it is not fanciful to regard it particularly as the eschatological virtue 'par excellence'. And it is hope, in its true Christian sense of assurance, that the world needs so desperately – the hope that only Christ can give.

In our own day preparing people for the liturgy has meant endeavouring to change a mentality. The reforms envisaged by the Council were thought by many of the bishops to be surprisingly radical. It surprised many who had regarded the liturgy as fixed and immobile that the reforms suggested went much further than changes or adaptations of texts and rubrics. What was needed was a change in attitude. Priest and people would need to re-learn the whole of the Church's understanding of herself as the instrument, teacher and guardian of worship and sanctification. They would need to know what was meant by 'celebration', by 'mystery' and by 'proclamation' with all the richness that these terms could convey only in the context of a Christian life lived to the full. Above all it has been appreciated that it is comparatively easy to change ways of doing things but much more difficult to change persons and attitudes. The

Constitution on the Liturgy (art. 11) has made this clear when it declares that to produce the full effects of liturgy 'it is necessary that the faithful come to it with proper dispositions, that their minds should be attuned to their voices and they should co-operate with divine grace lest they receive it in vain'.

The liturgy is not magic; it is of value according to the measure of faith and charity with which it is celebrated, and spiritual preparation for it is necessary for its fruitfulness. If at times a charge of lack of spontaneity may justifiably be levelled at its celebration it must be remembered that it is, of its nature, the 'Church at prayer'. Consequently, while always retaining its community character, it will always have to combine a delicate measure of sameness with one of immediacy. It has to speak to human hearts and minds, and those hearts and minds have to speak in common to their common Lord and Father. Mere externalism is as destructive of true liturgy as individual-istic self-centred piety. The joy of Christian celebration must be able to create as well as reflect the deepest convictions and human needs of all its participants. It must not be expected to do everything, for 'the spiritual life is not by any means limited solely to participation in the liturgy' (art. 12). The need for private prayer in order precisely to make the liturgy what it is intended to be will always have to be stressed, and while our Christian people need to be taught that consciousness of one another is an integral part of liturgical prayer, so is a prayerful silence to be understood as a means of sharing together in the mysteries that make us a people. Preparing the people spiri-tually for the liturgy demands an intense effort at self-prep-aration on the part of pastors.

Because of inflexible rules and rigid uniformity before the Council the celebrations of the Church's prayer were for most Catholics the reiteration of words and gestures which the tra-dition of centuries had made sacrosanct. Experience since the recent reforms has taught us to avoid two pitfalls. The first is that of behaving and thinking as though the reforms consisted in the substitution of one set of rubrics for another, of one set of texts for another. The other pitfall is that of disregarding all rules and authoritative prescriptions in the name of a new-found flexibility and adaptation to local needs. The priest will need to prepare himself by prayer, study and thoughtful care for his people in order to strike the right balance between legitimate flexibility and devout obedience. In order to do this he will see the need for a more and more profound consultation with those whose liturgical president he is. The liturgy is the worship of the whole Church and there are no mere onlookers. That is why the experience of preparing *together* for celebrations is so rewarding. If, in our own time, we are experiencing tensions and polarization of extreme positions in the Church we must look with confidence and faith to the future. The Spirit is directing the Church in its mission of worship and sanctification. If we find it difficult to resolve our tensions we need to remind ourselves that many tensions are inherent in the great mystery of the Incarnation and that 'Christianity must ever work to achieve the dynamic poise between -isms, with their impulse to become exclusivisms . . . As the worship of God (the liturgy) remains sternly God-centred; as worship by God's people, it is no less strictly man-centred. Each of us must judge for himself whether he is prone to one excess or the other. He can then also judge how best to use the liturgy as a corrective' (*Our Changing Liturgy*, C. J. McNaspy, p. 157).

4. The Place of Celebration

Austin Winkley

Introduction

Changes in the arrangement of church buildings are among the most tangible consequences of the renewal of our liturgy. This chapter deals with practical considerations of church planning, concentrating on those which affect worshippers.

Winston Churchill once reminded us that 'we shape our buildings and afterwards our buildings shape us'; therefore we must build wisely. Good architecture has the effect of supporting and egging on the users of a building. So we should still aim to make places of worship inspiring, doing this through a combination of practical insight and poetic expression. Although little will be written here of the aesthetic factor it should be understood that practical considerations alone will not give us the buildings we need.

Before looking closely at the church as a worship room it is worth reflecting on its potential as a multipurpose space. Many people have understandable qualms of conscience about spending large sums of money on churches when they are often used infrequently. Christian stewardship demands a responsible use of our resources. The facilities that can be provided by using a multipurpose space need to be carefully evaluated in relation to short and long term provision.

A multipurpose space is one designed to be used for several activities, for example a school hall is often constructed for assembly, physical education, dining, as a theatre, a meeting room, and for worship. It may be seen to work reasonably well for each purpose but a lot of noisy rearranging of furniture and equipment is needed to achieve the intended degree of flexibility. In addition to the labour involved we must not forget the volume of storage outside the hall floor area required to make it workable, and the visible wear and tear on the building and its furniture. The disposal of undesirable smells, particularly stale cigarette smoke and beer, is not easy. There are many subtle design characteristics of different spaces that make them what they are. It is not surprising therefore that we find in large schools not four multipurpose halls but purpose-designed spaces such as gymnasia, dining halls, theatres and chapels. We should understand therefore that the multipurpose building is to be avoided rather than considered the norm.

However in situations where it is necessary the community should be aware of the limitations and proceed thoughtfully to express in their building the Christian priorities which will still make it a church.

For the small Christian community a temporary hut can serve reasonably well for worship, bingo, socials and meetings, but if the parish grows, demand for other spaces will be generated and long term plans prepared for what has become known as 'a parish complex' containing almost certainly a place specifically designed with worship as its main activity.

Justification for such a scheme must lie in the conviction that the plant is necessary for the effective mission of that community. The particular considerations in designing a worship room are the main substance of this chapter, and it will be apparent that they can be achieved only to a limited degree in a multipurpose space.

The size of an assembly

How big should a worship room be? This major question has to be asked whenever a church is proposed and the answer has to be derived from several considerations; potential growth of the community, the amount of space needed by each worshipper, car parking provision, feasible expenditure and reflection on other people's ideals.

Over the years figures as varied as 100, 300 and 700 persons have been put forward both as ideals and more often as maxima for a parish assembly. In practice, while size does matter, the smallest practical group should be aimed at as it is easier to cater for. However it is not fruitful here to speculate about the complications derived from hypothetical budgets, priest/people ratios, size of parish etc., and it is more useful to underline other factors which might affect numbers.

A large assembly reduces mobility, and planning for more movement should be aimed for, not only in aisles but in the space allocation for each worshipper. 'Cost per place' has been a widely used but misleading rule of thumb for assessing value for money, but this has led to worship rooms being packed with seats in order to justify a particular expenditure. Of old, a standard pew place frequently measured 2' 10" by 1' 6"; a more realistic standard would be 3' 0" by 1' 10".

Rows of closely spaced seats should not be too long, say for eight to ten persons, and rows finishing against a wall or column should be avoided. The number of church places should not be equated with the number of fixed seats and kneelers provided; rather the number of fixed seats should relate to the maximum number required for the busiest Mass on say three Sundays out of four.

Any seats not used regularly should be removed to provide a maximum of open space. Permanent seating should not be provided for Christmas and Easter crowds as their needs can be met by temporary seats or by simply accepting that standing is normal for many worshippers on those occasions. Where existing churches are filled with seats, serious thought should be given to rearranging Mass times away from peak periods to shed the popular loading, and Saturday Masses should be considered for the fulfilment of obligations, as in other countries. The aim could be to have the area of a worship room related to regular seating by the ratio of about fifteen sq feet per person.

Such a basis can, for instance, provide seats for 250 people regularly, with a peak capacity including people standing of 750. If 400 permanent seats are fixed in the same space, capacity is reduced to about 600. Applying the misleading 'cost per place' rule to such a scheme, would the building be classed as cheap for 750 worshippers or expensive for 250?

Quite a different consideration affecting the size of new churches is the car-parking provision required by the Planning Authorities. They generally require one car-parking place per five pew seats; a more moderate provision is 1:10 but it is not unknown for the rule to be 1:3 where it is clear that a high proportion of worshippers will arrive by car. The cost of parking provision can be as high as a third of the cost of the building, so this is a powerful incentive to leave out permanent seats that are not required regularly.

Plan arrangements

The arrangement of church plans used to be simple to describe – the people occupied benches in the nave and side aisles and ministers occupied the sanctuary. All that was required of the congregation was physical presence and attention to the ritual. Now churches are planned in a variety of shapes reflecting the search for ways to make it easier for worshippers to participate. Despite the variety, no new set form has emerged. For a short period circular churches were in vogue, but the absence of a sensible place to read or preach in a central sanctuary soon showed that such a plan was ill-considered, however attractive the altar position seemed.

More successful as a geometric guide line is the horseshoe layout of seats with the sanctuary near the open end. It follows the 'natural' grouping of a crowd, unencumbered by furniture, watching a demonstration. This shape would be even more effective if people stood or sat on the floor. In the picnic position a fine sense of sharing is easily achieved. But in practice seating is considered necessary, so the different merits of straight and curved rows of seats need looking at. Curved rows enable members of the congregation to see each other, not only across the room but along the line; it is a far more unifying arrangement than straight rows of seats all directed one way. However, whether benches or chairs are to be used, the curved rows are difficult to achieve.

Planks of wood are not normally curved, connectors (required by fire officers) for chairs have to be very precise to give a regular curved line, and ideally the rows of seats should have different radii, but this prevents the standardization of components. Cranked benches are often the unhappy compromise where churches planned with curved rows of seats were planned without the full cost implications being appreciated. Cranked pews are better avoided and straight rows of carefully arranged groups of seats can make good plans.

The merits of one straight line arrangement that is often overlooked is that of the conventual choir. Designed for antiphonal prayer, it works well for its particular purpose. As choristers respond to each other and the leaders move about confidently, a strong sense of unity can be generated, within the limitations of straight lines. It is worth recalling that despite the confines of those limitations human beings with heads that pivot can direct the sense of their bodies towards the centre of activity with surprising dexterity. Many other straight line layouts can produce effective layouts.

When thinking of the respective merits of benches and chairs, it is worth noting that benches are heavy, so rearrangement of them is rarely attempted except for long-term change. Chairs are easier to move, benches have more rigid frames to attach kneelers to, but these hinder movement; hassocks do also and it would be much better if we could manage without them altogether. We have inherited rigid layouts. Our intention now should be to develop freer plan arrangements where people can move, see and be seen. Visibility is desirable because it strengthens communication but it is less important than in a theatre or cinema, as our aim must be designing for participation rather than simply for seeing. For example a sloping floor can help visibility but if it is too steep or stepped it implies an undesirable spectator provision; nevertheless a sloping floor can help a standing worshipper by putting the weight of the body on to the ball of the foot, giving a sense of forward projection rather than the static feeling produced by resting on the heel. A limitation of sloping floors is of course the need to fix seats to stop them moving.

Again, visibility may be improved if the sanctuary is raised above the seating area. But if it is too high, with the altar top set above eye level, then a cut-off occurs, and the celebrant appears to be behind a wall rather than standing before a table.

Entering and leaving church are activities which can either contribute to worship or detract from it. Sometimes people enter church before Mass with some reticence; they may then either move quickly through the porch and into a seat near the door, or be encouraged to move calmly, greeting friends and removing coats to a cloakroom before putting communion bread on the plate and proceeding hopefully to seats near the front. It is even practical to plan the church so that worshippers enter near the front seats -- thus presenting them with the unusual option of taking a front place or deliberately choosing to go further back.

A front entry plan can also have the advantage that the ministers enter and leave by the same door as everyone else, which expresses unity but also makes priest and people readily available to each other.

Even the after Mass crush can be exploited and provided for if large doors from the worship room give access to a reservoir space where refreshments are offered. Instead of the celebration ending in a crush, it can be extended in a reunion with friends, not only in the street outside but within the comfort of the parish complex.

Provision for particular groups within the church can strengthen or weaken the celebration. It is probably better if families stay together, but if babies or children are not happy or cause undue disturbance in the main worship room they will need adjacent spaces where part of the celebration can take a form more relevant to their needs. Such space could overlook the main room; but the image of the noisy 'cry room' where mothers with babies are herded together should be discouraged.

Choirs and musical instruments need special attention. They should be close to the centre of activity and have flexible space so that choirs, orchestras and bands of different sizes can fill an appropriate area without taking over as the centre attraction. Where an organ is to be installed it is worth remembering that organ pipes can be decorative, while instruments with loudspeakers are rarely so and require most careful siting.

THE SANCTUARY

With the disappearance of rood screen and altar rails this area is now only nominally separated from the rest of the worship room. A change of level or floor finish defines the space where the altar, lectern and president's chair are located. They, along with the font, are the major symbolic furnishings of the church. What they look like affects the quality of the entire space and their positions greatly influence the shape of the building. Most of the movement in the celebration takes place in the open areas between them, so each needs careful consideration as a centre of activity, related to the congregation, to other major and minor furnishings as well as symbolic objects in themselves. It is from these considerations that we have come to realize the weaknesses of long thin plans and circular ones.

The Lectern

Pulpits have gone but ambos have returned. Too often these are paltry structures, a sloping wood top on a flimsy leg. This 'place of the word' needs to be substantial, and while wood can be an adequate material, metal and stone are also suitable, often providing a closer link with the altar material.

The lectern position should be elevated in all but the smallest church and the reader seen to project his voice towards the centre of the assembly. It is better if there are no worshippers behind the reader and to that end the lectern can be positioned in front of, behind or to one side of the altar, but it should not block the congregation's view of either the altar or the president's chair.

The Altar

From recent tradition we have inherited long and shallow altars set against the wall. Depth was limited because the celebrant had to reach across the top to the tabernacle. Length was not limited by the need for circulation space at the ends; on the contrary it was encouraged by the assumption of three zones for the epistle, gospel and eucharist.

Much of the presence of the altar was achieved by backgrounds, namely gradines, reredos or east window. Now only canopies are available and these are difficult to design satisfactorily and costly to make. With the celebrant facing the people the altar must command presence by its location in the church and chiefly by the way people gather around it. An altar set high and remote may seem fitting as an altar of sacrifice but one set among the people will more readily express the image of the Last Supper table.

Instead of the long counter the free standing altar can be short and deep, say 6′ by 4′, or it could be the very commanding shape of five feet square, equally usable on all four sides. The practical height has also changed, being reduced from 3′ 4″ to 3′ 1″ so that people can more easily see the top surface.

Traditionally, altars are made of stone and this material is undoubtedly preferable to wood, but the latter more readily meets the need for flexibility. Metal legs may combine with stone or timber altar tops. The design should always be simple, yet profound and, ideally, a unique form.

The president's chair

The president is another manifestation of Christ's presence leading the people in their celebration, so his chair should be in a commanding position, seen but not over-elevated, and again not blocking the view of ambo or altar. As with the lectern, none of the congregation should be directly behind it. It is this requirement more than any other which makes the circular church impractical – there is nowhere in such a plan for the President's chair or the lectern to be positioned effectively. The advantage of asymmetrical layouts becomes apparent. Because of its symbolic character the president's chair, like the ambo, needs to be substantial. Ordinary dining chairs are inadequate except in the smallest of worship rooms. Often an old chair may be fitting even in a modern church, but the back should not be so high that it looks like a throne.

Secondary furnishings should be given the same detailed design considerations as the three major ones. Preferably the credence should not be free-standing as this can give it undue importance; a projecting or recessed shelf can provide a suitable fitting without overdoing it. A place for putting the money collection may be with the credence or a separate block may be provided, to avoid the custom of putting the collection on or below the altar. The use of *ad hoc* stools and side tables should be avoided as these detract from major furnishing which will have been thoughtfully designed. Candle holders, altar cloths and flower containers will all require new care in design and positioning.

The tabernacle

The place of reservation of the Blessed Sacrament should generally be outside the main worship space, as has always been the custom in cathedrals and churches where the office is recited. Until comparatively recent times the tabernacle has been considered central to a church and was often in the place where people like to pray privately.

There are advantages in making the tabernacle visible from and close to the entrance of the church but this may conflict with the need for access from the worship room.

According to local circumstances the tabernacle can be recessed in the wall as an aumbry, set on a stand or in a tower like the continental Sakramenthaus or, exceptionally, as a hanging pyx. It should no longer be set on an altar, unless, in existing churches, a tabernacle on a side altar is considered appropriate. In such cases the chapel itself may need freshening up with new colour and lighting. In reordering churches the existing tabernacle should be used in the new setting both to provide continuity with the old order and to save expense. Old tabernacle safes are well made and easily restored.

The font

Where a fixed font is installed this should not be in the sanctuary but stand in its own ground close by, where it can be seen by members of a congregation participating at baptism during a eucharistic celebration. In practice most of the sacramental rite will take place on the raised level of a sanctuary where everyone can see the child, with parents and godparents. The descent to the font for pouring of the water and the rising up again takes only two or three minutes, so it is not too serious if some of the congregation do not see that part. Symbolism is lost if the font is set in a high position rather than a sunken place; a high position can also detract from other centres of activity when it is not in use.

Traditionally fonts are carved from stone but ceramic or metal bowls may also be appropriate. Running water in the bowl is strongly symbolic of life, but the practical difficulties of keeping the water clean, pumps quiet, preventing flooding and meeting Water Board Regulations are not easily overcome.

In designing the church building and its furnishing the quality of the space will be greatly influenced by the materials used; what these are will depend largely on the size of the place and the budget, but the key to a good design lies in a true economy of means. This does not mean cheapness but the use of a few materials, avoiding variety for its own sake, and the greatest of restraint in using the more precious materials. This should ensure harmony.

Structure and lighting

The design of the structure and the method of lighting are

technical matters but the layman can readily grasp their methodology.

A worship room is a large space, so the walls must be stable and the roof structure deep and strong enough to cover the distance. It invariably adds to the quality of the space if the structural members are expressed rather than hidden. The lines of columns and piers merging with trusses, rafters and decking lead the eye of the observer along logical and harmonious journeys, stopping to rest and carrying through. The mood of the space will vary with the lighting. The design of daylighting comes before artificial lighting and must be considered in its own right rather than as the by-product of having windows, the shape of which will grow from multiple considerations including orientation, the quality of light aimed for, and external appearance.

Artificial lighting is more readily controlled, so anything is possible; but clever theatrical effects are rarely helpful.

The need for comfortable heating and ventilation, good acoustics and sound reinforcement are self-evident. With these there is no short cut to good technical advice. But the best made church requires thoughtful care and attention in all matters so, in rounding off this chapter, we should consider the image of the building as a whole.

These days a Christian community will have no desire to impose itself on the world, monumental office buildings have taken over this now questionable role of some historic churches with their 'nothing too good for God' message, but our new church buildings, even those limited in scale, will still express the priorities of the people who commission and use them.

Existing churches and their grounds need to look cared for. New churches may not easily be recognized as such and it requires sensitive awareness to ensure that the building fits in well in its neighbourhood. The sign of the cross is a meaningful symbol to mark it with and the cross must be well designed and sensitively located. Finally it must be said that a successful exterior is a controlled projection of the well-resolved interior. Both should speak for themselves.

5. Music and Pastoral Liturgy

Martin Hall

THE NATURE OF LITURGICAL MUSIC

It is not altogether surprising that in the re-examination of the liturgy at the time of the Second Vatican Council the role of music within the liturgy was also subjected to thoughtful re-appraisal – along with, it must not be overlooked, other art-forms which have through long traditional associations been inextricably involved with the liturgy itself.

The over-riding problem of music is that it does not conveniently exist in a permanent form as, for example, the plastic and visual arts such as architecture, sculpture and painting. It is of its nature ephemeral and requires constant re-creation. A successfully designed church building remains for a long period, for all to see and admire; its replacement is not undertaken lightly. Similarly, statuary and vestments, furniture and other adornments are 'one-off' items which, although needing financial investment at the outset, usually continue to give value and satisfaction to clergy and people alike, with only occasional need for renewal.

The great European ecclesiastical designers of the Baroque era, particularly those in the German states, recognized the role of music in their planning. This resulted in the devising of 'tonal architecture' in church adornment and the remarkable church organs of the period reflect this – not only in their perhaps extravagant structures but more importantly in their *sound*.

The finest instruments, however, still require a live, human agency if they are not to remain mute. As much, if not more, needs to be said of people, if only that vocal music has remained at the core of the liturgy for so many hundreds of years.

What I have to say in this chapter is based on the experience of a parish musician (a term I prefer to 'organist' or 'choir-master') over a period of some twenty years – a convenient period which both precedes and follows the liturgical 'reformation'. I have also had the good fortune to widen this experience as a member of a diocesan liturgical commission, which has afforded me the opportunity to work on practical sessions in other parishes, especially in those which for one reason or another either have abandoned, or are seeking to start afresh, the inclusion of music in their parish liturgy.

The use of music in church must always begin from the premise that its purpose is to add an extra dimension to the spoken word. It has of course other applications, which may be described as 'enhancement', since music can validly exist on its own, giving additional adornment to liturgical celebration in a 'background' sense (it must never be in the foreground). The ability of music to lift words on to a higher plane, however, cannot be over-stressed. It is my task to explain in a short space how this can be done simply.

The chief barrier to the acceptance of music, or music-making, in church is its necessarily subjective nature. The very act by *a* man (woman), *a* priest, *a* choir or *a* band of musicians often leads to criticism, adverse or otherwise, expressed or merely felt, which can quickly lead to considerations that have nothing to do with the liturgy. This stems from the fact that musical expression is a perfectly natural function (for most people) and often has emotional overtones capable of distraction, or, more problematic, associations with human experiences outside the spiritual. This powerful latent force must be harnessed if it is to serve the church in its role as 'handmaid of the liturgy'.

The introduction of the vernacular has, paradoxically, led to a falling-off in the 'adornment' of the liturgy. The pressures of pastoral life have also tended to stunt the growth of the diversity inherent in the new Roman Missal. I suspect too (as one less wise) that considerations of Mass timetables and other similar necessities have prevented many priests from taking the opportunity of putting into practice even a small number of the options available, let alone fully re-appraising the presentation of the liturgy in their churches.

It was perhaps one thing for the Council Fathers to reflect in abstract on what the liturgy really meant and how it might be enhanced *ad majorem Dei gloriam*, but another to realize how this might successfully be achieved in practice 'back at the parish'.

One aspect of the unreformed liturgy must surely be clear. It had become encapsulated in a highly formalized ritual, to the extent that by simply following pre-determined formulae the requirements of the Church appeared to be satisfied. This is not to say that many of these formulae were not of great artistic or sometimes spectacular merit, or even that they did not often fulfil the pastoral and spiritual needs of priests and people, but much of what was done was inevitably mechanical and took little into account except adhering to 'the book'. A personal experience will make the point. I can remember as a very young man in the 1950s reacting (no doubt over-sensitively) to my almost total involvement as organist in musical activity at the 11 a.m. High Mass to the extent that I felt that I must attend an earlier, low Mass, if the precept of Sunday observance was to be fulfilled; whatever else one was doing in the choir-loft, there was little opportunity for spiritual reflection, or union with the action of the Mass.

THE IMPORTANCE OF CO-OPERATION

The success or otherwise of music in any church in my view largely depends on the degree of rapport between the person entrusted with the music and his parish priest – unless there exists that *rara avis*, the enthusiastic priest-musician. I do not use that term pejoratively or even cynically; many parishes owe their musical tradition to such a one – the parish where I presently work being an example. But I am concerned to underline the principle (no doubt revolutionary to some) established by the General Instruction to the Roman Missal (73) that

'the particular preparation for each liturgical celebration should be done in a spirit of co-operation by all parties concerned, under the guidance of the rector of the church, whether it be ritual, pastoral, or musical matters.'

The United States Bishops ('Music in Catholic Worship', 1972) have commented further on this and I quote the relevant paragraph (no. 12):

'the planning team or committee is headed by the priest (celebrant and homilist), for no congregation can experience the security of a unified celebration if that unity is not grasped by the one who presides, as well as by those who have special roles. It should include those with the knowledge and artistic skills needed in celebration – men and women trained in music, poetry and art, and knowledge in current resources in these areas – men and women sensitive to the present-day thirst of so many for the riches of scripture, theology and prayer . . .'

These recommendations, some now ten years old, appear either to have failed or gone unheeded in many places. The ideas expressed in these quoted paragraphs have a continuing validity and I am concerned to show that they are neither idealistic nor even radical, when applied to the average parish situation. But they do require work, and planning.

I found early on (1968) that even a modest attempt to use the available options suggested by the Roman Missal involved the parish musician in far greater weekly preparation for a Sunday sung Mass, for example, than had ever been demanded by Tridentine practice, even where fairly elaborate ceremonies were the rule. I am persuaded, more than anything else, of the need to relate what is done to the celebration being prepared.

Intelligent interpretation of the provisions of the Roman Missal can reconcile musical involvement with the spiritual involvement of those taking part in the music-making, and more important, communicate this dual involvement to the other members of the assembly.

What kind of music?

The next truth possible of definition is that the music does not need to be elaborate to be effective; but it should be done to the best of the ability of those performing it. It follows that while simplicity is a pre-requisite, the music need not be dull. There is a dearth of good, simple music at present, and the advent of the vernacular has engendered a plethora of what a contemporary writer describes as 'abysmal slush'. There can be a parallel between bad church music and bad church art – the 'green plastic cheese' pocket-statuary sort of thing, for example. We may be incapable of providing art worthy of God, but we have no business to offer anything which offends a reasonable standard of taste.

In France, where these matters seem to be better organized, some three thousand vernacular hymns and songs have been published in the last ten years under the auspices of *L'Eglise qui chante*, of which it is estimated that about a hundred have found general acceptance in congregations for permanent use. This indicates the problem facing the church musician; in the Catholic Church in Britain the composer is in the position of his Anglican predecessors four hundred years ago at the Protestant Reformation. Unfortunately there are not so many men of the eminence of William Byrd and Thomas Tallis writing for the Church today and many years will pass before a corpus of good, new church music has been built up.

WHAT CAN BE SUNG?

Having said all this let us consider what in fact can be achieved with slender resources plus the will to make the liturgy come alive musically.

Too many churches have found the easy way out (it is, actually, a trap, because a dead-end) by adopting the missalette formula totally, especially those editions which offer hymns for each Sunday. The four-hymn Mass formula dates back to the Instruction on Sacred Music of 1958 and was introduced as an early attempt to furnish some vernacular moments in an otherwise entirely Latin celebration. I have known of at least one church where every Mass on a Sunday was 'adorned' with these hymns, supported by organists of varying ability or none. The 'musical' result was hardly inspiring, though no doubt the achievement was believed to be in the spirit of the 'new' liturgy.

There are certain parts of the Mass which should unquestionably be given musical priority over hymns. The simplest to begin with, the most effective, and the most involving of those taking part, are the responsorial texts. Of these, first and foremost is the Responsorial Psalm. A priest recently gave me his opinion that the spoken, or read, psalm is a 'disaster'. The most cursory glance at the Book of Psalms reveals that it was designed for singing, and it is no mere coincidence that the Jewish synagogal chants led to what the Christian Church knows as plainsong.

At this point the importance of the role of a cantor or leadsinger (man or woman) is worth stressing. The office and function of cantor are of ancient and distinguished origins. It may be convenient to provide a second lectern (a music-stand, draped at the front with a simple piece of fabric, will serve) on the opposite side of the sanctuary to the lectern proper – the lectern itself should not be used by a cantor except for the singing of the psalm. The people respond so much better to a confrontation; too many churches designed on Vatican I lines relegate the lead-singers to the back of the church. This is all right for music performed by a choir alone, when a degree of disembodiment may prevent distraction, but it makes no contribution to the ideal described by Bernard Huijbers, SJ of the 'performing audience'. The cantor should be regarded, properly, as a member of the sanctuary staff, as the servers and readers are. The idea that musicians are somehow interlopers needs suppressing at the earliest moment; at the same time the musician himself (herself) must not regard his/her particular task as of any greater importance than that of others carrying out a specific liturgical function during a celebration.

The responsorial psalm can be led by one singer, if necessary without any accompaniment. Faced with the transition from a sung Latin Mass to one in English in the space of a week I adopted the formula below (Ex. 1) for the psalm; together with Ex. 2 it provides music for every response in the Lectionary.

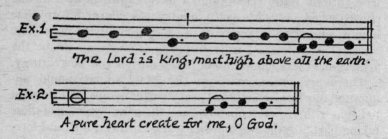

Ex.1 'The Lord is King, most high above all the earth.

Ex.2 A pure heart create for me, O God.

Of course it is desirable to vary the chant after a time – once the congregation has become used to the idea of responding. (At the end of this chapter I give a brief list of recommended music, and also of organizations from which assistance and information can be obtained.) Dom Gregory Murray OSB, who has done so much through the changing years to provide good, simple music for the Church, has formulated chants for the psalm verses which require little musical expertise; the same single singer is adequate for this purpose. Other chants are recommended: Dom Laurence Bévenot OSB was experimenting with English settings as long ago as the early 1930s, and Père Gelineau SJ needs no introduction from me. These three men have between them composed more usable music for the parish liturgy over the years than many perhaps musically more distinguished contemporaries.

The Alleluia after the second lesson follows, musically, as a consequence of the psalm. Acclamatory in character, it is of course a Gospel processional chant, but it tends too often to become an adjunct to the second reading, which it is not. A pause should occur between the conclusion of the reading and the intoning of Alleluia: at a solemn Mass this pause should be prolonged until the Gospel reader has asked blessing of the president and the procession is ready to move off. The example below is an extension of Exx. 1 and 2:

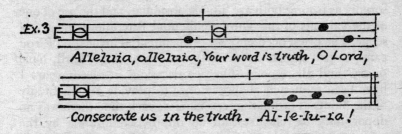

I have dealt first with the psalm and Alleluia if only because these are the most novel elements in the revised liturgy, as far as music is concerned. Other elements are often existing formulas given a new emphasis. Most notable are the various *Acclamations*. Very old in origin, they are properly the people's contributions and, once the principle of responsorial singing has been mastered, little difficulty need be encountered in including musical settings of the acclamations at a celebration. In addition to the Alleluia, four acclamations ought always to be sung: *Sanctus*; *Eucharistic Acclamation*; *Great Amen*; and the Acclamation after the *Our Father*. These are inevitably more successful if the priest's part immediately preceding them is intoned or otherwise chanted; failing this (and I accept that many priests prefer not to sing) a good lead-in from the organ and support from the cantor or other lead-singers should ensure maximum participation. Settings of the *Sanctus* exist (e.g. Tamblyn: *Community Mass*; Gelineau: *Festival Mass*) in which the melody is first sung by the cantor or choir and repeated by the people. Eucharistic Acclamations will be found in *Praise the Lord* (revised) and *Mass for All Saints* (Trotman), and are easily learnt over a few Sundays. The *Great Amen* sung is so much more effective a termination to the eucharistic prayer than a spoken Amen, particularly if the closing 'Through him . . .' is even simply monotoned by the celebrant; the people are prepared for what they must do and the *Amen* does not just catch them unawares. The *Our Father* itself offers an excellent opportunity for singing; there are settings available varying from adaptations of the Gregorian simple tone to the more eclectic and popular versions to be heard at many a school Mass these days.

The remainder of the Ordinary can be added as considered appropriate. The Kyrie and Agnus Dei can be sung responsorially as before; both are 'litanic' formulas, and the use of one of the variants of the Third Penitential Rite affords plenty of scope. The priest need only *say* the penitential invocation ('You came to call sinners . . .' etc.); the cantor sings 'Lord, have mercy' and all respond. On two occasions in recent years I have been requested at short notice to provide a sung Litany of the Saints at ordination ceremonies; each time there was no opportunity to rehearse and an improvised formula by the cantor was instantly responded to by a full church of four or five hundred people (they do not all come to the solemn sung Mass every Sunday, either!). The Agnus Dei can be sung to one of numerous simple settings and at first the people merely take up the refrain 'Have mercy on us'. The Gloria and creed are more ambitious; the new ICEL/ICET texts will, I am certain, provide composers with excellent material for simple settings. The Gloria may well be left to a choir of singers, especially on festal occasions, but the creed as a public affirmation of faith is a different matter. I have seen no satisfactory settings of the creed as yet, other than plainsong adaptations to English; the solution, adopted in my own parish for many years, could well be to stick to Credo III, again alternated between cantor and people. (This practice is specifically encouraged, along with the

Pater Noster and other parts of the Ordinary, in the Vatican's recommendations concerning retention of familiar Latin chants.) If time *must* be taken into consideration, then the creed had best remain said. Finally, the ministers' chants and appropriate responses are now to be found in the Altar Missals. With these added to the parts of the Mass already discussed, we have arrived at a complete formula for the sung vernacular congregational Mass.

I have quite deliberately refrained from reference to more elaborate music in the liturgy, supposing that where competent musicians are available less guidance is needed. Where choirs have become disbanded, or – almost as bad – an existing choir has entrenched itself in an opposed, Tridentine position so that what it does (or sings) has no connection with the ritual of the celebration, then insufficient notice has been taken of the underlying principles I have attempted to state earlier.

Enough has been said to show that a considered approach to music in the parish Mass can result in a true adornment of the liturgy once again. Dignity and solemnity can attach to Mass in a vernacular context, with the full participation of the congregation.

RESOURCES

'I do not have a musician in my parish, so we have no music.' 'The last choirmaster I had wanted to run the show.' 'I had a choir once, but they got fed up singing X's "People's Mass" every Sunday.' Remarks like these show the greatest practical problem facing the person who wants to make a beginning. Where can he find a cantor, an organist, or other musicians?

There must be one man (or woman) in every parish, who, if approached and properly instructed in the Roman Missal, could put one or two of the ideas I have set out into practice. If the priest or priests in a parish are prepared to have a go, so much the better.

There are three essential components in a sung Mass: priest (not necessarily the principal celebrant); people; and cantor or choir of singers. Between them they play a tripartite role and are all totally *involved* in the celebration. If an accompanist is needed (and an organ is not a *sine qua non*, however desirable) then there is surely one person within reach of every parish church in the land who can at least play the piano reasonably well. A piano adequately played is so much better than an organ indifferently played.

Regular attendance (loyalty, if you like) is almost more important than expertise. I will qualify that by insisting once again that however simple the music, the standard aimed at must be the highest attainable, otherwise the music becomes a hindrance if not a positive discouragement to the celebration and those taking part. At the same time, let us, as St Augustine bids, not allow ourselves to be offended by the imperfect while we strive for the perfect.

In conclusion, people will respond so much better, and progress be made, if preparation can be arranged. The ideal is for the cantor, or priest, to take a short (five minute) practice at the advertised starting time of Mass (not five or ten minutes beforehand or the stragglers-in will distract) to go over the psalm response and Alleluia for the day, and to encourage with a few brief words the participation of the people in the Ordinary, hymns or whatever else is to be sung by them.

BRIEF CHECKLIST OF MATERIAL SUITABLE FOR PARISH USE

Note: at the time of writing few settings of the Ordinary of the Mass using the new ICEL/ICET texts of Gloria, Creed and Sanctus exist. Doubtless existing texts will continue to be sung for a time, and some established settings will be re-issued with the new words to Gloria, Creed and Sanctus.

BOOKS: Bill Tamblyn, *Sing Up*, Chapman, London, 1969: a guide to singing in church
Music and Liturgy, the quarterly magazine of the Society of St Gregory
Music in Catholic Worship, document of the USA Bishops' Committee on the Liturgy, Washington DC, 1972
Music in the Mass, National Commission for Catholic Church Music, CTS, London, 1969

MUSIC: *Sing the Mass*, ed N. Kenyon, Chapman, London, 1975: a comprehensive music manual
Psalms for Sundays, ed K. Mayhew, Mayhew McCrimmon, 1973, 1974

Responsorial Psalms, various composers, St Thomas More Centre for Pastoral Liturgy. Published in grouped booklets

Music for Holy Week, Dom Gregory Murray OSB et al, Mayhew McCrimmon, 1973

Praise the Lord, revised edition, Chapman, London, 1972. The best general hymnal available

The Simple Gradual, ed J. Ainslie, Chapman, London, 1968

Community Mass, Bill Tamblyn, Chiswick Music, London, 1974

Festival Mass, J. Gelineau, Boosey and Hawkes, London, 1974

LATIN MASS: *Jubilate Deo*, Vatican edition, Catholic Truth Society, London, 1974

Congregational Sung Latin Mass, Association for Latin Liturgy, 1974

FOLK MUSIC: *20th Century Folk Hymnal*, Mayhew McCrimmon

ORGANIZATIONS from whom information and assistance may be obtained:

Royal School of Church Music, Addington Palace, Croydon CR9 5AD

Organ Advisory Group of the CMA, Mr John Rowntree, Addington Palace, Croydon CR9 5AD

Irish Church Music Association, c/o Catholic Communications Institute, Veritas House, Lower Abbey Street, Dublin 1, Ireland

USA Catholic Conference, 1312 Massachusetts Avenue NW, Washington DC, 20005 USA

Society of Saint Gregory, Hon. Sec., Addington Palace, Croydon CR9 5AD

Association for Latin Liturgy (*not* the Latin Mass Society), 11 Barton Close, Cambridge

St Thomas More Centre for Pastoral Liturgy, 9-11 Henry Rd, London N4 2LH

Southwark Diocese Commission for the Liturgy, Hon. Sec., 34 Lucknow Street, London SE18 2SN

Consult your local Diocesan Directory, or the national Catholic Directory, for details of other diocesan liturgy commissions, who may run courses for readers and musicians in your area.

6. Movement in Liturgy

Frances Collins

Why movement?
In all cultures throughout history, tribal and folk dancing has expressed the basic themes of life itself, and has therefore remained constant in its fundamental forms. Its central interests are few, and this provides a basic unity and simplicity. Obviously, the religious dimension of life is one of the great central themes for expression which can encompass the whole gamut of human emotions and reflect the whole of human experience.

Movement is natural to a young child, and he will find little difficulty in mastering the necessary skill and discipline to enable him to take an active part in celebrating the liturgy. Children are often curious, original and resourceful – one often sees them 'acting out' situations in everyday life – and by creating expressive movements through which they can contribute and respond to the liturgy, one can lead them into the experience of involvement in the worshipping activity of the community. This should be an experience which children can enjoy, and this is appropriate because the liturgy is essentially a celebration of the joy which the risen Lord has given to his people. But this should not be restricted to little children. Teenagers, and adults too, can express themselves through movement.

What is movement?
In general, movement can be random or given form and shape so that it can express specific ideas and themes through motifs. Dance is movement that has been shaped in order to make it into a powerful, expressive language. It utilizes the whole human body in such a way that the body can be thought of as the primary human language. This is especially true, and can be seen to be so, in the case of children, whose earliest exploration of their world and of themselves is through the medium of the movements of their bodies. But dance is bound up with

66

rhythm. This can be either regular, with a steady beat, or it can take a freer form, in which case the dance is more like our natural movements. Regular patterns of rhythm can be established and sustained by hand-clapping, foot-stamping, etc. Dance, then, can be thought of as being a particular form of language.

Movement in the liturgy

Now let us look at the liturgy. Fundamentally any liturgical act is the same as David's Dance before the ark. It is an attempt to communicate with God and to open ourselves to God's communication. Our own twentieth-century western liturgy bears the marks of that over-concentration on words as a means of communication which is the hallmark of a literate culture, the Protestant liturgy, perhaps more so than the Catholic, and the reformed Catholic liturgy more so than its predecessor. Even so significant movement remains. We kneel, we make the sign of the cross, we bow; the celebrant is more privileged in this matter than the congregation, he has more to DO.

If we are fearful that the introduction of movement into the liturgy means the intrusion of something new or strange – let us begin with what is already there. Let us advert to the fact that there is movement and that it is *significant* movement. There is no practical reason why the priest at the consecration should raise his eyes upwards – he does so because he is imitating Jesus; and the action of Jesus at the Last Supper surely embodied his deep feeling of trust and reverence for his Father. That is what the gesture means – that is what the celebrant must try and mean. That is what the movement of the gesture will help him mean and feel.

The argument for movement having an important place in the liturgy lies precisely in its suitability for expressing emotion, and I trust none of my readers regard emotion as 'out of place' in our relationship with God.

A first step in any restoration of movement must be to begin with what we already have. So we must begin by taking the gestures at present written into the liturgy and making sure that their meaning is understood. Secondly, that they are well done. This brings in a principle which I have not so far mentioned, namely that human gestures are not only meaningful, they are also aesthetic. They can be done in ways which contradict their meaning or ways which enhance it. The difference between a bob and a reverent genuflection, a true sign of the cross and a vague flapping of the hand, is obvious. It is here that one must be willing to look for advice from the professionals in the same way as the preacher or the reader does.

Having begun in this modest way and tried to help one's congregation and the altar boys to understand that movement can be prayer, one may perhaps move tentatively towards thawing out the present liturgy from its somewhat immobile state. There are two important reasons for starting with children. The self-consciousness and emotional inhibitions of adult congregations are formidable obstacles upon which a frontal attack may well be disastrous, and therefore contrary to the whole purpose of what one is doing – the quite simple innovation of the sign of peace has demonstrated this. Secondly, children need movement. They are still innocent of the original sin of verbalization. They express themselves happily and fluently in movement and they can enter into something which calls for movement far more fully and for a greater length of time usually than they can listen. Moreover, they learn far more deeply from movement than through words.

Obviously, the main area for experiment here is in children's Masses and school Masses. But parish clergy might like to reflect on the possibility of introducing a few simple gestures or actions for children into any Mass at which they are present. The Offertory Procession is one that is already gaining ground. There must surely be other possibilities worth trying.

So far I have been commending a relatively small, though I believe very important, revolution in the use of movement in the liturgy; use which is a possibility for the future; much more elaborate and extensive use of movement has been an important element of the liturgy. Two categories may be mentioned though there is not a hard and fast line between them. They are the *ritual dance* and the *ritual mime*. Again it is useful to point out that these things are only apparently foreign to our present liturgy. One has only to think of such occasions as the Paschal Vigil, with the lighting of the new fire; the procession with the Paschal Candle; the unveiling of the cross, to realize that dance and mime are already present in the liturgy at least in a vestigial form. It will take a long time to extend and develop them, but it will be valuable precisely for the same reasons as ritual gesture: it will enable the Christian people to enter into the Christian mysteries and the drama of salvation at a deeper level than merely rehearsing it in words. One danger that will have to be guarded against will be the spirit of performance and the attitude of a spectator. The participatory liturgy that is the keynote of the Vatican II reform must not be imperilled – but having said that, one must ask whether a careful use of dramatic mime would not serve to convey the message of scripture more effectively than the repetition of verbal passages however well chosen. One cannot help feeling this particularly on occasions such as the Easter Vigil liturgy when listening to the readings can become an ascetic rather than a religious exercise.

Lastly, the phenomenon of significant movement in fact is proof of the fundamental axiom of Christian theology – the nature of man as an embodied person – an axiom of which the doctrines of the incarnation and resurrection are permanent witnesses – because man is an embodied person. God can only meet him if the word is made flesh, for the flesh is where human beings meet – because he is an embodied person, and he can only be saved as such.

Practical notes: the language of movement
The Language of Movement is made up of the natural actions of the body with the many variations possible, thus providing a rich source of material.
Basic movements which can be used in gesture during the Mass:
1. The up-down dimension – rising and sinking – or rising to praise and sinking to adore. The action consists of a reaching upwards above the head and a lowering of the body to the floor.
2. The side to side dimension – opening and closing – or turning to one side and then to the other and closing in a gesture of prayer. The action is a widening and extending away from the centre of the body; and a narrowing and drawing of parts towards the centre.
3. Forward-backward dimension – the action is an extending forwards, and a drawing backwards of the body: e.g. a re-action of the group in response to the priest when he says: 'The

Lord be with you' (priest uses the side to side dimension, in turning first to one side then to the other as he opens his arms to embrace all the congregation). Response: 'And also with you' from the people, who could take a small step forwards joining their own hands in gesture to the priest: i.e. each individual replies in a unison group to the words and gesture of the priest; they then step backwards to their starting position.

All these movements can be extended in their appropriate dimension either upwards with a leap or a jump; outwards with a complete turn; and forwards or backwards with either an increase or decrease of speed and pathway. Basically, though, one must also be concerned with weight transference: moving the body weight from one part of the body to another; loco-motion: travelling over the ground from one point to another; elevation: getting away from the floor and arriving back on to it; gesture: a pattern in the air, usually made with arms or legs and turning: a constant change of direction.

How to vary the movement
Movement takes place in time – that is, not only in duration of time but in the type of action, whether the movement is sudden or sustained.

Movement takes place in space – that is, in a small space or a large space; and the action can be curved or straight (flexible or direct). The *shape* of the movement can be round, angular, thin, or twisted.

Movement takes place with weight – that is, it can be firm or gentle in action; or light or heavy in sensation.

Movement takes place with tension – this may be greater or lesser; vigorous or delicate.

Movement takes place with flow – it can be continuous i.e. having an on-going quality; or bound i.e. having the quality of stopping at any moment.

Movement takes place at different levels – it can be high, medium or low.

Movement, then, can go forwards and backwards, side to side, up or down, diagonally; it can turn, jump etc., use a lot of space or just a small amount.

Movement is very much concerned with relationship to people – that is, we can do the same as somebody else, we can mirror their movement, we can follow their lead, respond to their action, break away from them, or be cornered in a group situation on our own etc.

Movement provides an intimate link between what emerges as visible to an observer, and the inner experience and feelings of the person moving. It is an expression of feeling and thought linked to the communication of a particular idea. A person, then, moves with an embodied mind.

A few hints on dance composition for those with some knowledge

1. PLACE TO START. Making a dance is very much like writing a composition: first find something to say, then say it as well as you can. In selecting a movement to state your case, consider the short, concise actions of children. Here are phrases clear as crystal, uncluttered with clichés or tricks. Cut through the surface of your movement, trim it down, uncover and simplify the source of reaction. Explore movement until you find a movement phrase that excites you, that seems fresh and right. Impose an order in what you have to say in movement, an order that will illuminate your point of view.

2. OUTLINE. Choose one movement phrase that seems important enough to be a theme. Clarify its rhythmic pattern, count the underlying beat, and make a note of it even if you just say that it is made up of three seven-counts, one five-count and a three. Let the movement establish the count. Manipulate your movement theme in space until you have found just the right design and space relationship. Don't forget where and how the movement begins, where it goes, and where it finishes. Make a sketch of the floor and air pattern.

3. FORM. Examine the way you use your energy. For instance it may be that the first two seven-counts are smooth and sweeping while the third retards to a stop. At the end of the statement of the first theme another decision must be made. Do you want to repeat it? Should you vary it? Should you develop a new theme? Something must happen. Eventually you will need a resolution and an ending. Consider the theme: the body shape; floor pattern; group shape; relationship of the group and individuals: is there a trio? a duo etc.? Is the dance

dramatic, i.e. does it tell a story and therefore must have a climax? Is it ritual, in which case it will probably be more formed and repetitive and also in unison? The form, then, must have variety and balance.

4. PITFALLS. Each movement must *mean* something, so do not try to fill the space with just any kind of movement. Have contrast, but not too much or too little. Don't wander from the subject. Don't compose a movement beyond the performers' ability either in technique or in expression. Make sure the movement is large enough to be seen. Never let the dance go on long after its point has been made. Finally, seek expert advice if you possibly can.

7. The Liturgy and Art

Patrick Reyntiens

I should like to start with three quotations.

'Pythagoras. Only the mystical conception of geometry could supply the degree of attention necessary for the beginning of such a science. Is it not recognized, moreover, that astronomy issues from astrology and chemistry from alchemy? But we interpret this filiation as an advance, whereas there is a degradation of the attention in it. Transcendental astrology and alchemy are the contemplation of Eternal truths in the symbols offered by the stars and the combination of substances. Astronomy and Chemistry are degradations of them. When astrology and alchemy become forms of magic they are still lower degradations of them. Attention only reaches its true dimension when it is religious.'
Simone Weil, *Gravity and Grace*, Routledge & Kegan Paul, London, 1952

> O Merlin in your crystal cave
> deep in the diamond of the day,
> Will there ever be a singer
> Whose music will smooth away
> The furrow drawn by Adam's finger
> Across the meadow and the wave?
> Or a runner who'll outrun
> Man's long shadow driving on,
> Break through the gate of memory
> And hang the apple on the tree?
> Will your magic ever show
> The sleeping bride shut in her bower,
> The day wreathed in its mound of snow
> And Time locked in his tower?

Merlin, from Edwin Muir, *Collected Poems*, Faber, London, 1960

'L'art chrétien n'estpas un espèce de genre—comme on dit "art byzantine" ou "ogival", c'est par le sujet où il se trouve et par

73

l'esprit d'où il procède que l'art chrétien se définit . . . c'est l'art de l'humanité rachetée . . . tout lui appartient, le profane comme le sacré.'

Jacques Maritain, *Art et Scholastique*

In an important letter to *The Tablet* some years ago the late David Jones pointed out that the (then) new liturgy was a hazard, if not a positive menace, because it deeply disturbed the form and inherited patterns of ceremonial prayer, and the calling to mind of things past. To a mind as original and illuminating as David Jones', with its acute sense of history and the importance of myth, the danger then lay in a generation's carrying out with indecent haste reforms which, from the point of view of culture, let alone cultus, entailed grave ecological risks. The reforms have been pressed through, and it is in the light of the subsequent post-tridentine scene that we should survey the possibilities of liturgy and art.

The turning point of David Jones' letter[1] was the affirmation that if there is no artefacture there is no Christian cult. Man is a sign-making animal and signs are significant; if there is no evidence of signs it is reasonable to infer that there is no structure of belief and communal memory capable of stimulating a valid sign language. If the quotation from Simone Weil at the head of this chapter is applied to the same problem as David Jones is talking about we begin to see the outlines of a great divide in opinion, and practical action arising from that difference of opinion. Not only opinion, but outlook and vision.

So far as can be seen, from the time of the revolution in mathematics in the seventeenth century, a gradual dilapidation of traditional metaphysics has come about, of which the result so far is the emergence of 'modern technological man'. Is technological man capable of making significant gestures based on a belief and a culture quite outside his own terms of reference? No indeed; and why should he be? Civilization based on utilitarianism (the only common bond in the plural society), cannot make signs valid for the expression of truths of another order altogether. The fundamental meaning, and the immediate vocabulary, are alike simply not there to con-

[1] See appendix to this chapter, p. 79.

struct signs out of. It is the inherent impossibility of the Church's calling on contemporary civilization for signs that it is unable to furnish, that makes David Jones' plea for the retention of the Church's corpus of culture convincing.

Because it is an old corporate structure dating from the time when the cult of memory was of practical worldly importance (apart from its intrinsic attachment to Christian cultus) the Church is almost the only recognizable social body which is deeply committed to memorabilia, outside of the useful and the frivolously pragmatic. Unfortunately the two categories, as a matter of history, can, and have, been confused: the nineteenth century in general and the gothic revival in particular, can be instanced. The employment of the gothic idiom could be seen as a psychological regression into fantasy in the face of developments in civilization which could neither be faced nor digested.[2]

Again the Gothic revival could be seen as the Church's participation in a pragmatic charade or costume parade; there are those who see significance in the coincidence of the constitution of the English hierarchy and the opening of the Great Exhibition. Significantly, perhaps against expectations, it was Cardinal Newman who opposed the gothic revival as something superficial and transitory, and he has been proved right.

[2] The whole a-memorative movement in art and architecture and engineering against which the Church was in reaction gathered momentum in the course of the nineteenth century and found eloquent expression in some of the courses of study in the Bauhaus (1919–29).

Memorative art would always seem to make use of the easiest means of production at its disposal. One can parallel the use of mass-manual skill in the production of phoney historical artefacts in the nineteenth century, *because it happened to be there*, with the particular use of electronic mechanisms for the production of historic music on modern record players. It is one of the quirks of civilization that the arts of recall have transferred themselves largely from the visual, as in all ages prior to the twentieth century, to the aural. As a result, we see no more immorality in listening to reconstructions of fourteenth- or sixteenth-century music than the Victorians experienced in sitting in reconstructions of fourteenth- or sixteenth-century churches. This slide of memorative association from one art form to another has only barely been hinted at by David Jones: but even if it *is* an interesting phenomenon in itself, it could not repair the destruction of an organic memorative structure, once the beginning of erosion is under way. The structure of the Church depends for the transmission of truth on a sophisticated calling-to-mind technique involving all arts. What seems so undernourished and deficient today is the extent and vocabulary of the technical means at the Church's disposal to effect anything. See Frances Yates, *The Art of Memory*, Routledge and Kegan Paul, London.

But from another point of view the gothic revival can be seen as the first attempt of the Church to constitute an admittedly pragmatic corpus of artefacture in the face of western civilization's recession from the Christian cultural position. It is from this point of view that the psychological aberration of the gothic revival still holds some historical relevance.

If technological man is incapable of *poiesis* how can the Church ask for help from such a culture without compromising her position? The cultural situation is far more advanced in decay than it was a hundred years ago; since the 1939–45 war, the more avant-guard the art forms, the more hermetic and undecipherable the message: the split between the avant-guard and his Church is deeper. It is impossible either to use art (but this is to reduce art to a negotiable commodity) or to enter into the train of thought that makes such art convincing, except in an individual capacity, individually investigating, and responding to the arcane messages of a seer, the artist.[3] Obviously if all Church art is concerned with corporate anamnesis the rapprochement with the avant-guarde is impossible except by individuals who are personally highly gifted in knowledge, intelligence and sympathy, such as the late Père Couturier and the present Dean of Chichester Cathedral.

Owing to the revolution in architectural calling-to-mind (there is no calling-to-mind in modern architecture) the vocabulary of space and projection and void along the wall surface has been virtually eliminated, making it impossible even to place traditional works of art such as paintings, statues and areas of hand-decoration (e.g. mosaics, and the like) without their taking on an air of over-exposure and self-consciousness. And further, the atmosphere and ethos of the modern Art Museum has penetrated the sub-conscious to such a degree that any art exhibited under those conditions tends

[3] I see it as the tragedy of modern civilization to exist without a transcendental metaphysic. I am well aware that to hold such a position would be to invite attack from members of the Catholic Church even. Nevertheless it is a melancholy fact that it seems only in times of war that the necessary fusion takes place when the 'sign and what is signified are one' (David Jones) and this is implicit in everyone's attitude at that time. It is a matter for infinite regret that the fusion does not take place except in isolated individual cases during peace, and this may well be the significance of the Church's role in wartime: for the first time people turn to an organization which has always preached self-transcendence in however old-fashioned and inadequate a manner.

to give the impression of being in process of peripatesis. We are apt to get uncomfortable if art does not move on. That consumer ethics apply to the arts in almost all museums is by now a commonplace, but it is an indication of a radical change of mind in the idea of the role of the work of art. This shift of emphasis has spread its influence far outside museums.

If the Church turns to its own rules of liturgical art it may avoid gross errors of taste and false theology but there is no possibility of an energetic and vital aesthetic coming from rules designed simply as a filter against aberrations. There is nothing positive about the rules and advice laid down on the ordering of churches so far as art, so far as *poeisis*, is concerned.[4] That this is evident can be proved by the number of Catholic churches in England which are unassailable from a liturgical point of view and yet are appallingly inadequate in every other way. Perhaps this phenomenon is truly an expression of the relationship between the civilization the Church is forced to make use of to put her message across and the traditions of Christianity. Only too often is the new church a botched job because the decision makers, priest or laity, do not know whom to go to. They do not know whom to go to outside, but they do not know whom to go to inside themselves either.

If the purpose of the new liturgy is to make quite explicit the message of Christ's coming, and all that that entails, to a people who have no means of understanding the language the Church has hitherto used, it must be said that the word 'liturgy' has been given far too restricted a meaning. All is reduced to the written word and that in itself is badly written. Unfortunately the most explicit *literary* quality of the new liturgy gives no positive mandate for exploration in any other dimension. Admittedly English culture has been predominantly aural since the sixteenth- and seventeenth-century revolution in aesthetics (one of the subsidiary results of the Reformation) but that is no excuse not to begin to explore other channels. However the exploration of other channels depends on the laity primarily for its direction and force, and the laity is simply not adequate for the job.

Inevitably the Church is the victim of the poverty of lay

---

[4] Too often indecision and indefinition are passed off as benignitude or liberalism, especially in the sphere of art and liturgical applied art.

culture on the one hand, and the overdrawing of her own cultural credit on the other.

To repair ecological damage takes a very long time, and this goes for situations of spiritual and cultural damage no less than geographical. If the liturgy is going to be an expression of the aliveness of peoples, of congregations, it must concentrate on the synthesis of inherited values and free extemporization coming from the laity. In this synthesis lies the hope of repair. Of course the education of laity and clergy in aesthetic as well as liturgical matters is urgent and must have priority. Unfortunately there is no evidence that training in knowledge, love and discernment in contemporary art and architecture (or indeed in the past or present traditions of ecclesiastical art) has any place in the average curriculum either of school or seminary.

The proper balance between memory and innovation will only come about by cultivation in charity of human relationships: then problems will be seen to be concrete and not abstract. After all, art arises as a result of human relationships and contacts. Whilst there is every reason for not heedlessly doing away with the past, even the gothic revival screen or statue that gets in the way, the strong sense of preservation inherent in the Church should be balanced by opportunities of spontaneity and expression on the part of people. This is not only difficult for parishes to rise to (inadequate cultural background, gross self-consciousness and so on) but, so far as the visual is concerned, it is extremely difficult from an administrative point of view. There exists at diocesan level no administrative possibility of coordinating various efforts which might be beyond one parish or deanery to put on. Such simple possibilities as a diocesan Christmas poster are beyond the means, imaginative, administrative or financial, of the average curia. However, something must be initiated, and soon.

A period of experiment in visual art is badly needed where the (by now) fixed norms of the liturgy are given life by being interpreted with spontaneity and enjoyment. Mistakes or wrong emphases will not matter if the heart and head are rightly orientated. It is the nature of ephemera to pass. Fear of experiment and spontaneity arises from the Church's past concern with the fixed expression of belief being permanently attached to the body, the physical matière, of the place of worship. This concern can never be denied especially in the face of the dangers that David Jones has drawn attention to, but it can, and must, be enlarged and expanded in all ways possible if the Church's message is to survive. It is on this survival that civilization depends if it is to avoid the only transcendental experience open to a utilitarian civilization, namely the prosecution of war.[5]

[5] Too often truly religious artists both inside and outside the Church are thrown back to the conviction that only by individual lyrical response can the message of transcendence be conveyed, having lost all faith in the validity and fecundity of canonic forms of art-belief-expression largely through seeing the existing inadequte or inept patronage of the church.

APPENDIX: DAVID JONES' LETTER TO *The Tablet* 7 DECEMBER 1967

Sir: Gratitude is, I think, owing to Miss Alexandria Zaina for her letter published in *The Times* of November 4th, for that letter gives frank, dignified and moving expression to a sense of frustration and loss felt by so many, who, for a complex of reasons, remain silent.

These feelings regarding what the reformers of the Roman Liturgy have already accomplished and made operative (with every indication that this is but a beginning) are by no means confined to Catholics, for that liturgy was a visual and aural liaison with the formative things of this island and of the religion-culture of the entire West. Hence the sense of anxiety among those who ask why the loss of so integral and, as was imagined, entailed a heritage, should, with extraordinary haste, be considered an unavoidable and pressing necessity by those responsible, that is those

Bischopes and bachelers, bothe maistres and doctours
That han cure under Criste and crounyng in tokne.

That the Catholic laity should, generally speaking, have remained acquiescent, is understandable for there is an innate reluctance to meddle with affairs that can be and are only decided upon by the 'maistres and doctours'.

In any case, in any matter, sacred or profane, it is highly embarrassing to remind the cobbler that there's nothing like leather.

However, the situation is now such that no matter to what degree we approve of the proverb 'every man to his last' (and the present writer holds that saying very dear – nearer a precept than a counsel) we are unable to rid ourselves of concern for what is being shaped on the ecclesial lasts, owing to the following considerations.

The Christian cult rests solidly on the presupposition that man is a sacramental animal: hence the Christian belief that the Eternal God, *Deo vero de Deo vero*, 'placed Himself in the order of signs'. You can't have 'signs' or 'sacraments' of any sort whatever without an involvement in *poiesis*. And the Catholic priesthood and those to whom it ministers are committed to an act of *poiesis* whereby sign and what is signified are one.

All of this is alien to the thought-forms of positivist technological man. That is to say it is at odds with the civilizational phase in which we chance to live.

None the less it is to this sacramental principle that the Christian *ecclesia* is committed. And it is by that commitment that She unconsciously asserts the validity of all signa-making, all extra-utile acts, all *poiesis*.

That much was ratified and made explicit at the festal board in the Upper Room in the Roman procuratorship of Judaea by the young hero 'þæt wæs God Ælmihtig' when in 'his habergeon: HVMANA NATVRA' woven for Him by the pliant *puella*, the gladius-pierced Mother, he, by manual acts and spoken words made certain material things, other. Hence: no artefacture, no Christian cult.

There is, I submit, a certain reluctance, not least among Christian ministers, to accept this fact and its implications.

Though it is quite impossible in a brief letter to do more than suggest that there is a connection, however unconscious, between this reluctance and the prevailing determination to be rid of the hieratic language of the Western rite, to change the rubrics which stressed the sacral character of what is either a profound and un-fathomable mystery or nothing; to transfer the emphasis from propitiatory Sacrifice to 'commemorative meal', to somehow diminish whatever most evoked the numi-nous; to abandon the modal Chant – that most superb of art-forms that the West has given to the world and which, incidentally, leads us back to the modal chant used in the Cenacle . . . as also the laticlaved tunica of the deacon, the planeta of the celebrant, lead us visually back to that world of Antiquity.

'By a love of things seen' some were, at least occasionally, 'drawn to a love of things unseen'.

Will the changes, no matter how well intended, but entailing so vast a loss, aid us, conditioned as we are all to this or that degree by the desacramentalized world in which we chance to live, to be more drawn toward those 'things unseen'? That is the question being asked by many touching what has already been imposed. Soon, apart from sound-recordings, we shall hear no more *Kyrie*, *Gloria* or *Agnus Dei*, or *Lauda Sion*, or *Salve Regina*, or *Dies Irae* or *Dona eis Requiem*. Is it to be wondered that many are perturbed?

David Jones

PS Since writing the above, I have been studying the ICEL version of the Canon. This document confirms the worst apprehensions. Every vestige of sacred beauty has gone by the board and its deliberate omissions are more ominous still.

Part Two

CELEBRATING THE EUCHARIST

8. The Parish Mass

Harold Winstone

THE OPENING CEREMONIES

In any celebration it is important to make a good beginning. If the right note is struck from the outset, there is every chance that the celebration will be a fruitful and joyful one. If on the other hand the beginning is off-key, if it bears no conceivable relationship to what is to follow, then it will fail in its purpose and be in danger of becoming an arid piece of ritualism.

The purpose of these introductory rites (entrance, greeting, penitential rite, Gloria, and opening prayer) is 'to help the assembled people to make themselves a worshipping community and to dispose them to listen to God's word and celebrate the eucharist' (GI 24).

a. *The entrance procession*

The entrance procession is itself a sign, and like any other sign can signify different things according to the way in which it is done. It can signify, for example, that the priest is careless about his robing and the state of his vestments; that he has not bothered to recruit servers or regards them as unnecessary to the celebration; or that the servers have just been having a scrap in the sacristy. It can also signify that great pains have been taken with the preparation for worship, that it has begun with prayer and that everyone involved is recollected and has a lively sense of the value and importance of his office.

They go to the altar in their order:

1. a server with lighted thurible (if incense is to be used).
2. two servers carrying lighted candles and between them a server with the cross; followed by other servers who will be taking part.
3. the reader, who may carry the Gospel Book.
4. the celebrant and other ministers.

If incense is going to be used, the priest puts some into the thurible before the procession starts (GI 82).

On occasion, it may be possible to involve the whole congregation in this entrance procession. The people will then walk behind the servers and in front of the celebrant and ministers.

b. *The entrance song*

The entrance song is intended as a chant to be sung during the entrance procession. 'Its purpose is to open the celebration, to foster union among the people, to introduce the mystery of the feast or season, and to accompany the procession' (GI 25). It follows that great care should be taken regarding the choice of entrance song. Just any hymn chosen at random from a restricted repertoire will obviously not do.

'It is to be sung by the choir and people alternately, or by a cantor and the people, or by the people or the choir alone. The antiphon and psalm of the Roman Gradual or the Simple Gradual may be used, or another song appropriate to this part of the Mass, the day or the season, the text of which has been approved by the bishops' conference' (GI 26).

We come to the inevitable question: What is the ideal form of entrance song? The answer cannot be given in universal terms, but the question is nevertheless an important one. It must be particularized: What is the ideal entrance for this people, in this church, at this Mass, with these resources, on this day, in these circumstances?

The ideal entrance song will be one which stirs this particular people to a lively sense of being a real community come together to celebrate. How one achieves this ideal is a different question. The priest needs to know his people, their home and cultural backgrounds, why they prefer to come to this particular Mass rather than any other. The remark is often made that our urban parish congregations are so variegated that the individuals have very little in common with each other and therefore cannot form a true community. But is a completely homogeneous gathering either necessary or indeed desirable? The fact is that a sizeable crowd has come together to celebrate this Mass and if the priest is to respect these people he cannot do less than consider their needs and desires and ensure that from the very outset they are going to feel at home and relaxed and drawn together in a common joyful celebration.

There is nothing which characterizes a service so much as the kind of entrance song which introduces it. If the service begins with a good old-fashioned hymn sung lustily by congregation and choir, a newcomer to the parish will feel instinctively that this is going to be a straight-forward kind of service and not too involving. Then there is what we might call the 'cathedral worship' type of entrance. In a cathedral there is traditionally a long and stately procession of bishop, ministers and assistants to the accompaniment of spirit-awakening music sung celestially by the choir. This type of entrance is reproduced more or less successfully at the principal Sunday Service in many a local parish church, both Anglican and Roman. If it is well done we have the feeling that we are going to be uplifted in heart and mind as we worship God 'in the beauty of holiness', and witness a well-rehearsed and well-conducted performance of the Church's ritual. If it is badly done we resign ourselves to an hour's aesthetic torment.

Between these two types of entrance there are a great many gradations. Much new music is being written and is being 'tried out' in different parishes with varied success. The important thing is to bear constantly in mind the purpose of the entrance song as outlined by the General Instruction and to make every effort to ensure that this purpose is being achieved.

But what of those Masses at which for one reason or another there is just no singing? Does it make sense to get the congregation to recite a text? This was an expedient which first came into vogue with the Dialogue Mass. It is liturgically a curious development, seemingly based on two principles:

1. that if a scriptural text meant for singing cannot for any reason be sung, it should be recited rather than omitted, and
2. it is better for the whole congregation to recite it rather than an individual, as this makes for active participation.

The new Roman Missal does not on the whole give encouragement to this view, but it does nevertheless supply an entrance antiphon for every Mass, with this instruction: 'If there is no singing at the entrance, the antiphon in the missal is recited either by the people, by a group, or by a reader. Otherwise it is said by the priest after the greeting' (GI 26).

It would seem that the purpose of these entrance antiphons in the Missal is to specify the liturgical theme. In the Anglican Order for Holy Communion (Series 3) they are called Seasonal Sentences and their use is optional. In the Roman Mass the texts themselves are not optional, but only the way in which they are rendered. The priest, therefore, and his liturgical team, has to give some thought to the best way in which to render them in the given circumstances. The best way will be the way which best answers their purpose. They might well form part of the priest's introduction to the Mass, after the greeting. To say, as the CTS translation of the General Instruction of the Roman Missal does say, that the priest will use them only 'as a last resort', implying that he should first do his best to get someone else to read them, is to read too much into the Latin word *aliter*, which just means *otherwise*, i.e. offering *another manner* of rendition. There is no suggestion that one way is better than another.

c. *The veneration of the altar and greeting of the people*
'When the priest and the ministers come to the sanctuary, they greet the altar. As a sign of reverence the priest and ordained ministers kiss the altar; the priest may also incense it' (GI 27).
'If the cross was carried in the procession it is placed near the altar or in some other suitable position; the candles borne by servers are placed near the altar or on the credence table; the Gospel book on the altar' (GI 84).

The use of incense still has its appeal as a symbol of prayer: the prayer of the saints (Apoc 5:8), and now that the psalms are better known to the Catholic laity, many will be familiar with the words 'Let my prayer come before you like incense' (Ps 140:2). Then, too, it would be a pity to lose altogether the age-old association of incense with sacrifice. Among the Israelites the offering of incense on the altar was a part of the priestly office (1 Sam 2:28). Incense is probably the only ritual symbol we have which appeals to the sense of smell as well as sight. The sense of smell is a much neglected sense in worship and celebration.
It is not suggested that incense be used at every Mass. It will

make its impact if it is used on the more solemn occasions when it is desirable to have something in reserve to enhance the celebration.

'The priest then goes to the chair. After the entrance song, while all are standing, the priest and the people make the sign of the cross. Then the priest, facing the people, extends his hands and greets all present using one of the forms indicated' (GI 86).

The greeting is in fact an *exchange* of greetings and the fervour and genuineness of the response may very well depend on the sincerity of the priest's original greeting. A perfunctory greeting is not likely to elicit more than a perfunctory and half-hearted response. It is surely strange that after two thousand years of Christianity, Christians have still no universal form of greeting except the liturgical one: *Dominus vobiscum: Et cum spiritu tuo*, and now that we want to use it meaningfully we cannot agree on how it should be translated. The formula 'And also with you' seems to be the worst possible of translations. Perhaps when we become a more consciously pentecostal community a better translation will suggest itself.

The greeting is also a welcome to the assembled community. It should come across as such. After the greeting the priest or his deacon may very briefly introduce the Mass of the day (GI 86).

All such 'interventions', as they are called, need careful preparation. The intention is not to preach to the people at this stage but to focus attention on the celebration, i.e. the liturgical mystery that is being celebrated, or the character of the Sunday or the season. We must always beware of trying to put the liturgy in a kind of straitjacket. God will speak to his people in different ways. All that is required is a disposition to listen, an openness to the Spirit, an atmosphere of prayer and praise. This is what the priest's intervention should aim at evoking, not the atmosphere of the classroom. The readings which are to follow may very well have a moral or didactic theme, but this is not what is being celebrated. We are assembled to celebrate the covenanted, sacrificed love of Christ in the eucharist.

d. *The penitential rite and Kyrie*

The priest's greeting and introduction should conclude with an invitation to take part in the penitential rite. A variety of forms is available for this rite, so that it need never become stale with use. The third form given in the Roman Missal may be varied to meet the local needs and occasions. Alternatively the priest and his liturgical team may compose other forms based on the readings, the theme of the Mass or season, or on ideas taken from scripture.

If the 'Lord have mercy' is included in the penitential invocations, it need not be repeated after the absolution.

'This acclamation, which praises the Lord and implores his mercy, is normally sung by everybody. The people, choir and cantor all have a part in it. Normally, each invocation is sung twice, but may be sung more often if desired, and a trope (short textual insertion) may be incorporated in it' (GI 30).

On Sundays an asperges rite (the blessing and sprinkling of holy water) may take the place of the penitential rite. This rite has been revised for the new Missal and has become a very attractive and pastorally orientated piece of liturgy. Apart from the advantage of introducing the baptismal symbol of water at the beginning of the celebration of Mass, it has all the elements of good liturgy in that it involves movement, song and popular participation. The blessing prayers are shorter than in the old rite. Three alternative prayers are given, the texts of which are all very good.

e. *The Gloria*

Glory to God in the highest is 'an ancient hymn in which the Church, assembled in the Spirit, gives praise and entreaty to the Father and the Lamb. It is sung by the congregation, by the people alternately with the choir, or by the choir alone. If it is not sung it is recited by all together or in alternation' (GI 31).

It is sung or said only on Sundays outside Advent and Lent, on solemnities and feasts, and in special local celebrations.

The decision on whether or not at a particular Mass the Gloria is to be sung or merely recited is one which should be considered carefully by the parish liturgy team. We tend to think in terms of sung Masses and said Masses, but the distinction is not helpful. At every Mass we should ask ourselves if it would not be better to sing this or the other text, or whether it would not be relevant to sing a suitable hymn at any particular juncture. On the other hand we must never fall into the way of thinking that at a solemn Mass every possible text has to be sung. A balance has to be struck. The introductory rites of the Mass tend to be very cumbersome, and if they were all observed with the maximum ceremony they might easily overload the celebration. They are intended to lead into the Service of the Word, not to overshadow it. They are preparatory ceremonies, not ceremonies in their own right. All this has to be borne in mind when planning the celebration.

It is a pity perhaps that the same latitude has not been given in the Roman Mass with regard to the positioning of the Gloria as has been accorded in Series 3. In the new Anglican Order for Holy Communion the Gloria may be sung in any one of four places: at the entrance, after the Kyrie, before the Gospel, or after the communion.

f. *The opening prayer*
The opening prayer, or Collect, concludes the Introductory Rite. First 'the priest invites the people to pray, and together they spend some moments in silence, so that they may realize that they are in God's presence and may formulate their petitions' (GI 32).

The formal invitation to prayer ('Let us pray') may be amplified by the priest so as to give the people a starting point. It is unreasonable to expect people to pray in a vacuum. If they are invited to pray, they should at least be given some indication of what to pray about. Then the silence should be long enough to allow for genuine prayer on the part of the assembled community.

The collects are short, simple prayers, designed to sum up, not to replace, the prayer of the community. Because they are so short, they need to be recited slowly and prayerfully. The language, particularly of the ICEL prayers, is stark and unadorned; the expression neither rhetorical nor consciously poetic. They can be prayed in all honesty and sincerity and will convey only that degree of feeling which the user puts into them. In other words, they will not carry the burden of prayer, they will not do the praying for the community. They are designed merely as instruments of prayer. ICEL does however provide alternative opening prayers for those who prefer to use something more elaborate and poetic. These may be found useful in more intimate, small group Masses, but may be used at any Mass according to the choice of the priest and his liturgical team.

On ferial days throughout the year the Mass prayers may be taken from the preceding Sunday, from another Sunday *per annum*, or from the prayers for various occasions.

THE LITURGY OF THE WORD OF GOD

'Readings from scripture and the chants between the readings from the main part of the Liturgy of the Word. The homily, profession of faith and general intercession develop and complete it. In the readings God speaks to his people of redemption and salvation and nourishes their spirit; Christ is himself present among the faithful by his word' (GI 33).

All that has gone before should climax in the readings, but this is not always evident in our parish liturgy. Indeed after a searching penitential rite and an elaborate Gloria, the settling down of the congregation to listen to the readings might very well bring the feeling of anticlimax. As president of the assembly the priest must be aware of this danger and do all he can to obviate it. Sometimes a very brief introduction to the readings may be found helpful, something like 'And now God himself will be speaking to us, so let us open our hearts to receive his word.'

a. *The readings*
'In the readings the table of God's word is laid before the people and the treasures of the bible are opened to them. Reading the scriptures is by tradition considered a ministerial, not a presidential function. Hence the deacon – or, if no deacon is present, some other priest – should read the Gospel. A lector reads the other extracts. In the absence of a deacon or another priest, the celebrant reads the Gospel' (GI 34).

The main concern of the president should be to bring about such conditions as make it possible for God's word to be heard in the assembly with as little distraction as possible. Certain distractions, such as crying babies, may be unavoidable to a large extent, and anyway God can speak to us in the cry of a child. There are more fundamental causes that can impede the word of God.

The first, obviously, is inaudibility. This may be due to a defective public address system. In the past, speakers seem to have made themselves heard in church without this aid, but nowadays most churches have some kind of amplification system installed. In many churches, however, the system is either inadequate, faulty or badly designed, with the result that it is more of a hindrance than a help. Then the readers have to be trained to use the system properly; to know, for example, how close to the microphone they have to stand and how loudly and clearly they need to speak.

Unintelligent reading is another cause of irritation rather than edification. The priest who picks his readers at random just before the Mass is due to begin is asking for this trouble. Ideally the parish readers should form a group that will meet together in the course of the week to study the readings and make them the food of their life of prayer. They will then be able to read with conviction and reverence. It requires a great degree of humility to be a good reader in church. The self must be subordinated and become in every sense a servant of the word.

A brief thematic introduction to the readings can often be helpful, provided it is realized that in any event God will speak to the individual in his own way. We have no need to be over-anxious lest this or that point of instruction or doctrine be missed. A good president of the assembly can do no more than help to create conditions favourable for hearing the word of God. He cannot predetermine what God is going to say to each person present. It is probably a mistake to rely too heavily on themes. There is usually some thematic link between the Old Testament reading and the Gospel on the Sundays in Ordinary Time, but the second reading is the beginning or continuation of an epistle and may bear no thematic relation to any other liturgical text of the day.

Sometimes the readings can be enhanced by some form of dramatic presentation, such as the use of two or three readers taking parts, as in the reading of the Passion on Good Friday. A change of voice is always helpful and there can be no valid objection nowadays to women readers. The same reader should not normally read two lessons (including, as sometimes happens, the responsorial psalm).

The priest has a certain autonomy over the lectionary for pastoral reasons, but it should be exercised with great discretion. The Sunday liturgy should normally present the readings given in the lectionary for that Sunday. As regards weekdays, there is an interesting paragraph in the General Instruction which reads as follows:

'If the continuous reading is interrupted by a feast or special celebration, the priest should consider in advance the entire week's readings and, if the weekday readings which will be suppressed seem to be important, he may combine the weekday readings to include them, or he may omit the less important ones' (GI 319).

The liturgy of the word climaxes in the Gospel and this should be made evident by the ceremonies which herald its proclamation: e.g. the procession with the book to the lectern preceded by acolytes with lighted candles and accompanied by the Alleluia chant; the incensation of the book, etc.

'The liturgy teaches that the reading of the Gospel should be done with great reverence; it is distinguished from the other readings by special marks of honour. A special minister is appointed to proclaim it and he prepares himself by a blessing or prayer. By standing to hear the reading and by their acclamations, the people recognize and acknowledge that Christ is present and speaking to them. Marks of reverence are also given to the book of Gospel itself' (GI 35).

b. *Chants between readings*
Depending on the character of the reading, it may be beneficial to follow it with a period of silent prayer. 'Silence should be observed at designated times as part of the celebration, e.g. at the conclusion of a reading or a homily' (GI 23).

The responsorial psalm comes after the first reading and is an integral part of the liturgy of the word. It is ordinarily taken from the lectionary, since these texts are directly related to their respective readings. However, to help people to sing a responsory to the psalm verses, certain psalms and responsories have been chosen for use throughout the different seasons of the year and for the feasts of particular categories of saints. These may be used instead of the psalms given in the lectionary, or appropriate psalms from the *Roman Gradual* or the *Simple Gradual* may be sung (GI 36).

The Alleluia, or (according to the season) the Gospel Acclamation, is sung after the second reading. If there are only two readings in the Mass, either the psalm or the Alleluia or Gospel acclamation may be used. The responsorial psalm is to be said if it is not sung, but the Alleluia or Gospel acclamation if not sung may be omitted.

There is some virtue in reading the responsorial psalm if it is not to be sung, as it is a prayer in its own right and can be used as a prayerful meditation on the first reading. But it is doubtful whether it is at all helpful – and it is certainly not necessary – for the congregation to recite together the response after every verse. The response is a singing text, not a text for recitation. The continual repetition of a text, especially if it is not a very inspiring one, can become extremely irksome to an adult community. If they are to take any part at all in a recited psalm, it would be better if they recited alternate verses with the reader.

Better, of course, to *sing* the psalm and the response. Many good settings have been written for these psalms, with simple melodies for the response which the people can learn very quickly in a brief rehearsal before Mass begins.

c. *The homily and creed*
'The homily is strongly recommended as an integral part of the liturgy and as a necessary source of nourishment of the Christian life. It should develop some point of the readings or of another text from the Proper of the Mass of the day. The preacher should keep in mind the mystery that is being celebrated and the needs of the particular community' (GI 41).

The first thing to be said about the homily is that it does not exist in its own right. It is an integral part, not just of liturgy, but of this liturgy which is being celebrated on this particular day with these people.

Secondly, it is in no sense an interlude or breathing-space between two parts of a service. It is part of the on-going movement of the one celebration which, beginning with the proclamation of the word, will culminate in the embodiment of that word in the community through its sacramental union with Christ in the eucharist. The homily, then, should observe and assist this on-going movement. It should proclaim and make evident what God is accomplishing in his people through the liturgy that is being celebrated on this day.

The task of the celebrant as preacher is therefore no light one. He must be in command of the liturgical situation and be possessed with a genuine sense of occasion. He must know not only his liturgy, scripture, theology, etc., but also his people, for what he says must be accommodated to their understanding and their needs and concerns. He is a servant of the word and a servant of the people.

d. *The profession of faith*

'In the profession of faith or creed the people have the opportunity to respond and give assent to the word of God which they have heard in the readings and the homily, and to recall the main truths of the faith before they begin the celebration of the eucharist' (GI 43).

It is said by priest and people together, or if sung, is normally done together or in alternation. It occurs on all Sundays and solemn feasts, and may also be used on other specially solemn occasions (GI 44).

The constant repetition of a lengthy text Sunday after Sunday can have a very stultifying effect, and anything that can be done to vary the manner of rendition is all to the good. But it should be realized that it is a community act of faith which incorporates at the *incarnatus est* a common gesture of reverence and humility – a bow or, on the feast of the Annunciation and Christmas, a genuflection. This bow is not noticeable in most of our celebrations because the people's heads are already bowed – over their books. One should ask oneself if

94

printed texts of the creed cannot be dispensed with altogether. A community can very soon learn to recite or sing a text together without these aids. The very fact that one has sometimes to rely on the promptings of one's neighbours can help to make the profession of faith a more genuinely corporate act.

e. *General intercessions*
    'In the general intercessions, or prayer of the faithful, the people exercise their priestly function by interceding for all mankind' (GI 45).

The intercessions should flow from the readings, meditation and homily. They are not meant to be an extraneous insertion into our liturgy, bearing no relation to what has preceded and what follows. Christians meditating on the word of God will want at this point to vocalize their thoughts and express their concern for the needs of mankind in words inspired by their new understanding of the Christian message. Such a desire is inevitable in a priestly people.

The composition of 'biddings' is therefore a delicate operation and one which requires a high degree of sensitivity. In small-group Masses they can be spontaneous, but a high degree of 'articulateness' cannot be expected at a normal parish Mass, however open the community may be to the promptings of the Spirit. They should nevertheless represent the genuine concerns of the community, and as many parishioners as possible should be involved in their composition.

They should not be composed in prayer form, but in the form of invitations to prayer. They should state clearly and simply the intention for which the prayer of the community is asked.

'The priest directs the prayer: in a brief introduction he invites the people to pray and after the intentions says a concluding prayer. It is desirable that the intentions be announced by the deacon, cantor, or other person. The community expresses its prayer either by a common response after each intention or by silent prayer' (GI 47).

THE LITURGY OF THE EUCHARIST

a. *Preparing the altar and presenting the gifts*
    'At the beginning of the liturgy of the eucharist, the gifts

95

which will become the Lord's body and blood are brought to the altar. First the altar, the Lord's table, is prepared as the central point of the whole eucharistic liturgy. The corporal, purificator, chalice and missal are put on it. The offerings are then brought forward: it is desirable for the faithful to present the bread and wine . . .' (GI 49).

This dramatic expression of the people's involvement in the action of the liturgy dates from quite early times. Detailed regulations for it are given in the various Roman *Ordines*, but in the West elaborate offertory processions gradually died out after the twelfth century, except on certain occasions and in certain places.

The new Roman Missal has now restored them as a desirable feature of our parish liturgy. Attention must therefore be given to the way in which it is done. A slip-shod presentation of gifts will obviously not do. Either it must be significant and impressive or it is best omitted.

If the church is not too large it is possible to involve everyone in an offertory procession, though it will need a bit of organizing. The acolytes with lighted candles and other servers go to the table at the end of the church where the dish of altar-breads and the wine have been prepared. The altar servers will then take up the bread and wine and walk back to the altar behind the acolytes. They will be followed by the people bringing their offertory envelopes which they deposit in baskets held by sidesmen standing in the sanctuary on either side of the celebrant and other ministers. Meanwhile an offertory hymn is sung. The advantage of this method is that there is movement, and there can be no real celebration without movement.

Obviously a procession of this sort must be orderly and not too protracted. Where the congregation is a large one, or in a church which does not offer much room for walking about, other methods must be thought out. Parish groups, children, young people, etc., can be deputed to bring forward the gifts. It will still be a good idea to have acolytes leading the procession, and if incense is to be used the thurifer can also take part.

Certain groups in the parish may be able to devise a dance

or stately walk for the bringing forward of the gifts, and, provided it is well done, nothing is better able to enhance the mood of celebration.

The president should receive the gifts from the people with obvious gratitude. If only a small group has been involved and music rather than song has accompanied the procession, it may be very effective if the president pronounces the blessing at once. That is to say, he can take the dish of altarbreads from the giver and at once hold it up and say 'Blessed are you, Lord God of all creation . . .' Similarly, he can take the chalice of wine from the hands of the giver, get the deacon to pour a drop of water into it, and at once hold it up and say the prescribed blessing. The group then disbands and the celebrant and ministers put the gifts on the altar and perhaps incense them. There is nothing in the General Instruction which directs that the gifts be put on the altar before the blessings – rather the contrary, cf 102.

The celebrant then washes his hands and invites the people to pray that God may accept their sacrifice. He concludes this part of the rite with the prayer over the gifts.

b. *The preface and eucharistic prayer*
The celebrant now 'makes eucharist' in the official prayer of praise and thanksgiving – variously called the prex, canon, anaphora, and eucharistic prayer – which has its origin in the table blessings of the Hebrews which Christ himself recited when he 'said the blessing' over the bread and wine at the Last Supper.

The prayer is preceded by a dialogue which is also in the Hebrew tradition. For example, at the end of a ritual meal the father of the family would take up a cup of wine and say to those present: 'Let us give thanks to our God who has nourished us and by whose bounty we have life.' Those at table would then reply: 'Blessed is he whose bounty has nourished us and whose goodness is the source of life.'

The eucharistic prayer is described in the General Instruction as 'the climax and very heart of the entire celebration' (54). The celebrant's demeanour should make this clear from the very outset in the way in which he invites the people to lift up their hearts.

A decision has to be made on whether the prayer is to be recited or sung, and this must depend not on whether we are having a sung Mass or a 'low' Mass, but on what manner of presentation will highlight the prayer as 'the climax and very heart' of the particular celebration. If up to this point there has been a lot of music and singing, then it may be thought better to recite the eucharistic prayer slowly and prayerfully so as to make a fitting contrast to the rest of the celebration. On the other hand, the preface is a lyrical composition and, leading in as it does to the people's acclamation 'Holy, holy', this part of the prayer at least almost cries out to be sung. At a celebration, however, where there has been little, if any, singing the celebrant may decide that he can best highlight the eucharistic prayer by singing it rather than just reciting it. If he does so, he should render it lightly and joyfully, not ponderously and clumsily. Unfortunately, perhaps, a well modulated and trained singing voice is not one of the qualifications for ordination.

Another way of reminding the people that the climax and very heart of the celebration has been reached is by saying so before the introductory dialogue, and perhaps explaining briefly why the particular eucharistic prayer has been chosen for today's celebration. There are marked differences between the four eucharistic prayers that are currently in use, and any of these differences might influence the choice of one rather than another for a particular celebration.

The structure of the eucharistic prayer is based on the traditional Hebrew blessing prayers (*berakoth*). Such prayers (cf Ecclus 51 : 1–17) begin with a general statement of praise and thanksgiving to God, the creator of the universe: 'We do well always and everywhere to give you thanks.' They then state specific reasons for praising God here and now. These specific reasons are enumerated in our seasonal prefaces, culminating in what God has done for us through Christ our Lord. They then commemorate God's past mercies, not just as past and done with, but as ever present in their effects in his people: 'The day before he suffered (i.e. in the past) he took bread . . .' 'And so now, Father, we celebrate the memory of Christ your Son. We recall his passion . . .' This part of the blessing prayer is called the *anamnesis* – the memorial celebration. The prayers

then beg for God's continued help. This explains the inclusion
in our eucharistic prayers of intercessions for the Church and
commemorations of the living and the dead. Finally, these
prayers conclude as they began with a general statement of
praise and thanksgiving: 'all glory and honour is yours,
almighty Father, for ever and ever.'

Though based structurally on the Hebrew prayer of blessing,
a eucharistic prayer has the added dimension of being consecratory, i.e. by the power of Christ and the 'working' of the
Holy Spirit it changes the elements of bread and wine into
Christ's covenanted body and blood. For this reason all eucharistic prayers include at least implicitly an invocation of the
Holy Spirit, called an *epiclesis*. In the three new canons the
epiclesis is in two parts. Before the words of institution the
Father is asked to send his Holy Spirit on the gifts so that they
may become the body and blood of Christ. After the anamnesis
and offering, the Spirit is again invoked so that the Church in
receiving these gifts may itself be transformed into the body of
Christ.

The eucharistic prayer is specifically the prayer of the priest.
It is 'the prayer which he addresses to God the Father, through
Jesus Christ, in the name of the whole community' (54). Con-
celebrating priests have their part in this prayer, but the vocal
participation of the people is confined to the acclamations, i.e.
the *Holy, holy*, the eucharistic acclamation after the words of
institution, and the final, 'great' Amen. In some churches the
custom has arisen of making the final doxology ('through him,
with him,' etc.) a public acclamation. This custom, which
seems to have sprung from the genuine desire of the people to
associate themselves with this statement of praise, is clearly not
something that needs to be discouraged. It does not derogate
from the general principle that the eucharistic prayer is the
official prayer of the priest.

c. *Communion*

The rite of proximate preparation for communion begins with
the singing or recitation of the Lord's Prayer, the final invocation of which is expanded by the priest in what is called the
embolism, leading into the acclamation: 'For the kingdom, the
power and the glory are yours, now and for ever.' Various

'through compositions', i.e. musical settings for the whole rite, beginning with the invitation and ending with the doxology, have been composed and are worth learning, if only for the reason that they impose an obvious unity on what might otherwise appear a succession of prayers and responses.

This is followed by the rite of peace. 'By word and gesture the people pray for peace and unity in the Church and the whole human family, and express their love for one another before they share the one bread' (GI 56).

It is probably true to say that the effectiveness of the liturgical celebration *qua* celebration can be gauged by the readiness with which the people are prepared to make this gesture of peace with one another at this point. Some would advocate ritualizing the gesture or confining it to a friendly nod, avoiding physical contact (which is un-English except on the football field), but it is probably better to let it be spontaneous. It is normal and natural for people who are not very well acquainted to shake hands with each other. However, it is not normal for a husband to shake hands with his wife or with his small children. For them the natural thing is to kiss, and why not? It would be a pity if this gesture, which is a real break-through in liturgical celebration, should become formalized and stilted at the very outset.

In churches where there is no great spatial separation between priest and people, the priest himself can set the tone by moving among the people and greeting them with both hands, smiling at them as he does so, and making a special point of greeting the elderly, newcomers to the parish, those who have come back after long illness, small children, and reluctant teenagers. It does not really take up much time to do this, but if it seems to, let the choir sing 'Peace I leave' or 'Shalom'. Or the concelebrants or ministers (even the altar servers) can each take on a particular area of the church. With a little effort and genuine goodwill, it will not be long before the liturgical rite of peace welds the parish into a friendly and open community.

The breaking of the bread and the commingling is the third element of preparation for communion. 'The purpose of breaking the bread is not merely practical; it is intended to show symbolically that through communion we, though many, form

one body, because we eat the one bread of life which is Christ'
(GI 56c).

If this symbolism is really to be understood, then it is time we
used much larger hosts which can in fact be broken into many
fragments for the people. Nothing much is symbolized by breaking the priest's host into two, when he is going to consume both
halves himself anyway.

'During the breaking of the bread the invocation "Lamb of
God" is usually sung by the choir, or the cantor with the
people responding. If it is not sung it should be said aloud.
The invocation may be repeated as often as is needed to
cover the whole action of the breaking of the bread. The
concluding words are "grant us peace" ' (GI 56e).

Finally the priest invites the faithful to come to the Lord's
table to receive communion.

'It is important that the hosts given to the faithful should be
those consecrated in that same Mass, and that on authorized
occasions they should also share in the chalice. The reason
for this is that their participation in the sacrifice that is being
celebrated is thereby more visibly manifested' (GI 56h).

At this point, too, it is possible to manifest more visibly the
parish's pastoral care of the sick and the housebound. They
cannot be physically present at this Mass but they can nevertheless share its fruits, and those who *are* present can see this
happening and know that they are united in the communion
of the Lord with their sick and ailing brethren. All that is
needed is that the deacon, or commissioned laymen and women,
should be summoned to the altar at the time of communion to
be given the hosts which they will then and there take to the
homes of the sick and to those in hospital.

The manner in which communion is distributed to the faithful and received by them will depend to a large extent on local
custom and local decrees of the bishops. The General Instruction makes no mention of communion rails or of the posture of
the people in receiving communion. The personal preferences
of the faithful should be respected, and it is in any event wrong
to make an issue out of matters which are of relatively minor
importance. The important thing is that every Catholic who

believes himself to be in a state of grace should feel free to come joyfully and without inhibition to the Lord's table to share with his brethren in the meal of the sacrifice they have been celebrating together.

The communion song is intended to accompany the procession to the altar and to express the joy of the community. There is here the same degree of choice as that allowed for the entrance procession, with the same directive that if there is no singing then someone – perhaps the whole community – should recite the communion antiphon that is to be found in the Missal.

After communion there should be a period of silent prayer. In order to avoid unnecessary movement during this period, the sacred vessels may be put on a side table and purified after the end of Mass. The priest may introduce this silence with the words 'Let us pray'. This makes more sense than saying 'Let us pray' after the silence, as though the people had not been praying all the time. After an appreciable silence the priest rises and sums up the prayers of the community by reading the official prayer after communion.

Brief announcements may be made after this prayer, and these are followed by the blessing and dismissal. The new Roman Missal contains a rich variety of blessings and prayers over the people. The priest should be familiar with these and know when to use them.

A hymn may be sung to accompany the procession back to the sacristy. In general, it should be a joyful hymn of thanksgiving. There are some hymns to which one can clap an accompaniment. Children love these, and it is always gratifying to see people leaving church with smiles on their faces.

9. Children at Mass

Edward Matthews

My earliest memory of going to Mass as a child is of the taste.
Not the taste of the consecrated Host, as you might piously
expect, but the taste of the pew in which I was kneeling. I was
small, and occupying a place designed for a fully-grown adult.
My mouth most conveniently and deliciously found itself on
the same level with that part of the pew designed for elbows.
What more natural action than to suck and lick to see how it
tasted!

I can recall the flavour even today. Never was there a tastier
morsel than that ancient varnish, worn by the hands and
clothes of generations of worshippers. The pungent aroma of the
incense, billowing in great clouds from the distant sanctuary,
added to the sensation. Occasionally, in mid-suck, my eye
would be caught by the sight of my grandmother in the distant
centre of the church, following the Mass quietly and devoutly.

And there is the reason for my pew-tasting: the grown-ups
could see and follow the Mass well enough, but not so the
children. We were parked in a narrow side-aisle from which our
view of the sanctuary and all that was going on there was
obstructed by a couple of enormous pillars. In such a situation
what could we children do but find our own entertainment?
Mine was pew-tasting.

The point I am making is that there was no provision for
children at Mass. No provision, that is, other than being parked
in the darkest and least convenient part of the church. It was
the adults who were given the best places: it was only they who
could see and follow what was going on during the Mass. This
appeared to be the natural order of things and nobody questioned its correctness. The Mass was an adult affair, a 'mystery',
which children would not fully understand until they had
grown up.

Having said that, it must be admitted that the adults were
not much better off. Although they could see the action of the

Mass, their attitude was that of spectators. The little participation allowed was confined to the brief moment of communion and a sort of mental participation from a distance.

But times have changed, and that state of affairs has vanished from our churches (or it should have done). Participation, 'which is demanded by the very nature of the liturgy' (CL 14) is commonplace: clergy and laity now understand more clearly the different roles that they must play in the Church's worship – roles which are an illustration of the ordered structure of the Mystical Body (cf CL 26).

For ten years, however, the problem of children at Mass has remained. No amount of vernacular, simplified gesture, etc. is capable of producing the fruitful participation of children if that vernacular language and those gestures are adult in form. Admittedly, the children have a better chance of participating; but the difference between the old Latin liturgy and the newly reformed liturgy in adult form is narrow. To rectify this situation, to make it possible for young children to participate in the liturgy fully, consciously and actively (cf CL 14), the Sacred Congregation for Divine Worship, published, 1 November 1973, a Directory for Masses with Children.

Such importance is attached to this document that the Congregation has stipulated that it should be regarded as a supplement to the General Instruction on the Roman Missal (Directory for Masses with Children – hereinafter referred to as D – no. 4). This is important because it tells us that the Directory is not an optional extra, the application of which depends upon the personal likes and dislikes of the local community. Its inclusion in the Roman Missal as a supplement gives it a power and authority commensurate with the importance of the task it is designed to undertake. Nobody, priest or layman, who has the pastoral care of young children, can afford to ignore it.

Why the Directory?
I have said that there was a need for the participation of children in the Mass. That is a position which requires some justification because there are many people who would dispute it. Is it not enough, they would say, for a child to attend the adult liturgy and in that way develop a growing awareness and

love of it? To answer this objection requires a little thought: we cannot reply simply that 'it feels right'. There is a theological/liturgical basis to the Directory which we should examine.

First of all let us clear our minds of any one-sided view of the liturgy. One such view is characterized by those who see the liturgy as one big downward movement of God to man, and nothing else. Such a one would describe the liturgy as 'God coming to us, giving us grace, giving us confidence that something always happens once the "secret formula" is pronounced'. This passive attitude to worship is not uncommon. And why not? After all, God *does* come to us in the liturgy, we *do* receive grace, we *are* confident that the sacrament will achieve its effect. The trouble with that view is that it is too one-sided.

Equally unbalanced is the view at the other end of the spectrum which can see in the liturgy only a massive exercise in self-expression. In this view it is God who is the grateful recipient of man's favours. The reality of liturgy lies between the two extremes. It is the action of both God and man because it is the action of the Mystical Body.

Pope Pius XII, in the encyclical *Mediator Dei*, gave us the classic definition when he said that liturgy 'is the whole worship of the Mystical Body of Jesus Christ, that is, of the Head and its members'. The point to note here is the view of liturgy as a positive action: not a passive reception. In liturgy we do something.

Who are the 'we' who worship? First of all we are human beings – redeemed, but still human. Being human means a union of soul and body, so that without one or the other, man is not a complete human being. Liturgy must respect this duality by being neither a wholly interior act nor one of merely superficial action. The sort of worship we offer to God should express the nature of the people God made.

Worship is truly human – an act of body and soul. Therefore not only should it be 'spiritual', in the sense of it being an interior act, but it should also be physical. That is why words, gestures, movement, signs and symbols play an essential part in our liturgy. Without such use of the body it would be the action of disembodied spirits.

Take it a step further. Liturgy is the worship of God by a community – the Mystical Body. This involves relating to the

God we worship, and relating to the people with whom we worship – what some have termed the vertical and horizontal relationships within the liturgy. Once again we encounter a dual aspect: the Body is united with Christ its Head in a union which is real but spiritual, and this is manifested by the union of the other members of the community amongst themselves – a union which is physical because the members are human, have bodies and must relate to each other in a human fashion, in a way consonant with their nature. So, once again, the need for words, gestures, signs and symbols.

Liturgy is physical and spiritual. It is the worship of people as they are. There is no reason why this same principle should not be applied to children, the only difference being that the physical part of liturgy will have to be 'tailored' to meet their needs, to be a genuine expression of their faith and their encounter with God.

Baptism the key to worship
Although children differ from adults by reason of their age, in another sense they are equal with one another. The levelling factor is baptism; that sacrament ensures that all, young and old alike, are members of the Mystical Body of Christ. Age, or lack of it, makes no difference to status in the kingdom of God. When the apostles attempted to stop children from going near Jesus he was quick to reprove them, using the now-famous words, 'Suffer little children to come unto me.' We might apply those same words to participation in the liturgy.

The adult form of the Mass must be our ultimate aim for children because adulthood means maturity and a greater capacity to love God (cf D 21). Meanwhile we should be leading our children, slowly and gradually, to the point at which they can play a full part in adult worship. Just as normally you do not teach a child to swim by throwing him in at the deep end of the pool, so you cannot expect a child fully to comprehend the Mass if all he experiences is the adult form. Therefore children must be allowed to break through the surrounding cordon of adult liturgy and thus meet Christ in the liturgy on his and their own terms.

Baptism gives children the right of access to Christ in the liturgy. After the pouring of water in the baptismal rite there is an anointing with chrism which is a sign that the new Christian is a participant in the prophetic, kingly and priestly roles of Christ. Children are therefore sharers in the priesthood of Christ. They are true worshippers of the Father. It is the duty of the Church to see that the children are able to carry out their duties of worship in a manner suited to their nature (cf D 1).

Obligation of participation

Participation is not an optional matter: that is a conclusion that can be drawn from what has already been said. Vatican II expressed the idea in more forceful language when it stated that 'full, conscious and active participation in liturgical celebrations . . . is demanded by the very nature of the liturgy' (CL 14). Not a participation confined to one or two favourite parts of the liturgy, nor with only half of one's mind, nor with the totally unthinking habit of years, nor with a passive 'let-the-others-get-on-with-it' attitude. Participation must be 'full, conscious and active'.

The Council goes even further: 'Such participation by the Christian people as "a chosen race, a royal priesthood, a holy nation, a purchased people" (1 Peter 2:9; cf 2:4–5), is their right and duty by reason of their baptism' (CL 14). Baptism – there it is again. Thus even children have the right and duty of participation in the Mass. Can they do so in adult forms? No. Some adaptation is essential. Hence the need for the Directory.

Adaptation does not destroy

Adaptation means the application of 'tailored' forms of liturgy to particular groups, or circumstances. It does not mean the alteration or elimination of what is essential. Misunderstandings arise from faulty knowledge of what is essential and what is not.

Space forbids a detailed survey of what is open to adaptation and what is not, but there is no doubt that adaptation can go much further than most people realize. By and large, it is the internal structures of the liturgy which must alone remain constant. But even these can be expressed in differing words or gestures. The eucharistic prayer is an example of this fact: in recent years we have learned to become accustomed to at least four official versions. Their texts are different but each contains the identical structure. And so for other parts of the liturgy. Adaptation does not mean destruction.

So that, briefly, is what the Directory for Masses with Children is all about. It is the application of certain clearly defined liturgical and theological principles to the particular needs of young children of primary school age. The Directory deals with all aspects of the liturgical participation of young children, but the remainder of this chapter will confine itself to a consideration of children at the Sunday parish Mass. Further suggestions for Masses with children will be found in chapter 10 below.

Do we need special Masses for children on Sundays?

This is not an easy question to answer. Perhaps the question should be 'Is it possible to arrange a special Mass for children on Sundays?' Years ago there was so little happening on Sunday that getting children to attend one particular Mass was fairly easy. Nowadays it is far more difficult: there are so many distractions and entertainments that organizing a regular children's Mass can be a gamble.

Even if the gamble succeeds there remains a further problem. The family should be the basic unit of worship; separating children from their parents in order to organize a special Mass may be harmful in the long run (cf D 16). That is not to say that special Children's Masses on Sundays should be altogether ruled out; but they should be occasional rather than habitual.

Local circumstances differ from place to place and no definite rule can be laid down. The best solution would appear to be in an occasional special Mass for children, while ensuring that at *all* Masses at which a large number of children is present something is said or done to help them to participate in the celebration (cf D 17).

What we can do for children at Sunday Mass

So much depends upon the home background. You can produce the most wonderful liturgies, all light and joy, but without family love and prayer you may well be wasting your time. However, that requires consideration of its own. We will have to assume that all is well at home and our suggestions will be for the 'normal' Mass-going situation.

Troublesome children

In a passage which perfectly illustrates the pastoral nature of the Directory, special attention is paid to 'infants who are unable or unwilling to take part in the Mass' (D 16). Every parent knows all about that. The suggestion is that these children should be put in the charge of parish helpers. Here is a job for the girls of the local youth club, or an organization like the Legion of Mary. They should not only be child-minders but should also help in teaching the children to pray and take part in a simple liturgy. Naturally the religious part of the activities would not last as long as the adult Mass – perhaps five minutes at the most. The entire session is wound up by the children being taken into the Church for the final Blessing of the Mass: an important point in teaching both children and adults about the community.

This requires a lot of organization, but it is well worth while. The children are happy (most of the time), the parents have peace of mind, and the rest of the congregation is preserved from the noise of fractious children.

'A few well-chosen words'

Children should not be ignored, especially when there is a large number of them present at Mass (D 17). On most occasions it will be merely a matter of addressing a few remarks to them at important moments of the Mass. The celebrant's aim should be to help the children understand in a general way what is going on and what the particular Mass is all about.

The greeting and introduction to the Mass is the first and most obvious place for a few words with the children. After explaining briefly to the adults what the theme of the Mass is, it is a relatively simple affair to turn one's attention to the children. Simple words, simple concepts. Very often the children's theme will be quite different from the adults', yet both will be drawn from the same readings and Mass prayers. In other words, introducing the Mass to children may not be just a matter of putting the adult introduction in simple language. Many adult themes are unsuitable for children (e.g. social justice in the office, factory or workshop). Brevity is of the utmost importance: the introduction is not the place for a homily.

The homily is the next occasion for a few words to the children. Once again, simplicity and brevity are of importance. A five-minute homily to the adults should be followed by no more than two minutes for the children. It is amazing how much of value can be said in so short a space: it is also a good exercise in sticking to essentials.

A final natural moment for words to the children is at the dismissal, immediately before the Final Blessing. Three or four sentences about the Mass theme and a thought to go away with will be of great help and will make the children feel part of the celebration.

Direct participation

The older child has a lot to offer the community celebration. A children's choir can be the heart of a weekly celebration, leaving the adult choir free to lead the singing at another Mass. The children themselves enjoy the singing and they are made to feel important contributors to the celebration. Soloists may be used, particularly in leading the Responsorial Psalm between the Readings.

More ambitious is the playing of musical instruments. But a children's orchestra, simple and without frills, is not an impossibility: several parishes have proved it.

As readers, children have few rivals. Clarity, freshness, measured speed are hallmarks of their reading. More often than not they lack that self-consciousness which is so often the ruin of the adult reader. Yet we should never allow a child to read not understand. The ability to read and comprehension do not always go together. The proclamation of scripture demands faith – which is a form of comprehension.

Action

Young children are not much impressed by wordiness. Doing has more impact than saying. That is why singing in a choir or reading the scripture is important – both require action as well as the words of singing and reading. Therefore when planning a Sunday Mass for children it is not sufficient to select a few popular hymns, and let it go at that.

A good example of participation by action is the Offertory procession. It is a central act of the Mass; it is not merely a special addition 'to amuse the children'. Even better if entire families can take part together, showing in a small way that the Mass is the worship of the entire Church, young and old alike. Occasionally the children might offer gifts collected by themselves for the sick, the old or the homeless; these would be signs that the sacrifice of the Mass is accompanied by the sacrifice of our own lives.

Even drama can find a place in the Mass. Careful planning and rehearsal can produce mimes which illustrate and accompany the readings (particularly the Gospel) in a most effective manner. Some may think that drama in church is unsuitable: but it appears in a different light if you consider that the entire liturgy of the Mass is a form of ritual dance, or drama. Naturally great care must be taken not to allow the Mass to degenerate into mere play-acting. Good taste sees that it will not.

Special liturgy of the word
The Directory 'canonises' a practice which has met with much success – the withdrawal of children from the first part of an adult Mass in order to celebrate their own adapted liturgy of the word (D 17).

Required for this are a conveniently situated room or hall close to the church, a small band of helpers or catechists, and good timing. It works this way: after the opening prayer a solemn procession of children, carrying a Lectionary, makes its way from the Church to the near-by hall. There grown-ups (not necessarily a priest) lead the children in suitably simplified readings and hymns that they know. A special homily is preached by the best person available (again, not necessarily a priest), specially-simplified prayers of the faithful are used and the entire group returns to the church for the offertory.

Naturally, this provides greater scope for adaptation and goes a long way to ensuring that the children gather fruit from the proclamation of the readings. Upon this basic format can be built many differing forms of the celebration of the word.

As in all forms of liturgical adaptation, the danger is always present that the liturgy will take second place, with adaptation for its own sake coming first. But the danger must be faced. Careful, well-planned adaptation can only result in benefit for the children. Only through adaptation can we arrive at 'that full, conscious and active participation which is demanded by the very nature of the liturgy . . . this full and active participation by all the people is the aim to be considered before all else; from which the faithful are to derive the true Christian spirit' (CL 14). There lies the key to the Directory for Masses with Children.

10. The Liturgy in Small Groups

A. J. McCallen

INTRODUCTION

The Sunday parish liturgy has traditionally provided a 'natural' occasion for bringing together the members of the local church in all their variety. But recently the social unities presupposed by the parish structure have so weakened that, when people come together for Sunday Mass in an ordinary English parish today, they are met by a sense of disassociation rather than one of harmony. This is quite at odds with the spirit of unity that should be evident in the eucharist and we should not merely accept it as an unavoidable part of modern living. It may appear to be impossible or very difficult to achieve that sense of belonging together as a Christian community at prayer which makes it natural to come together for the liturgy, but we should not be resigned to the fact.

Fortunately there are signs that a new kind of parish community can be created, even if it takes time and effort. But the feeling of frustration with the existing parish celebrations has led many people to go back to the origins of the Christian liturgy and to re-express its essential spirit in contemporary forms. One of the results of this has been a massive extension of the use of liturgies for 'specialized' groups. In many of these situations, the liturgical community has simply been built on an existing social unity, and there seems to be no limit to the number of situations which can provide a natural foundation for a worshipping community. We now have house Masses, class Masses, folk Masses, 'handicapped Masses', 'deaf Masses' and very many others. To a very large extent they have proved to be a most valuable innovation with a significant contribution all of their own, for in our anonymous cities they have created a religious warmth that was sadly lacking, and by presenting the Mass in close-up they have provided a valuable source of instruction that could not have been given so successfully in other ways.

113

Naturally there have been some who have looked on eucharistic liturgies for small groups with great suspicion. They may have heard horrific tales from Holland – quite likely in a biased form – which led them to see the group Mass as a serious risk. Possibly this unease was encouraged by an out-dated theology of the eucharist which obscured the fact that *all* Masses are basically group Masses. Even now, it does not appear to be clear that *the Mass is first and foremost an occasion for Christians to come together in prayer to meet God the Father – as a group united round his Son, our Lord.*

For many people in this country, the 'Folk Mass' for young people was the first expression of this kind of liturgy. The Folk Mass was an ordinary Mass with a few new hymns in a modern folk style. It merely made use of one element in the life and culture of the young people so as to help them come closer to the central action of the Mass. The young people were being given the chance to respond to the call of Christ in their own language. To them this folk music was important, and as such had a part to play in their prayer life – just as much as the music of a previous age. The Folk Mass allowed them to make an offering of their lives as they were lived. One of the important things about group liturgies is that they help to relate life-as-it-is-lived with the sacred mysteries of Christ.

The use of modern music still helps a lot of school children to become *united* within the worshipping *community*. It can bring home to them that the Mass is concerned with coming to God *as a community.* We might expect this to be obvious at any Mass. But the recent history and practice of the Church seems to have obscured this basic fact. What a pity this is, for we will never persuade people to recognize the theology of the Mass 'as an expression of unity' if it is not evident in practice. It is a concept that cannot be grasped at a purely intellectual level. We must see for ourselves that the Mass is a community action, for no amount of talk will convince us.

The history of the Mass began with a small group of Christ's followers sharing a religious meal in the upper room in that house in Jerusalem. The early Christians do not appear to have felt any great need to depart from this style of celebration after the death of their Lord and always met for the breaking of bread *in their own houses* (Acts 2:46). Right up to the period of

Constantine the eucharist was normally celebrated in a domestic context. Only the provision of official church buildings in more prosperous times changed this pattern. It is interesting, however, to see that the religious communities of later centuries were quick to reverse the process and bring the eucharist back into their own houses.

In practice today, those communities who rely on a priest coming in for daily Mass may be getting only a part of the benefit of having Mass in their own houses. Often the 'convent Mass' is a subdued, even sleepy affair, performed in the early morning for convenience, with little congregational participation. This should not be true of the usual small group Mass, which should highlight the spirit of participation in the liturgy and bring the Mass to the people in 'close-up', revealing many details that are usually obscured by distance. Such a Mass demands a certain amount of preparation by all concerned, and this is something rather new. Many good priests are so well used to the presence of a mere handful of old faithfuls at their daily Mass that they do not feel the need to involve them in any tangible way. Over the years the Mass has become very little more than an act of priestly devotion. It may take a great effort to rethink this situation and to recognize more clearly that every Mass with a congregation is a Mass "for others."

The clergy need to develop a natural sensitivity to the liturgy – something which may take time and effort to achieve. Without this, however, it is hard to see how they can prepare and control a balanced liturgy in which people can participate as they should. This is a kind of creative skill which can only be perfected through careful attention. In the group liturgy, the celebrant must become conscious of his role as a leader – bringing the congregation together in prayer in the mystery of Christ.

A. THE LITURGY FOR YOUNG PEOPLE

(i) *Some general comments*

Masses for young people are hardly a new idea. For many years there have been Sunday Masses for young children in a lot of parishes, and many priests have celebrated Mass for the pupils of the parish school even as frequently as once a week.

The clergy have been lucky to have the support of their teachers even perhaps at the Sunday parish Masses. They relied on them to keep the children in order, but they rarely seem to have asked their advice on how to *involve* the children in the liturgy. Not many English teachers would have been reckless enough to have offered any criticism of this. They would not have felt adequate to discuss matters liturgical at a critical level. Nor did most priests feel any unease at this, working on the principle that the Mass was the Mass, irrespective of the state or age of the congregation.

It was a perfectly defensible opinion – to begin with there was not much that could be adapted, especially since England was not greatly influenced by the early stirrings of the liturgical renewal on the continent. Possibly children's prayers might be read during the Mass, and later on there might even have been the reading of a commentary on the action of the Mass. But while the Mass was in Latin and in silence, it was natural for the priest simply to push on with his own prayers at his own pace.

Suddenly everything has been changed – or at least a wonderful new opportunity for change has been presented to us. The use of English and a radical new flexibility built into the revised order of Mass has created a totally new situation. The use of language and the freedom permitted by this new flexibility tend to 'stand out' in the 'close-up' situation of the group Mass. But in the Mass for young children, especially in the school situation, they become absolutely critical.

In the past, it often seemed that priests were expected to be faceless in liturgical celebrations. They had their backs to the people, of course, which did not help, but there were deeper reasons for it than that. The personality of the celebrant did not have a place in the 'sacrifice of the altar'. It was a distraction, and needed to be kept out of the way. Even when the priest turned towards the people, at the *Dominus Vobiscum*, he was expected to keep his eyes downcast. This ideal of impersonality was not always achieved, of course. The personality of the celebrant could still intrude, especially through the style of his Latin pronunciation, or in the way he gave his sermon, but this was accidental. So when the Roman Missal of 1969 gave specific notice to the 'individuality of each eucharistic celebration', it was demanding something quite new from the clergy. It even suggested that the individual celebrant should *adapt* the liturgy to *suit the actual congregation participating in the Mass* (GI 3–5).

The General Introduction of this Missal made it quite clear that the local Conferences of Bishops were to establish norms, additional to those given in the Missal, 'to suit the traditions and character of the people, regions and various communities (GI 6). Some conferences made it their business to follow this suggestion as soon as possible. Others asked the Holy See to provide more specific guidelines on how to do this. The Directory for Masses with Children appeared in November 1973 to meet this precise demand.

This Directory has an importance extending beyond the confines of the specific group for which it was prepared (pre-adolescent children). The document bears testimony in detail to a whole new flexibility of style and a remarkable degree of adaptation. It is something of a 'model' document which translates the spirit of the 'new' liturgy into practical effect. As such, it endorses the principles of flexibility and adaptation right across the board, not merely among the very young.

Faced with a Mass for young children, this flexibility can be both a challenge and a strain for the celebrant. He cannot hide behind a 'correct way' of doing the Mass, perfect for all times and all places. The correct way can only be discovered by looking at the actual situation in which Mass is to be celebrated. Many priests may feel over-exposed in this situation – not least because children today are only too ready to be critical anyway. But this should not deter them from making a decent effort. It would not be wise to suggest that Masses for young people should be left to those special people who have a natural talent in this field. No doubt some people are much more suited than others to working (and praying) with young people. But it should not be impossible for most people to learn to avoid the main pitfalls and to make an effective gesture in the right direction.

The Directory makes it clear that a liturgy for children requires preparation. Effective preparation begins with a few simple and basic questions: who are the children involved in this particular liturgy; what age are they; have they anything in common; what resources can they call upon?

Yet many parish Masses for children appear to be little more than relics of the past. Even if the children do attend them, they do not receive anything specifically geared to their age. It is often hard to see what is the purpose of these liturgies and for whom they are intended. They may be a well-intentioned gesture towards the parents, especially of the very young children in the parish, and I think they are recognized and appreciated as such. But the liturgy has hardly been allowed to fulfil its potential.

In many ways, we are somewhat behind continental practice in this whole field. It was the experience on the continent of preparing liturgies for young people over several years which laid the foundations for the practical norms of the Children's Directory. Within a year of the publication of the Roman Missal of 1969, the French Episcopal Commission for the Liturgy was able to publish a carefully considered document on the whole subject of Masses for small groups, giving special attention to young people. No doubt the large-scale Catholic youth groups in France focused attention on the need for suitable liturgies for the young. We do not find the same kind of situations in this country – except in a few summer camps or among the scouts and guides. In England, only the Catholic schools have provided a fruitful situation for the development of a liturgy for the young. Most of what is to be said in the rest of this section will therefore concentrate on the school situation. No doubt many of the ideas proposed can be developed with equal effect in other situations.

Within our schools there are obviously many different and distinct groups of young people. Going by age alone, it is possible to recognize several divisions within the years between five and sixteen, which are taken account of in all the other areas of school life. There are the infants and lower juniors, from the reception class upwards, who are only just coming to terms with school. There are the upper juniors, and beyond who are rapidly growing into adolescents. There are the older pupils who are already looking beyond school towards adult life. We may feel it is unnecessary, or at least an impractical burden, to take account of each of these groupings with their own peculiarities in our presentation of the liturgy. But if we do not take notice of the differences between each age group, we are simply wasting an opportunity of building on what the school already provides. There are, of course, schools planned on radically different lines from those I am thinking of, and these will make quite different demands on us. But most of our schools do reflect these divisions and we are foolish not to build on what they offer.

If we want to introduce the very young children to the Mass soon after they first arrive at school, we will need to find a different approach from that used with even their eight-year-old brothers and sisters. Yet you will find places where these very little ones are gathered together for Mass with children up to the age of nine or even eleven, and expected to get on with things as best they can. I was recently present for such a school Mass in a church only a few days after the beginning of the Christmas term. Several of the 'babies' simply cried throughout the whole operation. Probably some of them were unhappy enough at being separated from their parents for the first time without being made to go into a strange, cold church building for Mass – perhaps also for the very first time. I suspect that the differences that we actually encourage in our schools between one age group and another are so great that Masses for the whole infant and junior school are best limited to a few occasions such as the beginning and end of term.

Often we think of a small group Mass as being limited to a mere handful of people, between eight and fifteen in number. In the classroom situation, this is not likely to be a viable figure. The size of individual classes will usually increase that number to twenty or even thirty children. This *can* be too many, and it may be worthwhile looking for a natural division of a large class into smaller units. But we should not forget that young people can sometimes be embarassed and even silly when they are broken down into very small groups, and they may feel more comfortable together with a slightly larger number of their friends.

Most schools do not have their own chapels, and it is very likely that the place for Mass will be the classroom itself with the benches pushed back against the walls. This can be a distinct bonus, for it brings the liturgy directly into the daily life of the class. Some people would call it a disadvantage, on the grounds that it reduces the liturgy to yet another classroom lesson. Some would even say that it takes away all sense of the holy from the liturgy and lacks dignity and beauty. It is surely up to the celebrant and the class teacher to make sure that neither of these drawbacks is allowed to spoil the liturgy in practice.

Nevertheless, I would not like to suggest that a church building should never be used. The classroom Mass can appear to be so different from the Sunday parish liturgy that it may be of real value to recreate the same kind of celebration within the traditional church building, to bring home the authenticity of what is done in the classroom. Often the problems of time and distance from a convenient church will make it very hard to do this. But if it is possible to make use of a church occasionally, this should not put a strait-jacket on the Mass. It is sad to see teachers trying their hardest to encourage young people to take part in a church service, only to find the clergy objecting and even refusing to allow everything they do in the normal school liturgy. If the church is to be used, it seems ridiculous, for instance, to refuse to allow the use of musical instruments like guitars or trumpets. It may in fact be necessary to go much 'further' than this. We may prefer to use a side altar rather than the main altar of the church, so that the children can come closer up to it. We may even find it necessary to bring in a suitable table to take the place of the altar just for the occasion, if it is impossible for a convenient arrangement to be found within the existing organization of the building. The church building should not be allowed to be an obstacle in the way of the liturgy. It should indeed be a positive help in the satisfactory presentation of the eucharistic celebration.

(ii) *Five to ten-year-olds*

The Directory for Masses with Children warns against making Mass for children 'childish'. This is a very real temptation in the way of priests and teachers who are trying to bring the Mass to those in the infant school. It is true that the best in modern teaching literature is well able to keep the balance between stimulating the powers of imagination in the child and merely falling into sentimentality. But a great deal of infant material (especially in matters religious) is excessively infantile – even for infants. The Directory reminds us *not* to be infantile in our celebration of the liturgy. The children themselves go rapidly through several stages of development over these years, and it does no good to encourage them to associate religion with the babyish things they are so quickly outgrowing. Even so, the Mass has to be interesting – even 'entertaining' in the best sense of the word – if it is to hold the short-lived attention of the small child. It must also communicate a special atmosphere and meaning if it is to become more than one lesson among others.

Perhaps those at the very bottom of the infant school (often more concerned with toilet training than spirituality, at least at the beginning of the first year) are hardly ready for a class Mass. They cannot go to communion and may well take much more instruction (and respond more prayerfully) within a short, simple, informal bible service. It might be best to leave the composition and direction of the whole thing to the class teacher, though the priest has much to offer by his official presence. The usual form of songs, a simplified reading from the scriptures, a little talk (perhaps in the form of a story) and a prayer, ending with a blessing, would seem to be quite sufficient.

Even when the first traumatic school year has been completed and the routine of school life has been accepted, we are still dealing with a very young age group with all their limitations. Young children are usually not blessed with over-much staying power of concentration. When a priest visits a class, he may be a familiar friend or an interesting stranger, and as such may be able to command more attention than his performance deserves. However he can quickly lose that attention when he begins to speak at a level beyond the children's understanding. The problem of concentration is hardly new: but whereas an older child may 'turn off' quite wilfully, at this stage he may simply not be able to control his wandering mind except in fits and starts. There are after all many things more interesting than doctrine and liturgy at this age.

The words to be used in the liturgy pose a lot of problems for these children. Many of them get very little conversation at home and are limited to a very poor vocabulary. They may not understand much, even when they actually listen to what is said. It is important to be simple, using short sentences, watching for 'responses' and asking questions to find out what is being taken in. If a particular subject is tackled from several different angles, it is more likely that something will get through. Fortunately words are not the only means of communication. Music, art work, and even movement are all acceptable and effective means of getting the message across. Probably no children's liturgy could succeed without the use of one or more of these, and the younger the child, the more he or she will find it easier to respond to the non-verbal.

But, of course, all of this requires preparation – within a limited timetable. This is one good reason why school Masses should be limited in number. It is not possible to prepare just any number of liturgies in this fashion. Some people seem to think that an unlimited number of Masses will bring about an unlimited amount of good (or grace). But the reverse can often be the case. It is better in these 'Masses of devotion' to take full advantage of the resources of our schools gradually to create an awareness of the inner reality of the eucharist, so that later on in life, each child may have the desire for a fuller and informed participation in the ordinary parish liturgy. When we present a class Mass, we are in one sense 'selling' the Mass, by trying to convince the child that liturgical prayer has a natural place in his life.

If the Mass is to be made to suit a particular group of children, priests and teachers will need a basic grasp of the liturgical form of the Mass. This is less complicated than it may sound. It does not mean that we need to be expert Masters of Ceremonies or Professors of Liturgy. But it does demand more than the knowledge that 'the Mass is a sacrifice' and that 'the change in the bread and the wine can aptly be called transubstantiation', however significant these truths may be. Rather it is necessary to know what is the purpose and significance of the entrance rites, the priestly prayers, the liturgy of the word, the preparation of the gifts, the eucharistic prayer, the communion rite and the conclusion of the Mass. Only if we can see the Mass in balance, as a framework which must be filled out in due proportion, can we then adapt the Mass to suit each situation.

Other people in this symposium are considering the place of music, movement and art, and I presume that it will not be difficult to take advantage of their comments in the school situation. Apart from making a few comments of my own on the choice of music, I only wish to emphasize the need to use everything we can to create a sense of colour and beauty and joy in our celebrations.

I appreciate that people will nearly always differ on the relative quality and beauty of individual pieces of music. I personally find that most children respond to a surprisingly wide variety of musical material, from the quiet meditative piece of orchestral music to the swinging melody from the Charts. To a large extent, the quality of the music and the extent of its use, and the whole business of instrumental accompaniment, from glockenspiels to guitars, will depend on what each school itself has to offer. Music can be a basic element in liturgies for young people, and should not be underestimated. However, I particularly wish to make a plea for attention to the lyrics. Children may go for the tune, but we should not overlook the words. Many folk hymns, popular though they undoubtedly are, are no more suitable for little children to understand than the hymns of centuries ago. Yet the lyrics are part of the liturgy and should themselves be suitable to the age of the singers. One popular song, probably sung in hundreds of schools, instructs the singer to 'cast his worries on Christ'. I wonder what a seven-year-old would understand by this! On the other hand I would not like to recommend indiscriminately the use of those children's songs written specifically for young children. Some of them are equally undesirable because of their childish words and tuneless melodies. Sometimes it may be best to encourage the children to write their own songs to their own tunes or to their favourite melodies. With guidance, they can produce some very attractive results.

It does no harm, in any case, to take the children through the songs line by line, to make sure they grasp the meaning of the words. The celebrant can usefully refer to the words of the songs in his homily to bring their meaning home yet again. We need to approach the songs we use in the liturgy with a critical eye. Music is not merely decorative in the liturgy, it serves specific purposes. The entry song draws the children together into a united worshipping community. It also draws attention to the theme of the Mass or to the current liturgical season. The Gloria or song of praise should *proclaim* what it means. The song or psalm which follows the readings should be a prayerful response to the word of God. The acclamation before the Gospel is a joyful welcome to the word of God. The offertory song accompanies the offertory procession. The Sanctus, the acclamation and the Great Amen involve the children in the Great Prayer itself. The communion song should express the shared happiness and devotion of children who have been joined together by Christ. The final hymn looks ahead to the continuing presence of Christ in their daily lives.

It is good to see that the Children's Directory specifically permits the rewriting of official texts, such as the Gloria, Sanctus and Agnus Dei, to allow them to be sung to appropriate musical settings (D 31). There is no reason now why these 'difficult' responses should not be sung in addition to the other hymns. Some of the available settings of these pieces are popular with children and fit naturally into the children's liturgy.

I have suggested that the entrance song should reflect the theme of the Mass. It may help if I immediately explain why there is often so much emphasis today on the use of themes in group liturgies. The Mass has only one ultimate theme, and that is the celebration of the death, resurrection and second coming of Christ. But it remains useful in each individual Mass, as in other liturgies, to use different specific ideas or images as a kind of way in to the mystery of Christ. These ideas and images give useful coherence to the liturgy of the word and to the music. They can also be a source of colour and beauty when they are expressed in visual terms by decorating the priestly vestments with cut-outs, or by putting up photographs and pictures on the classroom or church walls. In this way it is possible to have a Mass about water, or a Mass about trees, or even a daffodil Mass or a red Mass – each featuring these distinct elements in a special way. It is up to the celebrant, however, to ensure that in the end each Mass is clearly seen to be a 'Jesus Mass' first and foremost.

In a Mass for very young children, quite ordinary things can create a sense of occasion all by themselves. For instance, it may be a good idea to arrange with their teacher for them to go and wash their hands before the Mass begins, to put them in the right frame of mind for something special. They can then come back into the classroom together in a little procession and go straight into the Mass itself. Or again, they can stay inside and prepare the teacher's table to make it suitable for its special use as an altar table. They can arrange the altar breads for communion on the paten. Possibly something more like real food than the ordinary hosts could be used on these occasions. One large altar bread suitable for breaking into many particles, enough for everyone, would be even better. This might allow the sign value of the fraction before communion to be effective. Most adults, let alone their children, are puzzled by the statement declaring that we all share *one* bread, when in fact we each seem to receive something quite perfect and separate in itself. I sometimes wonder if the offertory procession, preceded by the individual placing of the altar breads on the paten, doesn't even encourage this.

The classroom should be decorated with the children's work. This is a special occasion, and there should be a festive atmosphere. The celebrant contributes to this by his dressing up in special clothes. Another way of beginning Mass can therefore be the actual vesting of the priest in front of the children, as he explains the origin and purpose of each of the different garments. Then he can call the children to pray with the sign of the cross, and the greeting, before going into the first song.

The entry rites of the Mass are very flexible. They are intended to concentrate our attention on what we are going to say and do. Very little apart from the collect prayer is essential, though it would obviously be pointless to leave everything else out. After the sign of the cross and a greeting, it is natural to say a few words of introduction – but this should not be overdone. Then there can be an act of penance – perhaps sung in the form of a short litany or dialogue. The American bishops recently expressed concern lest this become merely a public confession of sins or an examination of conscience. They emphasized the fact that the Kyrie is an act of praise to the Lord who shows us mercy, not a wail of self pity (see the account given in the *Southwark Liturgy Bulletin*, October 1974, p. 1). Perhaps they were also concerned to avoid the excessive extension of the penitential rite out of all proportion to the other entrance rites.

Although I cannot see much advantage in young children singing the full text of the Gloria, it may be desirable to make occasional use of a simpler text to emphasize from the beginning of Mass the importance of thanksgiving and praise.

The entrance rite ends with the opening prayer of the priest. 'Let us pray that . . .' says the celebrant, and tells the children to be quiet and still for a moment. Even the youngest child should be encouraged to shut his or her eyes and concentrate for a few seconds. The more noise and activity there is in the liturgy, the more there is need for moments of real silence. Children should be trained from an early age to expect a degree of silence in the Mass and to appreciate its value.

The presidential prayers of the Mass are somewhat complex pieces of writing based on stylized Latin originals. I think everyone agrees that these must be considerably simplified if they are to be made suitable for young children. The Directory for Masses with Children warns us to avoid 'anything alien to the literary genre of the presidential prayer' (D 51) but I suspect this is not intended to be as restrictive as it sounds. The Introduction to the Roman Missal 1969 tells us quite simply that the opening prayer *expresses* the *theme* of the celebration and addresses a *petition* to God the Father through the mediation of Christ in the Holy Spirit (GI 32). This merely demands that the prayer be addressed to God the Father, in the name of Jesus, and that it should be a prayer of petition on the theme of the Mass. It also follows that it should be reasonably brief and formal in tone. I personally feel that there is no need to retain the long prayer endings. Even if there is no mention in the body of the prayer of the work of Christ or the Holy Spirit, it is sufficient to end with a simple – 'Father, we ask you this for the sake of Jesus your Son', or even 'Praise the Father, the Son and the Holy Spirit for ever and ever'.

All three presidential prayers: the opening prayer, the prayer over the gifts, and the concluding prayer, should be written in the form of a petition. The second of these will also obviously include a word of offering, just as the third may include a word of thanksgiving. But they should not be prayers only of offering or of thanksgiving.

The liturgy of the word can present many problems. I have not found that the original texts of the scriptures speak very directly to young children, even with a certain amount of editing. Faced with this, I myself have tried to provide a collection of considerably simplified texts which will prepare children for the originals. Other people have preferred to re-express the scriptures in terms of mime or drama. If this is well under control, it can be very telling. But it carries the risk of growing so big that it spoils the internal balance of the complete liturgy. I often feel that it is better to keep mime and drama for non-eucharistic liturgies which can be completely built round them. However, a less radical division of a scriptural text into several parts and the use of choral speech is perfectly acceptable – and traditional – and it can provide a satisfactory compromise between a full-blown playlet and a solitary, lone reading (D 47).

I am sorry the Directory did not support the use of simplified versions of the scriptures more enthusiastically. I can see that some versions are so far from the originals that they are hardly likely to lead children 'to read the bible and appreciate the dignity of the word of God for themselves' (D 47). But I am convinced that some kind of judicious editing and paraphrasing is necessary. As more simplified texts become available, it should be more easy to recognize the wheat from the chaff.[1]

The Directory allows great freedom in the choice of readings for Mass. It merely requires a reading from the Gospels, and even this can be read by a child (D 41–47). The responsorial psalm can be replaced by a suitable hymn, and this is a great concession, for the psalms are hardly the prayers of childhood. The Directory also stresses the importance of a short homily. Whether it is by introductions to the readings or by a little discussion afterwards, it is essential that the meaning of the scriptures be made abundantly clear and relevant. Even so, although this is one time when the teaching function of the liturgy becomes more apparent, the liturgy of the word should not degenerate into just another lesson. The Mass is a celebration. The priest who can tell the class a short story with a moral may keep the whole thing in balance, providing instruction and 'entertainment' at one and the same time. But if the celebrant really feels he cannot get on the right wavelength, he should ask the teacher to take his place.

[1] Alan Dale's version of the Old and New Testaments, *Winding Quest* and *New World* (Oxford University Press) provide a good starting point. There is also Sister Monica Mary's volume of Family Mass themes (with homily notes), available from the Portsmouth Catholic Education Centre; several volumes of Mass themes from the Grail at Pinner, and my own lectionary for young children, *Listen!* forthcoming (2nd edition) from Collins Publishers in 1976.

The liturgy of the word ends with the prayers of the faithful. The children, even the youngest, can take the fullest and most active part in these. It does them good to have to prepare them, for by doing so they begin to learn the basic notions of liturgical prayer. These prayers are to be addressed to God the Father or to Christ – but not to our Lady or to the saints. They should not be merely an excuse for untutored free expression; children can usefully be taught what is required. Of course, the prayers do not have to be polished, the language and the spelling can be left as rough as they come, so long as the children grasp the basic idea of how to express in words their prayers of asking and giving thanks.

To a small child, God is either all or nothing. It is hard for him or her to appreciate the way God seems to work. The child may demand that God stops a war or a famine, as if to suggest that God only does what he should when we tell him. It may be helpful if we teach the child to pray that *people* do *what God tells them* so that *they* themselves stop the fighting and provide for their neighbours in times of starvation. This is all part of teaching a child to pray.

It should also be remembered that the first part of a bidding prayer is an intention for prayer, not a prayer itself. If we allow the child to rush through the intention and the response ('Lord, hear us etc.') as if they were one, we may confuse the issue. It is better to allow a slight pause before the response so that everyone else can stop and pray for themselves. The response itself could also well be changed to something more simple like:

Reader: Lord,
Children: Hear our prayer.

Next comes the preparation of the gifts or 'offertory'. It has been recommended that we prepare the altar from scratch, even to the extent of putting the altar cloth on the bare table at this point. I have never found this very convenient. But one way to symbolize our preparations can be to place the candles on the altar table at this point rather than at the beginning of the Mass. Where there is plenty of room, it is also most effective to move everyone from the place where the liturgy of the word has been celebrated to the place where the liturgy of the eucharist is to occur. But I must admit that in practice few classrooms would be big enough to allow this.

Bread and wine are obviously the chief gifts. But there is

room for other things to be brought to the altar table, such as those connected with the theme of the Mass, or simply related to the children themselves (such as their written work or their drawings, which can be placed on the altar table itself). In these cases, it may be desirable to compose extra blessing prayers on the pattern of the two existing models: for example – 'Blessed are you, God our Father, for you have given us our hands to write and draw in these work books. Blessed be God for ever.'

Finally, the Pray, brethren can be reduced to a simple 'Let us pray . . .' and the offertory prayer can become a short word of thanks to God for his many gifts and a request that he accept our offering.

Before going into the eucharistic prayer, it is good for the celebrant to stop for a few moments of silence. Then a word of introduction can remind the children of what is about to happen. We are, as it were, revisiting the Last Supper between Jesus and his friends. It is something very special and a great privilege, and we thank God our Father for his kindness.

We are still waiting for a eucharistic prayer for children. But there is good reason to hope we will not be waiting for much longer. We need a prayer that will give scope in the preface for mentioning other reasons for praising God apart from the work of Christ. We also need texts that will allow more vocal participation by the children themselves during the priestly prayer. It is not at all impossible to maintain the distinctive role of the celebrant whilst allowing considerably more opportunities for making a response. Indeed the responses could be used to break up the prayer into its component parts and reduce it to more manageable proportions.

For the time being, it is helpful to bring the children forward to stand round the altar table for the eucharistic prayer. They will quickly respond to the idea that they are like the apostles round Jesus and will have a taste of the unity for which Christ prayed. They can always return to their places again later so that they can come up for communion in a single file if this is required. The children can also genuflect with the celebrant, or kneel at the consecration. This can be a most effective way of emphasizing the holiness of the occasion without necessarily spoiling the unity of the whole eucharistic prayer.

The Great Amen which brings the eucharistic prayer to a close should never be thrown away. The celebrant must prepare for it by saying, or singing, the doxology with gravity and strength. Then it will be simple to achieve a convincing Amen in reply. Amen is a very short word to express so great a response, and it can be over and done with before it has even begun. Even when it has not been possible to use a sung version of the Doxology and Amen, I have found it useful to repeat the word, Amen, three times – in the way that many of the musical settings do – so as to emphasize its importance. This might sound affected with an adult congregation, but is perfectly acceptable with a junior group.

The communion rite falls into three parts: the Our Father, the sign of peace, and the breaking of the consecrated host. The Our Father can be sung, and there are some attractive settings of it already available. With preparation, the sign of peace can easily be performed with great success with small children – they enjoy it in fact – it's fun, but they also appreciate its meaning, especially when two scrapping partners find themselves next to each other. A handshake or a smile or an expression like 'let's be friends' says everything that is needed.

I do not find the Agnus Dei very helpful in Masses for young children. The whole concept of the sacrifice of the innocent animal is a hard idea to explain. If we take away the Agnus Dei then we should also rephrase the 'Ecce Agnus Dei . . .' This can then become something like: 'This is the Risen Christ, we are happy to be called to his supper', or 'This is our Lord, the Bread which comes down from heaven . . .' However, even if the Agnus Dei is removed, it is still necessary to break the host into pieces, and this should be done with deliberation, even adding a suitable comment or prayer such as: 'This bread is broken into many pieces so that the one Christ may come to feed us all.'

During communion, we are asking a lot if we expect young children to remain quiet and recollected throughout. It is better to keep them happily occupied by singing together a simple song or refrain, or by listening to a restful piece of music on a tape or record.

The Directory does not say anything about communion under

both kinds, so it may be worth remarking that it is untrue that young children cannot do this reverently. I have seen children who have just made their first communion receive the Blessed Sacrament under both kinds with no trouble or disrespect. With a class teacher specially authorized to assist with the chalice, it would present no problems at all.

After communion, we should make sure there are a few moments of silent prayer before the concluding prayer. Next there is a final opportunity for a brief comment, reminding the children of one of the ideas from the liturgy of the word. Then comes the blessing. Occasionally it can be good to make up an extended blessing relating to the Mass theme. The Mass is finally brought to a joyful conclusion with a cheerful song.

I know some people who have read the preceding pages will accuse the Directory for Masses with Children of making the Mass so simple that it takes the mystery out of the eucharist. I can only disagree. The mystery of the Mass does not depend on dimly understood expressions or puzzling, even ambiguous language. The mystery of the eucharist is the mystery of Christ himself, in his death, resurrection and second coming. I sug-- gest that this is quite deep enough in itself to satisfy anyone without the distractions of obscure language and symbols.

(iii) *The ten-year-olds and upwards*
I have spent a lot of time in the last section considering in detail the adaptation of the Mass for a particular age group, taking full advantage of the freedom permitted by the Directory for Masses with Children. I consider a great deal of what was written there applies equally well to many other situations where a small group of people come together to celebrate the liturgy of the eucharist. However, there is little need to prove the desirability of a similar approach in the present section, for there is a natural continuity between the two age groups under consideration. But, as always, we need to make certain modifications to what was said in the previous section to re-adapt the liturgy to the *changing* needs of the children themselves.

We need to help these children to develop their prayer life beyond that of the little child. Today the sense of wonder that we find in childhood is often dispelled very early in life, and

the natural sense of God and the spiritual can disappear with
equal speed at the same time. The classroom liturgy has something to contribute towards preventing this from happening.

During the early school years the liturgy can fit naturally
into a very flexible timetable where it is easily related to the
other areas of learning. As the children grow older, it will be
necessary to fit the liturgy into a more strictly organized routine
within a precisely articulated syllabus which includes R.E. as
one subject among several others. I think the liturgy can be
made into an essential part of the R.E. Syllabus, and indeed
some recent life-experience syllabuses almost seem to *demand*
the support of the liturgy to bring home the spiritual message.
A planned use of classroom liturgies, including the liturgy of
the Mass, can help to reinforce this spiritual teaching by turning
it into prayer. In any case religious education extends beyond
theology and morality. The information given in a religious
lesson *needs* to be re-expressed in prayer. Classroom liturgies
within the ordinary R.E. periods can provide structures of
varying degrees of formality to achieve this. With the use of live
or recorded music and carefully chosen or specially composed
prayers, with religious and secular readings to suit the theme
and occasion, it is possible to create something fresh which
puts the truth of Christianity into real life.

This age group can often surprise you with a demand (and
an apparent satisfaction) for a more formal celebration of the
Mass than that required by their juniors. It may be quite
sufficient to encourage their participation in vigorous singing,
and to provide *brief* linking passages between one section of the
Mass and the next. They seem to approve of the way in which
some priests 'talk their way through the Mass', joining the
different parts together into a single unity. It's a pity that a
lot of priests do not take advantage of the many opportunities
in the Mass today for introduction and comment. The children
themselves will, of course, continue to perform the readings and
write their own bidding prayers as before. In some schools the
development of new skills may open up new areas of participation that were simply not available before. Instrumentalists
who can really play may bring something very special into the
music of the liturgy. The ability to sew may allow the girls to
create or decorate their own vestments. It is good for all these

secular attainments to be related to the life of prayer by their use in the liturgy.

It should be possible to make good use of the liturgy of the word at this age. It may still be desirable to use *New World* or *Winding Quest* rather than the original texts of the bible. But at all cost, the scriptures must be shown to be relevant, and no just a collection of strange out-dated stories. A good short homily has a special part to play in this. Sometimes a secular poem or reading, or a piece of recorded music can provide a valuable comment on the word of God. Priests and teachers have the challenging task of helping their children to draw together their previous religious experience, so that they can build on it for the future. We have to try and deepen their faith and under-standing of things which were previously taken on trust. The liturgy should not be left out of this process.

It is about this time that many of the children start to find difficulties in going to communion. Sometimes this is caused by well-meaning parents or grandparents who pass on their own misconceptions regarding the necessity of confession before communion. An apparent inability to remember to fast for the stipulated time can also reduce the numbers quite unnecessarily. Many children who are eager to take a full part in the school liturgy will simply never attend Sunday Mass and may con-sider themselves barred from the sacrament. Others may feel unworthy or embarrassed at doing something so explicitly sacred.

First of all it is essential to convince the children of the im-portance of communion within the Mass. Secondly it is worth developing whatever ideas they may have about the sacredness of the eucharist, and to emphasize the fact that none of us are exactly worthy of approaching the table of the Lord, but that Christ himself invites us to come because we *need* his support. It should be possible to answer all the different excuses for not going, without seeming to be indifferent to the sacredness of what is done, or to the very real problems of human sin and unworthiness. We should take care not to create further obstacles in the way of meeting Christ in the eucharist. We can easily cause the children who 'cannot' go to com-munion to feel 'unjustly' excluded, especially if they are in a minority.

One would have hoped that the child who has grown up with the Mass in English and has been taught in the school to love the liturgy, should not find any difficulty in recognizing that the Mass makes sense. In practice, my own experience suggests this is far from true. No one has to explain to a schoolboy why it is that a game of soccer or rugby proceeds from one stage of the game to the next. The action of the game may be quite complicated, but there will be no difficulty in seeing the match as a whole, when it comes to an end. This can hardly be said of the Mass. The inner logic of the liturgy often does not seem to come across, and the Mass often seems to be reduced to an apparently endless succession of irrelevant details.

This problem may take a long time to solve, but the class Mass provides an ideal situation in which to do something about it. Mass schemes such as the one provided by Sister M. Travers in *The Shape of the Mass* (Burns & Oates, 1970) can provide a useful plan of action to achieve this. My own method of tackling the problem is less elaborate: I have worked out a simple plan of the Mass, giving its several component parts in the order of their appearance, with a short comment following each section, outlining its place within the whole Mass. (See below for one version of this.) In doing this I make no claims to have said everything about the eucharist. But I can give each child a copy of the whole thing to read. I can also use the exact words to introduce each section of the Mass during the actual classroom celebration itself.

Once again, of course, I am stressing the need for liturgical sense, and some people will think that I am being merely academic. But it remains a fact that we will not really satisfy young people in the end merely by brightening up the liturgy. We must make it make sense, and make sense in their own lives.

WHAT HAPPENS AT MASS

(1) HYMN/IN THE NAME OF THE FATHER/GREETING/INTRODUCTION
We come together as God's family at prayer gathered round the priest.
(2) PENITENTIAL RITE/COLLECT PRAYER
We ask God our Father to forgive us and prepare us for Mass.

(3) LITURGY OF THE WORD

(READINGS) We listen to God, who speaks to us in the words of the Bible.

(RESPONSORIAL PSALM) We pray together by joining in the PSALMS or songs.

(THE PRAYER OF THE FAITHFUL) Then we pray in our own words for the help we need and thank God our Father for taking care of us.

(CREED) On Sundays we show we believe in God's love by saying this.

(4) THE PREPARATION OF THE GIFTS

We prepare the bread and wine for Mass, and ask God to accept them with our prayers.

(5) EUCHARISTIC PRAYER

We remember that God our Father has been good to us in many ways, but most of all by sending his Son, Jesus, to live with men on earth, (PREFACE), and we thank him with a song of praise. (HOLY, HOLY, HOLY).

We pray to the Holy Spirit to bless the bread and wine.

We go back over the Last Supper and meet Jesus again. (CONSECRATION).

Then we thank God our Father for Jesus, who died for us, and was raised to life so that we could live like him, and we pray that Jesus may come back again to take charge of the world we live in.

Finally, we ask the Holy Spirit to change us and make us all into a holy family of God.

And we end the EUCHARISTIC PRAYER by joining together in the GREAT AMEN.

(6) OUR FATHER/PRAYER FOR PEACE/BREAKING OF THE BREAD

We prepare ourselves to meet Jesus in holy communion, and we ask him to help us live together as friends who share the life of Christ.

(7) HOLY COMMUNION

Jesus comes to feed us with his love.

(8) THANKSGIVING/BLESSING/FINAL HYMN

We thank God our Father for holy communion and ask him to bless and protect us so that we can go out from the Mass and share the life of Christ with others.

(iv) *The last few years at school*

The fourteen–fifteen-year-olds start to make new demands on the liturgy. If they were older and were engaged in further education they could expect special provision to be made for them in the university or college chaplaincies, should they wish to take advantage of it. But little attention is paid to them in the meantime. It could be argued that they should not be treated any differently from adults. After all, it is said, once upon a time these people would already have been working in adult jobs. We forget, however, that our whole education system sets out to extend the learning life of even the ordinary child well beyond previous limits, and with this has come an automatic extension of the years of uncertain change and development.

Some young people in this group will be perfectly at ease in their home parish liturgy and make no complaints, apart from the occasional grumble at boring sermons and dull music. It may be that they have already reached the level of maturity which allows them to remain untroubled by the limitations of the parish situation. On the other hand, they may have become merely apathetic.

Many young people, unfortunately, vote with their feet and simply stay away. A school liturgy can provide something specially geared to their demands. It may be sufficient to present them with a Mass that is simple and flexible and quietly prayerful, with a few carefully chosen words after the readings. If this is done within a school break-time, there will be no compulsion, and the people who come can be made to feel relaxed and yet involved. It may be worth going beyond this, however, to try and explore the needs of a particular group in depth. There is a dearth of information about what has been done in this area. People have either not managed to think this one out very far, or else they have chosen to remain silent about their efforts.

Early in the Directory for Masses with Children, we are told that a fully Christian life is unthinkable without sharing in the liturgical action which brings the faithful together to celebrate the Paschal Mystery (D 8). This is certainly none too obvious to many young people in the fourteen–seventeen age group. Whatever their previous understanding and appreciation of the Mass (which may have been limited) they now seem to need convincing all over again of the value of liturgical prayer.

Perhaps the Mass cannot do this by itself adequately. It may be necessary to begin at the very beginning with the need for prayer in general, and lead on from there to the value of prayer that is shared with others: only then would one be ready for the eucharist. So many priests in different situations speak about the great desire for prayer among groups of young people, that we cannot merely dismiss this age group as prayerless. But I would not like to suggest that this desire for prayer will always be very obvious on the surface. Real development in this area may require a lot of guidance and support. In practical terms this may well demand the formation of some kind of discussion/ prayer group which can work towards a eucharistic celebration at its own pace.

If someone has been able to take such a group through several productive sessions, I would hesitate to suggest the way in which he should proceed. No doubt the group's own requirements will already have made themselves felt. I can only suggest the following comments, on the grounds that they have proved useful to me in the past.

I have found music usually features significantly in these celebrations. It is surprising how many modern secular songs provide serious comment on the world in which we live, and it isn't difficult to make use of them in prayer. Records (and record players) create all kinds of problems when they have to be used during the liturgy, and it may be much easier to have everything collected in the right order on tape. A tape recorder is easier to handle.

There needs to be a fair amount of silence in the midst of all this noise and activity. Silence is just as much an essential part of liturgical prayer as it is of 'private' prayer, and there should be plenty of time for quiet meditation in common. Apart from silent prayer, there's obviously need for written prayers suitable for the celebrant to use. This is a situation when it would be desirable to make use of a more extended collect, in which the priest can draw together the various concerns of the people present and concentrate them into a united petition to God the Father. The ICEL translation of the 1969 Roman Missal provides many examples of the extended form of opening prayer, and I have recently noticed some American publications which provide other examples of the same thing. (For example, *Eucharistic Liturgies*, Gallen, Newman Press.)

Although we all know we are put in contact with the word of God through the word of the scriptures, we often find ourselves growing a little deaf to the urgency of his call. It would be nice to think that we will have already taken our young people to the point where they can devote the patience and concentration to simply reading or listening to the scriptures in a spirit of prayer. But in fact, they are often merely bored by the familiarity of the text, and do not bother or know how to go deeper. A secular reading can provide a way in to a well-known passage, and highlight (or contrast) its meaning. Poems and songs are very useful things to have around, for their value as introductions or commentaries to the readings from the holy scriptures. I can never understand why so much feeling is generated against secular readings in this context, for they are not aimed at supplanting the word of God, but only at creating a new approach to it.

There may be little need for an extended homily after so much in the way of commentary and introduction. Some people favour a 'dialogue' in which everyone can take part, though I personally find them unsatisfactory, either going on too long or drying up before they get anywhere. Nevertheless, the Directory for Masses with Children recommends the idea for use with young children (D 48) and it may be of equal value here.

I hope in time there will be new eucharistic prayers more suitable for flexible, informal situations like this, where several people may even be seated round a large table with the celebrant. However, the priest can even now achieve a fair degree of effect if he speaks one of the existing prayers by heart – as if he were saying it for the very first time.

Obviously the sign of peace has a special significance under these intimate conditions. Equally, the breaking of the host into enough pieces for everyone to receive from the 'one bread' can be very telling. Communion should be under both kinds, and there should be a period of silent meditation afterwards, before the blessing.

(v) *Parish Masses for young people*

If you have struggled through the preceding pages, you will have a fair idea of what can be done to involve young people in the Mass. But of course the parish situation may not allow the use of many of these suggestions. To begin with, there may not be any single cohesive group of young people of a similar age on which to build a special liturgy. There may also be a number of people in the parish who will strongly object to any noticeable adaptation of the public Sunday liturgy.

Whatever the case may be, if we are to have a special Mass, we must ask ourselves whom we are trying to help. Some parishes with lots of young people have already discovered the difficulty of arranging a Mass that is suitable for the *whole* age range, and are beginning to see the need for two distinct liturgies, one for the younger children and another for teenagers. If this is possible, providing something for each group on alternate Sundays, for instance, it may be easy to go straight ahead with some of the things that have already been suggested in the previous section.

One way of avoiding undue criticism may be found in choosing a completely new time for these children's liturgies, a time that will not disturb the people who attend Mass at other regular times. If the new time (and style) is well publicized in advance, there will be no excuse for those who come to criticize the use of a guitar or the changing of a prayer or reading.

The amount of preparation for these liturgies will be restricted by time and talent. Outside the school situation, we can no longer rely on its enormous fund of resources and expertise. Unless we have a parish school that can help us, we must develop our own resources independently. If there is to be singing, and there should be, we need a leader-group of singers and instrumentalists to support the others. If there are to be children reading at Mass, we will need people to prepare them to do this effectively. The same is true of the prayers of the faithful, the offertory procession, the use of visual material to decorate the church building, or the use of recorded music and all the rest. It takes a lot of effort if we are to involve more than a handful of altar boys.

In a parish with one priest and a small congregation, a

special liturgy for children may be impractical. Even so, we should not allow the children to be forgotten completely. The Directory for Masses with Children specifically reminds us not to let the children feel neglected (D 17). The Directory suggests that it may be possible in this situation to divide adults and children during the liturgy of the word and the homily, giving the children something more suited to them in a separate place from the main church (D 18). Then they can return to the main church at the offertory – perhaps bringing the offerings of bread and wine with them in a small procession. I suspect that most young people would prefer not to be segregated from the rest of the community in this way, but I may be wrong.

I know that some priests would be happier to keep their congregation together and to substitute for one of the official readings a simpler version of the scriptures and then attempt to pitch the homily at the level of understanding of the ten–twelve-year-olds. Those who do this tell me they find that many adults like this themselves. Unfortunately, this approach can be very restrictive, especially today when people are asking for more than mere exhortation in the homily. Everything, of course, depends on the preacher's own style. Some priests can begin their homily with a minute or two specially geared to the children before pursuing the same idea to a deeper level for the sake of the adult congregation. Each person must work out his own solution.

One specific way of showing our concern for young people in the liturgy is by using their music. I know that many older people dislike the use of folk music in the Mass, but it is surprising how quickly they can get used to a selection of modern words and tunes. I suspect that a good mix of the old and the new with 'Lord of the Dance' rubbing shoulders with 'Sweet Sacrament Divine' may go a long way to keeping everyone happy.

B. THE LITURGY FOR HANDICAPPED PEOPLE

(i) *The physically handicapped*

There does not seem to be very much written about liturgy for the handicapped. Perhaps this is because in the past there was not very much done for them in the liturgy anyway. In the revised ceremonies of the anointing and pastoral care of the sick, the Church has provided a visible sign of her concern for all the sick, including the physically handicapped. This is very encouraging. No doubt most parishes will eventually provide a liturgy for the anointing of the sick several times each year. I hope that a special provision will be made to involve the physically handicapped in these ceremonies. Perhaps in time the anointing of the sick will also be equally open to the mentally as well as the physically handicapped.

People with a physical handicap, even if it is severe, will often be unwilling to claim extra attention. They frequently want to live as normal a life as possible – including a normal prayer life. They may well reject special treatment. It may not be easy to find out where their genuine needs lie. They may simply require help with transport, or a ramp to get their wheel-chair over the steps leading up to the church. They may have a sight or hearing deficiency and need a place at the front of the church near the altar where they can see and hear what is happening. Many physically handicapped people attend specialized state schools during the years of childhood and adolescence, and may not be very well instructed in their faith. They may, therefore, need (and appreciate) further religious education to help them to participate more fruitfully in the liturgy of the eucharist.

A person who develops a serious physical handicap in adult life may suffer a terrible blow to his morale. He may find it hard to reconcile himself to his condition. This could be a suitable occasion for a house Mass 'for the sick'. From time to time, priests should make a point of talking in their homilies about the hardship and suffering caused by sickness, and they should remind the community of its responsibility to visit and care for the sick and handicapped.

(ii) *The mentally handicapped*

The mentally handicapped (who are often physically handicapped as well) present different problems. Many of them will be in residential care, though it is wonderful to see how many parents try to keep their children at home as long as possible, often until they themselves grow too old to continue. It may be impractical to arrange a liturgy to suit the Catholic patients of a large state-run residential establishment. But families and friends may be pleased to bring their own relatives to the local church on Sunday if it is suggested to them, and they are made to feel welcome.

I believe that the work of Jean Vanier has opened up new areas in this question, for in his own communities he stresses the particular value of sharing the liturgy with handicapped people. Up to now, my own thinking has led me to feel that the most useful service we can offer the people in residential establishments is that of visiting. If we, the members of the liturgical community, take the trouble to welcome the handicapped into our lives by our visits, then we indirectly involve them in our liturgy as well.

We may have something more specific to offer those who stay at home and the people who look after them. The term mentally handicapped covers a great variety of disorders extending from the case of a child who appears to be totally paralysed in mind and body to that of the mongol child and even of the SSN child and their adult equivalents. Each of these requires a different approach, which can only be discovered through personal contact.

Up and down the country there are several voluntary organizations dedicated to helping mentally handicapped children or adults and their parents. The Catholic Handicapped Children's Fellowship is one of these.[2] Although the CHCF is a national organization, it is made up of local groups who offer a variety of services for the children. The members of the local group will be in contact with the handicapped people in their area and will know them at first hand. They may also organize Masses for them.

Basically there are two reasons for having a liturgy for the mentally handicapped. First of all it is a good thing simply to bring these people physically to Christ, even if we do not expect them to respond in a conscious manner – though in practice we may be surprised at the degree and the warmth of the response which occurs. A severely handicapped person may still be able to establish a personal relationship with others and therefore,

[2] Secretary, Miss Marguerite Donnelly, 2 The Villas, Hare Law, Stanley, Co Durham DH9 8DQ.

presumably, with Christ as well. Secondly, and of equal importance, we need to bring their parents and families to Christ, with all their joys and sorrows. Some of them may have drifted away from the Church while they were struggling to come to terms with this personal tragedy. Others may actually feel rejected by their local church because of the criticisms they suffered when they did not manage to control their children in church. Even those with strong faith who do endure need all the encouragement our prayers can offer.

Each liturgy is bound to be different from the next. Some groups provide occasional Masses for the parents and children in their own parish or deanery – often concentrating more on the needs of the parents than on those of the children. Surprisingly enough, if priest and congregation are relaxed together, the children will often be quite content and relaxed as well, even without special attention. Other groups arrange special Masses for the whole of their town as often as one Sunday a month or provide house Masses in the homes of the parents. Churches are not always the best places for this kind of liturgy – they have benches that get in the way, awkward pillars that children can walk into and they are big and cold places where the noise of the children will echo, and where parents may feel ill at ease.

Regular liturgies can provide the opportunity for a gradual exploration of a child's religious potential. At one end of the scale a child or adult may only experience the warmth and colour of a living celebration. The rhythm of music and the flickering of candles may be all we can provide for them – the rest must be left to Christ alone. At the other end of the scale it may be possible for some children gradually to become so familiar with the Mass that they even begin to desire to meet Christ in holy communion. They may not be able to express their faith in words, but in the warmth of a family liturgy they may be able to establish a relationship with Christ which could not be achieved elsewhere.

In the Fellowship to which I belong, every attempt is made to emphasize the colour, brightness and friendliness of the liturgy. Comfortable chairs are arranged in a semi-circle around the altar table in a large room, in a local college of education. We have had a simple vestment made for us in white material on which colourful patterns can be sewn, reflecting the theme of the Mass. We use bright, rhythmical music, and many of the children are able to join in with percussion instruments. The scripture readings are very simple and quite short. (I've been quite surprised to find my own lectionary for junior children, *Listen!*, has proved quite useful in this connection.) Some of our children have said their own bidding prayers and taken part in the offertory procession, though I must admit they have been known to bring more than the customary gifts to the altar! If the children have not been able to go to communion, and as yet many of our children do not, we arrange for the priest to go to each of the children in turn to give them a blessing so as not to leave them out of this important part of the Mass. Also at this point we have tried giving them each a small present or a picture of Christ or a badge which could be pinned on their clothing. Then after the Mass we always have tea and cakes and biscuits for everyone, which provides a pleasant conclusion to our celebration.

These Masses are clearly intended for the benefit of parents as much as for their children. They therefore fall under the category of 'Masses for children in which parents participate' (D3). The children feel at ease with their parents and friends and like to stay with them during the Mass. It also pleases the parents greatly to see their children participating in the prayer of the eucharist. It is clearly not easy to keep the balance between the requirements of both children and adults, but the enthusiastic support of the parents encourages us to feel that we are on the right lines. As always, the homily presents special difficulties. You can often catch the attention of the children merely by speaking to them individually by name. They like this and they take notice, but I must confess that since the homily has to be kept very short, it leaves very little time to say anything directly to their parents.

(iii) *The deaf*

The old low Mass was largely a silent Mass. The new revised liturgy of the eucharist is a much more wordy affair – perhaps excessively so. This creates problems for the person who is becoming rather deaf in old age. We therefore need to make special provision for the 'hearing of the word' by those who suffer from this disability. The reader who is self-conscious and does not want to 'show off' can end up by being totally inaudible. The celebrant who does not enunciate his words clearly might as well not speak at all. We must adapt our voices (and our buildings) to achieve this essential level of audibility, so that the hard of hearing are able to participate in the liturgy.

However, my main concern in this short section is not primarily with the hard of hearing. I wish to consider a quite distinct group of people, namely the profoundly deaf. The profoundly deaf are people who are born deaf or who suffered some disease very early in their life which radically effects their hearing. A large proportion of these people are more than just deaf; their hearing deficiency creates a barrier which may impair intellectual growth. In many cases this can be very serious, reducing language to a minimum and severely restricting the power to think in the abstract. New methods are making it possible for an increasing number of profoundly deaf people to lead a normal life. But in the past, the profoundly deaf remained cut off from the rest of society – and from that society's church, and this is still true to a large extent. If it were not for the work of a small number of chaplains for the deaf in various parts of the country, the profoundly deaf would be left virtually outside the church – in spite of a long history of Catholic involvement in the education of the deaf. The profoundly deaf would prefer to be normal members of society, but their hearing deficiency has often forced them to keep their own company or to find their friends among people with a similar deficiency. Probably this is a reason why so few people are aware of the serious effects of this handicap.

It would be impossible to give an adequate picture of all the things which can be done to make the liturgy live for the profoundly deaf. The Association for the Catholic Deaf of Great Britain and Ireland[3] provides regular courses to help priests understand the thought patterns of the born deaf and to make use of 'signing' in the Mass. I hope in time that the Catholic Deaf Association will produce its own collections of texts suitable for the eucharist and other liturgies, including eucharistic prayers and model readings. All that I can do here is to draw

[3] Secretary, Rev. A. Tomaney, MBASW, 9 Jesmond Park West, Newcastle-on-Tyne NE7 7DL.

attention to the need for liturgies for the profoundly deaf and to list a few of the problems involved in creating them.[4]

The adult person who was born with a major impairment of his hearing is often very limited in his use of language and this has an effect on his grasp of abstract thought – which is very serious when you remember how many abstractions there are in basic Christian theology. Unlike children who will understand later what they have learned today, they may *never* understand some things. Of course this does not mean they can understand nothing, but it does demand that if we are to speak effectively to the profoundly deaf we must employ concrete thought and expression. A vivid story with plenty of colour is likely to say more about the life of Christ or how to be a good Christian than a logical abstract talk on the same subject. Even 'signing' or finger spelling will be useless, if the original material is complex, abstract, and wordy. Another thing to remember is that the adult deaf are not children, but grown ups. They have the experience of adults (and their problems) and do not want to be treated in a childish manner. I must say from my own experience that trying to be simple, concrete and adult, all at the same time like this, has had quite a beneficial effect on the way I speak at ordinary Sunday parish Masses.

The deaf are very keen to express the idea of community in a concrete – even physical – manner. Their particular sense of togetherness seems to last among themselves right throughout life. The 'sign' of peace, for example, is natural to them. Though they may be rather conservative in their religious practice, nevertheless they take great pleasure from participating actively in the liturgy wherever this is possible.

[4] I cannot myself adequately treat the further problem of confession for the deaf, but I feel it is necessary to draw attention to the difficulty of confession in this 'deaf' situation, if the sacrament is to be anything more than a 'handing in' of a written list of sins and the silent reception of the absolution. It has been suggested to me that only the provision of full-time deaf chaplains on a large scale will make it possible for the clergy to get to know the deaf over a long period and speak to them in their own language, and so be able to tackle this problem.

(i) *Introductory remarks*

It's quite a shock to look back to 15 May 1969 and the document from the newly created Congregation for Divine Worship on Masses for special gatherings. It is good to see that this, the very first document produced by the Congregation, was concerned with *new directions* in the liturgy, but how different in spirit it is from the Directory for Masses with Children of only four years later. The document is full of fears that bizarre novelties will infiltrate the Order of the Mass. The local bishop has to be approached in each and every case where Mass is to be celebrated outside a sacred place, and a report of the proceedings is to be sent on to him later. Fortunately within the year Cardinal Heenan in this country made his own position very clear. Talking about house Masses he wrote: 'We offer the Mass in our house because we realize that the home is a sanctuary fit to become the setting of the most sublime act of worship . . . the Mass brings us together as a family. It is a perfect beginning or end to our group meetings and presents to us a perfect opportunity of sanctifying our homes.' (*The House Mass and House Groups*, FSA, January 1970). As a result, it has not taken long for house Masses to become a normal part of parish life in most areas.

I would like to look at house liturgies under three headings. It seems to me there are three distinct good reasons why the Mass should be celebrated in a domestic setting. It may be for the sake of someone who is sick or perhaps for the old or even for the dying. It may be on the occasion of a family celebration; or finally, and perhaps most important of all, it can be an occasion for building up the communal and missionary spirit of a parish or district.

(ii) *The liturgy for the sick*

There's nothing very new about house liturgies for the sick. First Friday or even weekly communions for the sick are a standard part of English parish life. The old form of this ceremony was very brief and it frequently took place during a rushed visit as the priest hurried from house to house trying to fit everyone in. Unfortunately many priests have already greeted the new ceremony with alarm, complaining that it will take too long and is unlikely to be appreciated by old people who are deaf. It is now possible to use lay ministers to bring communion to the sick, and this should release priests from being overburdened by excessive numbers. It should therefore be easier now to spend more time with each individual person. As for the problem of deafness, only a small proportion of the sick people we visit are so deaf that they would not appreciate what we are saying. I think they deserve to be given at least the chance of using the new ceremony with its richer content.

The new Rite of the Anointing and Pastoral Care of the Sick is a very full document which will take quite a time to be assimilated. I hope it will not be simply dismissed out of hand. I particularly hope that priests will make full use of the wide variety of texts it provides. I myself have been well satisfied over the last two years with the dignity and prayerfulness of the rite for communion of the sick. It reflects the entrance and communion rite of the Mass and should help people to relate holy communion outside Mass to its origin and foundation within the whole liturgy of the eucharist. I have found that people really appreciate the dignity of this rite, not least because it gives them the opportunity of praying quietly with their priest for a few minutes. It is a little longer than the previous rite – though not excessively so – long enough to encourage other members of the sick person's household to join in, whenever they can, and even to receive communion themselves. When this happens the ceremony ceases to be a merely solitary business and becomes an expression of the Christian community at prayer.

During the course of a long illness, especially when a person is dying, it seems only obvious to try and celebrate the Mass itself in the sick person's house if he or she is willing. Some people will simply not like the idea, and we should respect their feelings. But if they would like a Mass and are well enough to take the strain, the eucharist can provide a wonderful occasion for prayer that they can share with their family and friends around their bedside or in their living-room. If the sick person is weak it might be better to have a very quiet Mass with only the immediate family present, perhaps in the mid-morning for example, before the sick person becomes tired.

I have found here as on other occasions that the simplest arrangement is for the priest to prepare a Mass kit, and to bring everything for Mass himself. It is surprising how many people do not even have a decent white table cloth suitable for the occasion. It may be a good idea to explain to the lady of the house just what is required for the Mass and then leave it to her to say if she can provide anything herself.

I personally feel the need of great simplicity in the arrangement of a house Mass. Some people still prefer to use altar stones, even portable altars, but they are not necessary and are often both unsightly and awkward to use. Tall unstable candles can be an absolute menace, but a colourful vase of flowers can be very welcome. Elaborate vestments often look hopelessly out of place in a small modern room (and dirty vestments, including chasubles, look twice as dirty when the priest is close to the people). It is interesting to see that the French bishops some time ago allowed the use of the alb and stole without the chasuble 'in the interests of the simplicity and *dignity* of the Mass' (Note de la Commission Episcopale de Liturgie, *Messes de Petits Groupes*, page 12, February 1970). As for the position occupied by the congregation themselves, this must depend on the size of the room. Some people would find it easier to sit throughout, others would prefer to stand. The sick person may find it necessary to remain in bed.

The state of the sick person and the mood of the people will determine just how much active participation is possible. I know of one recent occasion when a lapsed Catholic who was present at a Mass for a sick friend left the room in tears at communion time and busied herself in the kitchen. Clearly she was too emotionally involved in the situation even to be present to the end of the Mass. I can mention another occasion of a Mass for a dying man, which was attended by a non-Catholic grandson and his wife who had probably never been to a Mass before and could hardly be expected to participate fully in the usual way. Each situation is different, but it is a fact that many people who will not read a scripture reading or say a bidding prayer at the Sunday parish Mass will be ready and willing to do either in the situation created by the house Mass.

The celebrant should remember that the elaborate gestures

and movements suitable in the parish church can easily appear merely quaint within the average-sized room of an ordinary modern house. The profound bow or genuflection can look like something out of the Mikado, rather than an expression of reverence. Even the movement of the arms or the expression of the face must be taken into account. There are no hard and fast rules to achieve what is required, but the celebrant must take the trouble to do more than merely transpose the grand Sunday liturgy into the domestic situation.

It may be desirable to include the anointing of the sick in such a Mass after the homily, as long as it is not going to extend the ceremony to a burdensome length. The new rite for anointing and pastoral care of the sick describes in detail how this is to be done. Such a Mass can bring comfort and strength to the sick people and their families. I know of one recent house Mass and anointing that happened to take place within an hour or two of the patient's death, which seemed to transform the whole sorry business of dying into something dignified and holy for the people who were gathered there. It is wonderful to experience the working of the liturgy in this way.

(iii) *Domestic celebrations*

Recently, the National Liturgical Commission of England and Wales discussed the possibility of creating a Betrothal or Engagement Ceremony. Several drafts of the proposed order of service were put forward, and on each occasion it was pointed out that this ceremony could usefully be performed in the house of one of the two people to be engaged, rather than the church. Putting to one side the value of such a ceremony in itself, this makes me ask the question why do we not more frequently 'celebrate' in a religious manner our special family occasions within our own homes. Perhaps some people do, and solemnize all sorts of occasions from a baptism to a housewarming in this fashion. But these people are fairly exceptional at present. This may, however, change in time.

There appears to be only one disadvantage in this kind of 'social' house Mass: it can be divisive. The eucharist is concerned with a community which extends beyond the family unit, and it would be wrong for the Mass to be allowed to create separatist groups within a parish. The Mass could have a snob value in this situation and some parishioners are quite capable of using it for this unworthy purpose.

In practice much of what was said in the last section (and before) applies equally well here. We should try to achieve a liturgy that is warm and sympathetic while still being dignified and prayerful.

(iv) *Building up the parish community*

I sometimes think we try to renew the parish liturgy by starting at the wrong end. People are told they are the Christian community at prayer when they come to Mass on a Sunday, even though they may consider themselves anything but a community. Many of them look on the revised Roman Rite of Mass as a translation of the Tridentine Mass with a few changes, and wonder why they feel so dissatisfied. They may come to Mass diligently, and would be horrified at the thought of missing, but they would never look for the connection between the forty-five minutes they spend in church on a Sunday and the rest of the time they spend 'in the world' during the week. These are problems that will perhaps never be solved from the pulpit. Perhaps they go too deeply to be solved at this level. It may take a much more immediate experience of the liturgy to allow people to come to terms with what amounts to a whole new understanding of the local church and its liturgy as an expression of a missionary community.

Most parishes can be divided into small areas on a geographical basis, and if we can develop a simple sense of community at this level, then we will already have created the basic units of the larger *parish* community. The liturgy is only one thing among several others which will promote this basic sense of community, but it has its own distinctive part to play. The Christian community is nothing if it is not a prayerful community, and the preparation and the actual celebration of the Mass in each area goes a long way to establishing this fact. The practical execution of this kind of Mass is bound to be controlled by the life style of the people involved. In one area a short series of discussions leading up to a house Mass might be ideal, but hopeless in another. Each situation will have to be judged individually; it is no use making great demands on people if they are not going to be fulfilled. But if the liturgy is part of an overall plan for building up the community, then we should be able to find ample opportunity to prepare each Mass with the people involved in the way best suited to them.

A parish that has its roots in a community rather than a church building is likely to draw attention to itself, especially in an anonymous urban area. A Christian community which is concerned to build up the Body of Christ is very likely to extend its concern to those outside the Church and draw back a response from outside. This is the basis for a truly missionary Church, and if we are ever to enter into the spirit of the new missionary rite of Christian initiation of adults then we will depend greatly on this local area grouping for support in the various stages of initiation from the pre-catechumenate right through to the ceremony of baptism itself. It would be reasonable to presume that many of the liturgies proposed in this rite will be performed in a domestic setting, perhaps at the very level at which contact was first made with the local community.

CONCLUSION

I hope this chapter has suggested a few ways in which the liturgy can be adapted to suit the needs of particular groups of people. I have suggested a few specific ideas which may help others to do this – though none of them are very original. But I hope I have managed to go a little deeper by drawing attention to some of the controlling principles behind our changing liturgy. Despite the freedom which is built into liturgical forms today, I do not think that liturgy is a 'free-for-all'. We adapt the liturgy not just for the sake of change but to draw a particular group of people more effectively into the mystery of Christ, taking care not to upset the internal balance of the liturgy. We make use of ordinary human experience not to destroy the holiness of the Mass but to create a genuine eucharistic celebration which will help to transform our human lives. We involve people actively in the Mass not to belittle the ministry of the priest but to make clear that the eucharist is the shared action of the whole people of God united in prayer.

11. Some Urban Problems

Harold Winstone

In spite of all that we read about the break-up of family life, the home is still the cell of human society and of the Church's life.

In the towns many people are living in cramped conditions and there are many tensions and pressures which make life extremely difficult for these families. Young people tend to opt out of living with the parental family and at a relatively early age leave home either to get married or to live with friends in rented accommodation. Economic necessity forces wives to go to work as well as their husbands, and in consequence children are left in the care of other people for long periods of the day, or are left to their own devices.

In these conditions only rarely does the whole family sit round the table for a common meal. Evening meals are served canteen-fashion. Each member of the family takes his plate to his favourite stool and watches the television programme while he eats. There is rarely any thought of prayer.

How can one begin in these circumstances to think about liturgy in the home? It is a miracle if one can get these people to come to church. But that is just the point. Many of them no longer come to church, or come only rarely, and then what they experience is so unlike anything that goes on at home that it seems completely unreal, a different world. Either we must relate to them in their homes or not at all. Their children may not even be attending Catholic schools.

And so we visit them in their homes. What to do? To pass the time of day with them? To check up on their religious practice? To preach to them? None of these methods of approach will get us very far. All we can hope to do is to bring them some realization of the presence of God. Every time a priest or a parish sister or catechist enters such a home the visit should be something in the nature of a celebration. More often than not they will be offered a cup of tea, and here is a heaven-sent opportunity. They should accept it only on condition that everyone has a cup of tea or a glass of orange or something. Then, when the drinks are handed round and they have everyone's attention, they can hold their cup in front of them and say something like this:

Blessed are you, Lord God of all creation.
You have given us this drink as a sign of your love for us
to refresh us in body and revive our spirit.
Blessed be God for ever

Everyone should then be encouraged to say 'Blessed be God for ever', and then with conversation, laughter and gaiety proceed to take their drink. This is only the rudiments of a prayer-meal, but it is a real celebration for all that and will transform the visit into an occasion of spiritual profit, much more effective than a sermon.

There are obviously many other ways of achieving the same result. One way is to turn up at a child's birthday party, either by invitation or co-incidence and to bring an awareness of God's loving presence into that situation. If he keeps any records at all, a priest will know the birthday of most children in his parish. It will be in the baptismal register or on the school application form or on the baptism certificate produced before first communion. One of the parish catechists could keep a diary of birthdays of all the children in the parish.

Most families, however slip-shod in their religious practice, seem to welcome the idea of a house blessing, and here again is a good opportunity for a religious celebration. The keynote, however, must always be one of joy and gaiety. A solemn celebration is a contradiction in terms.

Happily there still are families in our parishes where the faith is alive and lived, where there are family prayers and family celebrations of the major liturgical seasons and feasts. In these families the parents themselves can be taught how to celebrate with their children. They can come together in groups and exchange ideas and learn how to organize a prayer-meal, for example, and how to involve their children in all the necessary preparations for such a celebration. When someone is sick they will know how to prepare the room and the patient for the visit of the priest or commissioned layman who comes to bring holy communion, and the whole family will help to choose the readings and take part in the prayers.

Whenever they have a celebration they will extend invitations to their friends and neighbours and in this way perhaps bring in those children from other homes where prayer is rarely thought of. They will do this particularly when they have a house Mass.

The house Mass is becoming increasingly popular today and is proving a very effective means of 'Christianizing' the lives of our people. In some parishes visiting is done systematically in areas. When the whole of an area has been visited, the people of that area are called together for a house Mass in one of the homes. Invitations are written out and delivered by the host family. This family also chooses the readings and prayers and hymns, and after the Mass they provide tea and biscuits so that their guests can stay on for a while for a friendly discussion. Needless to say, the whole family is involved in the preparations for the Mass. They decorate the room, prepare the table and provide the candles and the cruets, etc., and may even provide the wine and learn how to bake unleavened bread.

Priests who celebrate house Masses of this kind must learn to adapt themselves to this new situation. Many of the trappings and techniques of a church Mass are inappropriate in an ordinary living-room. The priest's vestment will be of the simplest kind and his whole demeanour will be one of homely simplicity – yes, like Christ sharing a meal with his disciples.

Most of the time he will sit rather than stand, and the people will be seated around the table. Or, if there are too many for this arrangement, the priest will sit at a low table and the people sit round the walls of the room with the children squatting in front of them on the floor or on cushions.

The homily will be in the nature of a dialogue, with everyone present sharing their thoughts. There will be silent prayer. The intercessions will be spontaneous, each one asking for prayers for sick or distant or departed relatives and friends. The children will sing their own songs and take a lively part in the kiss of peace. Communion will be under both kinds. Over all there should reign a spirit of joy and peace, and a lively awareness of the presence of Christ.

People have remarked that after the experience of a house

Mass of this kind they have understood much better what the Mass is all about and their Sunday Mass has in consequence taken on new meaning and become much more fruitful.

Those teenagers who tend to cut adrift from the family and live a sort of gang life in clubs, discotheques and coffee bars present an entirely different problem. For them we need young trained leaders who will dedicate themselves to living their kind of life with them, and who will bring them together in groups and help them to see for themselves the worthwhileness of living a truly Christian life. The need for such leaders is very great indeed and we have hardly begun recruiting for what is very definitely a specialized vocation. If we had only one such leader in every urban parish we would be making some headway. As it is many of these young people are drifting away and we leave them to their own devices, hoping that in the providence of God they will find their way to a stable marriage and return to the practice of the faith. We are expecting a lot.

Catholic Youth Clubs can do much to alleviate the situation, but still everything will depend on the leaders. There are very few clubs where the priest would be welcome to come in one evening for a club Mass organized and participated in wholeheartedly by the young people. In most clubs he had better not try. Unless the initiative comes from them he is in any event wasting his time.

We should be training leaders now, not just in the techniques of running a youth club, but in relating as Christians to these young people and devoting several years of their lives to helping them to live genuinely Christian lives and to find the God who gives joy to their youth.

Part Three

CELEBRATING THE OTHER SACRAMENTS

12. Initiation

Christopher J. Walsh

A. BAPTISM

'Those who, through the Church, have accepted from God a belief in Christ should be admitted to the catechumenate by liturgical rites. Then, when the sacraments of Christian initiation have freed them from the power of darkness, having died with Christ, been buried with him, and risen with him, they receive the Spirit who makes them adopted sons, and celebrate the remembrance of the Lord's death and resurrection together with the whole people of God' (Decree on the Church's Missionary Activity 14).

In this description, which would have been familiar to the early Church, the Second Vatican Council reaffirms the traditional understanding of Christian initiation as a unity and a process. It is not something achieved with a trickle of water one Sunday afternoon but a progressive entry into a commitment and a relationship, marked at each stage by a liturgical celebration, and culminating only in a communion of life with Christ and his people in the eucharist. Becoming a Christian is a conversion, a growing adherence to Christ in faith and sacrament over an extended period of time. For a long time in the West it has customarily begun with infant baptism, been deepened and made explicit by a Christian upbringing and education, and completed in first communion followed eventually by confirmation. But increasingly in the future we may expect it to resume its classical and more intelligible sequence of personal conversion and faith growing to maturity during a period of catechumenate and reaching sacramental climax in a single celebration of baptism, confirmation and first communion. This adult pattern is the paradigm to which we must look to understand the meaning and consistency of Christian initiation. The infant pattern, despite its incidence, is not the liturgical norm but rather a common exception.

Baptism, the first and basic sacrament of initiation, must not be regarded as an extrinsic operation, something done to us which simply frees us from original sin and fills us with sanctifying grace. As long as this popular but simplistic understanding of it persists, the entire reformed liturgy will be suffered and resented as an academic irrelevance and a pastoral imposition. A first priority, then, is to restore among clergy and people a richer and more adequate appreciation of the meaning of baptism. The outlines are provided in the introduction to the new Order (nn. 3-6) and should be driven home in preaching and instruction at every level.

Baptism is the sacrament of that *faith* which enables us with the grace of the Holy Spirit to respond to the gospel of Christ. It is therefore the Church's primary concern to bring catechumens, parents and godparents to that degree of real and active faith by which they can commit themselves to Christ in a new covenant relationship. This explains the restoration of the catechumenate, the instruction of parents, the emphasis on the liturgy of the word and the baptismal profession of faith.

Baptism is also the sacrament by which we are incorporated into the *Church*, the living temple, the royal priesthood, and the holy people of God. It is the sacrament of rebirth in the Spirit which makes us adopted children of God, so that we share in his divine nature and are drawn into the inner life of the Trinity. Of its nature it involves us from the very beginning in relationship and solidarity with others, and so can never be a purely private affair.

All these effects are achieved by the power of the *Paschal Mystery* of Christ's death and resurrection, which liberates us from death in sin to life in God. In baptism we are united with him in the likeness of his death, buried with him, and rise to new life with him through his resurrection. But what is celebrated in baptism is the beginning of a process, a way of life. The response of faith and conversion, the assimilation to Christ in his Paschal Mystery, is the work of a lifetime. It must be deepened, carried forward and authenticated day after day in lives of love, service and witness, whereby we die to sin and self in order to live for him.

The initiation of adults

The restored rite of adult initiation is one organic liturgy celebrated in a succession of stages. Conversion to the living God, commitment in faith to Christ as Lord, is something progressive and cumulative. Faith grows over a period; baptism as the sacrament of faith assists and carries it forward at each stage by liturgical celebrations which express and activate the grace of the sacrament. The catechumenate, then, is not merely a preparation for the sacrament, it is an integral part of it.

EVANGELIZATION. The liturgy of initiation begins with the admission to the catechumenate, but before candidates are ready for this they must have come through the stage of evangelization, a period of search and enquiry in which they hear and respond to the Good News and experience their first leanings towards the Christian faith. Such initial inclination will normally result from contact with a Christian community and exposure to its life. The responsibility of the Church to such 'sympathizers' is therefore one of example, welcome and dialogue. Informally, and in ways appropriate to the time and circumstances, the local church should offer such people opportunities for conversation and friendship, for information and reflection without obligation or pressure, and above all for experiencing at close quarters the spirit and way of life of the Christian family. The atmosphere should not be that of an enquiry class or a statutory marriage instruction but more that of a family welcoming a new neighbour or a prospective son-in-law. In no circumstances should the catechumenate be begun without this relationship being established, not only with the priest but with a representative section of the community, especially with genuine Christian families. Only then will 'sympathizers' come to realize that Christianity is not simply an intellectual assent to a system of beliefs but a style of life and relationships in a community of shared faith.

ADMISSION. When the candidates are ready to indicate publicly their initial conversion and their desire to become Christians, they are formally admitted to the catechumenate in a liturgical rite whose principal feature is the marking of the candidates with the sign of the cross signifying their first commitment to

Christ, their entry into the household of the faith, and the Church's acceptance of responsibility for them. The service begins at the church door. After being questioned on their motives for presenting themselves, the candidates declare their readiness to follow Christ, and their sponsors together with the whole congregation declare their readiness to help them. The priest then performs a first 'exorcism', asking God to withdraw them from the power of evil. He may accompany this formula with either the traditional breathing in the face or the more acceptable extension of hands. The solemn signation then takes place, and may be followed by some symbolic rite of acceptance into the community – either the traditional gift of salt or, more helpfully, the gift of a crucifix or medal. All are then invited into church for a brief service of the word. After the homily each may be given a copy of the gospels, and the rite concludes with bidding prayers. A delightful rubric suggests that they should not disperse immediately but stay for a social get-together with the faithful.

CATECHUMENATE. Coming to faith is more than just the individual's response to God's call. Both call and response are mediated through the community. Only when the candidate's faith is 'socialized' and integrated into that of the community, the possessor of God's promises, can it find security and shape. The catechumenate, then, is not simply a series of doctrinal instructions, but more especially a formation in Christian attitudes and values, an acclimatization to a rhythm of prayer and worship and a whole way of life. It is for this reason that on admission to the catechumenate each candidate chooses a sponsor from the local community, ideally someone with similar interests and background to himself, who will accompany and support him through all the stages of his initiation, discuss his problems with him, and introduce him into the life of the local church through his own family and circle of friends.

The period of catechumenate, of its nature, may last months or even years, depending on the time needed for the individual's faith to mature. It should consist in individual and collective catecheses, accompanied and strengthened by participation in worship, so that instruction in doctrine may be matched by growing familiarity with the mystery of salvation. Candidates should be encouraged to attend regularly at the liturgy of the word (long known as the 'Mass of the Catechumens'), but since they do not yet share in Christ's priesthood and may not yet communicate it is inappropriate for them to remain for the rest of the eucharist (the 'Mass of the Faithful'). The Order also provides a series of minor 'exorcisms' and blessings for use *ad libitum* at any stage during the catechumenate by the priest or deacon or whoever conducts the catechesis.

ELECTION. When, after consultation between clergy, catechists and sponsors, the catechumens are at last judged ready to proceed to baptism, they are admitted ('elected') to the next more intensive stage of preparation, described in the Latin text as 'purification and enlightenment'. This will normally coincide with Lent, the community's preparation for the Easter sacraments. This is a decisive stage, a definitive application for baptism and the Church's acceptance of their seriousness and suitability. The increasing tempo of the liturgy indicates that this time is to be devoted to a more intensive spiritual preparation and recollection, rather than to further instruction.

It opens with a service of 'election and inscription' on the first Sunday of Lent. After the homily at Mass, the candidates are presented by the one who was responsible for the catechumenate. Their sponsors are first questioned about their progress and suitability, then the catechumens themselves are questioned about their motivation. They then sign their names as a commitment to baptism, and are 'elected' or admitted for baptism at the coming Vigil. After concluding prayers they are dismissed and the Mass continues.

On the third, fourth and fifth Sundays (or on intervening weekdays) the traditional 'scrutiny' liturgies are celebrated. As in the early Church this forbidding name does not indicate an examination of the candidates' doctrinal competence but a solemn form of prayer and imposition of hands aimed at liberating them from the power of sin and encouraging them in their adherence to Christ. The fact that they normally take place at Sunday Mass means that the whole community is able to support them with its prayers and special biddings. During this period, too, the words of the Lord's Prayer and the creed may be formally committed to them in special services for which readings and prayers are provided.

BAPTISM. Candidates are urged to spend Holy Saturday in recollection and, if possible, fasting. Where possible they should assemble together during the day to repeat the Lord's Prayer and creed, to receive the 'ephphetha' sign on their ears and lips, and the preliminary anointing on their hands or chest with the oil of catechumens. All of these are optional ceremonies. At night they will assemble with the whole community to keep the Vigil, in the course of which they will be baptized. After hearing again the history of salvation in the liturgy of the word, they process to the baptistery during the singing of the litany, where the bishop or presiding priest solemnly 'blesses' the water with one of three splendid prayers of thanksgiving which recall the natural and biblical symbolism of the element. Regular exposure of congregations to these texts should do much to counteract the widespread and superficial understanding of baptism as merely the washing away of original sin. Then, after renouncing Satan and professing the faith which they have been making their own for several long months, they are baptized. The new Order, while allowing the customary pouring of water, makes clear its preference for baptism by immersion – if not of the whole body at least of the head – in such a way that it may be understood not just as a rite of purification but as the sacrament of assimilation to Christ (*Praenotanda*, 32). In several recently built churches the baptistery incorporates a pool in which the candidates may stand while water is poured over their heads, or they are ducked under a jet or trickle of water – which seems about the best combination of symbolism and practicality. In most of our existing churches such arrangements would be entirely out of the question. With the usual style of font or with provisional bowls of water the best that can be achieved is a ducking of the head. If it be objected that this would be a ludicrous procedure with inelegant results – splashing, spluttering, water on the floor and ruined coiffures – one can only reply 'So be it', that this is what it is all about. Baptism should be traumatic; and very wet.[1] To stress this

---

[1] Cf Theodore of Mopsuestia, Baptismal Homily III, in E. Yarnold (ed.), *The Awe-Inspiring Rites of Initiation*, Slough, 1972, p. 201.

point is not to question the validity of small quantities of water, but to switch the emphasis from the essential minimum for exceptional cases to the desirable optimum for normal cases. The entire sacramental and biblical symbolism of water summed up in the blessing formula, the image of dying, being buried and rising with Christ, if it is to be experienced and not just believed, surely demands something more than an apologetic thimbleful of water.

But not even water and immersion can symbolize every effect of baptism. The water-baptism is followed by two brief explanatory rituals,[2] each symbolizing an aspect of the sacrament. The sponsors first clothe the neophytes with a white gown to signify that they have put on the new man in Christ, and then they hand to each neophyte a candle lighted from the Paschal Candle to signify that they are now children of light.

CONFIRMATION AND COMMUNION. Unless grave reasons make it impossible, the sacrament of confirmation is celebrated immediately. The neophytes are brought before the bishop or presiding priest who explains to them that now they are reborn in Christ and become members of his priestly people it remains for them to receive the gift of the Spirit which will conform them even more closely to Christ, and enable them to be witnesses to his resurrection and active members of the Church. He extends his hands over them, invokes the sevenfold Spirit upon them and anoints them each with chrism, after which he greets each with a sign of peace.

The Mass resumes with the prayer of the faithful in which the neophytes, as newly accepted members of the priestly people, should have an active part. For the same reason they should be involved in the procession and preparation of the gifts which follows. Special mention is made of them in each of the four eucharistic prayers, and before they receive communion for the first time – in both kinds – the celebrant may remind them that this first communion is the climax of their entire initiation, the foundation and centre of all their subsequent Christian life.

[2] Also by an anointing with chrism, as in infant baptism, if for some serious reason confirmation is not to follow immediately.

Adaptation

This is the normative rite of adult initiation. Each episcopal conference is to prepare its own version based on the Roman model but adapted to the needs of its own country and taking account of local customs. It may, for instance, dispense with certain ceremonies (like some of the exorcisms, the oil of catechumens, the ephphetha, etc.) and provide alternative formulae where options are indicated. The priest, or catechist, too, has considerable liberty not only to choose among various options but often to substitute formulae of his own and to construct a liturgy suited to the particular circumstances from the elements and models provided.

In addition to the normative rite the Order also provides a 'simpler form' of adult initiation according to which the whole liturgy may be condensed into a single celebration with the optional addition of just one or two out of all the catechumenal services. However, this reduced rite may only be used in exceptional cases, for serious pastoral reasons, and in each case requires the specific permission of the bishop. And even when it is permitted it presupposes that the candidates will have undergone an adequate period of formation and will have acquired a familiarity with the life of the community. It should be celebrated preferably during Sunday Mass, with the active participation of the congregation. Finally it must be stressed that it would be clearly contrary to the mind of the Church to resort to this shorter form habitually, as it would deprive the candidates of the liturgical and spiritual support to which they have a right.

Normally the full rite should be timed to conclude with the Easter Vigil, though for 'grave pastoral necessities' it can be celebrated at other times. The 'election' service should accordingly take place on the first Sunday of Lent, but the admission service can be celebrated at any suitable time. What is important is that candidates should never be rushed into it, and it would seem best, where practicable, to wait for a group to form who could be prepared together. If numbers permitted, two or three dates in the year could be set aside for admission services in the cathedral (as with confirmation) or in each deanery.

Organizing the catechumenate

Many will be tempted to dismiss this entire liturgy as impractical, unnecessary, artificial and excessively complex, something which could only have been devised by academics and
romantics quite out of touch with pastoral realities. But they
should be reminded that the catechumenate was successfully
restored in France as long ago as 1953, and that the leader of
the group which produced the new rite has had twenty years'
experience of running such catechumenates. Organized catechumenates exist in every diocese in France and are staffed
by qualified personnel.[3] In the city of Paris alone there are
some thousand trained lay catechists and as many again in
training. And it is not unknown for hundreds of candidates to
be admitted to the catechumenate in a single ceremony, and
quite common to see tens of catechumens baptized in a cathedral
or city church at the Easter Vigil.

Of course needs and conditions are by no means identical in
this country. But we talk often and feelingly of our 'post-
Christian society'. If such it is, then the restoration of a genuine
catechumenate is absolutely imperative as part of the re-
organization of the Church for mission. And as the new Order
for infant baptism becomes better known and is taken more
seriously, an ever-increasing number of people will have grown
up without baptism, even though linked in one way or another
with the Church.

We shall need properly constituted centres for the catechumenate, under the direction of specialist priests, religious
and catechists. At the moment, and for a long time perhaps,
they would be impossible and unnecessary at the level of the
individual parish, but they should certainly be contemplated at
the level of the deanery, city or pastoral area in our conur-
bations and densely populated dioceses.[4] The network of
Catholic Marriage Advisory Centres provides an obvious

[3] Cf F. Coudreau, 'The Catechumenate in France' in *Worship* 42 (1968), pp.
223–41, and Various Authors, 'Evangelization and Catechumenate in the Church
around the World' in *Concilium*, vol. 2, no. 3, February 1967.
[4] There is admittedly the possibility of some conflict between the need for large-
scale organization to ensure realistic numbers and the desirability of a progressive
insertion during the catechumenate into the life of the local parish. But it is neither
inevitable nor insuperable. It is here that the role of the sponsor is so invaluable in
introducing the candidate into the life of the local church – at all levels.

model. They would obviously need to be extremely flexible, providing classes, discussion groups, reading programmes, etc., at a variety of levels, which would cater not only for the committed but also for the curious, not only for catechumens but also for those baptized but never brought up as Catholics, and perhaps, too, for Catholic parents and sponsors being prepared for baptism of their children. Catechists would need a thorough and demanding training, but it should not be necessary to point out the enormous positive advantages and other potential uses of such a corps of trained and committed lay people in the local church. (Again the training of marriage counsellors provides a useful model. Diocesan catechetical centres would have something to contribute, but much work would be needed, and a reorientation away from child-centred to adult-centred catechetics on a scale that has scarcely been contemplated yet in this country.)

The baptism of infants

Until 1969, as is well known, the Roman liturgy had never possessed a rite of infant baptism. In the early Church children were brought for baptism at the Easter Vigil along with adults. (The revised liturgy of Easter Night makes explicit provision for this once more.) When infants came to outnumber and eventually replace adults as the normal subjects of baptism all that happened was that the adult rite with all its stages was gradually run together into a single service and performed for children (who were still addressed as adults) at any time their parents or godparents brought them, and normally the sooner the better. The Second Vatican Council demanded for the first time the preparation of a rite which would take account of the fact that those to be baptized are, in fact, infants, and which would bring out more clearly the roles and duties of both parents and godparents (CL 67). The new rite of infant baptism (1969) is a single service, but comprises four distinct stages each conducted in a different part of the church.

(i) It begins with a rite of welcome at the church door, where the priest greets the families on behalf of the assembled congregation and, having put them at ease, asks what names are to be given to the children and what are the expectations of their parents in bringing them for the sacrament. He addresses both parents and godparents on their responsibilities, and then traces a cross on the children's foreheads to signify their belonging to Christ and the community's acceptance of responsibility for them. Since, in fact, this responsibility will be exercised principally through the parents and godparents, he invites them to sign the children in the same way.

(ii) All now process to their seats for a brief liturgy of the word. This is designed to arouse the faith and commitment of the parents, godparents and congregation, not of the babies, who may be taken out, if necessary, so that the word may be heard. Volunteer babyminders should be provided by the parish so that mothers and godmothers may not be deprived of this liturgical opportunity. One or more readings may be chosen from a wide selection provided. They should be chosen with regard to the circumstances and needs of the families involved, and should not be invariably the same. A psalm or hymn may be sung in response. The priest should then give a brief homily, explaining the reading(s) and applying it to the situation of the hearers. The rubrics do *not* regard the homily as optional, and the very nature of the occasion indicates the necessity of at least a few words to elicit and give shape to the faith which the families will soon have to profess publicly. Bidding prayers follow, in the preparation and delivery of which the families could be involved. They end with the invocation of the saints (parallel to the litany in adult baptism) during which the babies are brought back. This section of the rite concludes with a prayer of 'exorcism', asking that the children may be delivered from evil to become temples of the Spirit, and an anointing on the chest with the oil of catechumens.[5]

(iii) The next stage of the rite takes place at the font. As in the adult rite, the priest first blesses the water with one of three solemn formulae of thanksgiving and praise, declaring the rich salvific history and symbolism of water. Then the renunciation of sin and profession of faith are demanded – not of the infants or their 'spokesmen' as in times past, but of the parents and godparents speaking for themselves. Their profession is then ratified by the priest and congregation together, expressing the

---

[5] This is a rite which local episcopal conferences have the option of dropping. Despite the difficulties over anointing (cf infra) and the danger of confusion with later anointings, the English bishops have decided to retain it.

solidarity of the believing community into which the children are baptized. This should be one of the high points of the whole rite. For reasons which will become clear, everything should be done to heighten its impact. The formula provided is fine, strong and clear, and should be proclaimed by the whole assembly with deliberation and vigour. When proper resources are available (an organ and confident congregation) it could be replaced or reinforced by a stirring rendering of Newman's 'Firmly I believe' or some comparable hymn. On no account should we allow the occasion to be frittered away in confused mutterings or pusillanimous music.

The baptism itself now follows with the usual formula. Once again the text envisages immersion. In fact this should be easier to manage with babies than with adults. Few there are, even among a celibate clergy, who have never witnessed a mother or nurse rinsing a baby's hair at bath-time. (Hold in one arm, dip head backwards and downwards into the water, with other hand ladle further water over the front of the scalp.) Needless to say, the water should have been warmed somewhat either before the service began or before it was brought in. Time and towels should be allowed for the godmothers to dry the heads, time during which the suggested acclamations or Easter hymns could very well be sung. The water-baptism is followed up by three explanatory rituals which express symbolically various aspects of the new life of the baptized. First their incorporation into Christ, the anointed priest, prophet and king is given literal expression in an anointing on the forehead with chrism. Then the new creation which they have put on in Christ is represented by the gift of a white garment, and finally their status as children of light, illumined by the risen Christ, is signified by a candle for each child, lighted from the Paschal Candle.

Even at the best of times anointing is a difficult symbol for us in northern Europe. We have little appreciation or experience of this sort of oil or this sort of use of it. And in this instance the difficulties are compounded by the ambiguity of the gesture in relation both to the previous anointing of the chest and to the subsequent anointing, a few years hence, in the sacrament of confirmation.[6] Whatever we are to make of it will not be made

[6] It is interesting that this anointing is omitted in adult Baptism when Confirma-

any clearer by employing miniscule amounts of oil and removing them instantly as if we had suddenly changed our minds or were ashamed of what we had done. In the bible, we are told, oil suggests richness and joy; let us at least be expressive and expansive in our use of it.

Likewise in the interests of authenticity the white garment should be a real garment, and having been given to the child should not be taken back again. The rubric recommends that the families themselves provide it. Failing that the girls' school or the needlework guild or other women in the parish have often been happy to provide a supply of simple shifts. The candle, too, should be something worth keeping as a memento of baptism, perhaps to light again at confirmation and first communion. Certainly it should not be a mean article from the votive rack, nor something that will be immediately pressed into service in the next electricity cuts. Substantial and pleasantly decorated candles are now commercially available.

(iv) Parents and children now process with lighted candles to the altar, where the priest reminds them briefly that the initiation of their children will not be complete until they have celebrated confirmation and made their first communion. The Lord's Prayer – the prayer of adopted sons – is then said by all together, and the whole liturgy concludes with a series of blessings, of the mothers, the fathers and the whole congregation.

Faith and infant baptism

The provision of a new rite evidently means that the practice of infant baptism continues to be regarded by the Church as normal and proper. It has, of course, been questioned at various times in history, and not only by Baptists. We would do well to recognize that it does pose a problem for the whole of our sacramental theology and practice. We customarily describe the sacraments as instructive signs: 'They not only *presuppose faith*, but by words and objects they also nourish, strengthen and express it; that is why they are called sacraments of faith. They do indeed impart grace, but, in addition, the very act of

---

tion is to follow immediately. Evidently the compilers of the rite were aware of the ambiguity and possible confusion.

celebrating them disposes the faithful most effectively to receive this grace in a fruitful manner' (CL 59; my italics).

It must have occurred to most of us that infant baptism can only with difficulty be reconciled with such a description. To celebrate the sacrament of baptism in the absence of any such faith or response would appear to be a meaningless piece of 'magic', not rendered any more intelligible by appeals to invisible effects in the supernatural order. But this would be to forget that adult responses and adult relationships are not the only ones having any reality or value. Surely God is just as capable of forming a relationship with a child, albeit a unilateral one, as is any human parent or adult. In infant baptism God begins to communicate himself, to accept the child as a member of his Son. As in every sacrament this communication demands a response, but the response can only be given to the extent that God is recognized and his grace personally and consciously accepted. The communication is begun in the expectation that the child will come eventually to respond for himself. The divine and the human contributions to the encounter are not simultaneous. But if the response never does take place, there is no encounter and the sacrament remains permanently crippled and frustrated. And so it is that the Church insists that there must be a reasonable and well-founded expectation that the child will grow up to make his own response, if baptism is to be celebrated at all responsibly. When such confidence does not exist, infant baptism would be indiscriminate, something condemned by Bishop Hensley Henson as 'indecent in itself, discreditable to the Church, and highly injurious to religion'.[7]

In medieval Christendom, perhaps in parts of Ireland still today, one would be justified in making a general presumption since, no matter what the home background, the ethos and structures of society would provide the growing child with an environment of faith and Christian practice in which he could

---

[7] As A. M. Henry has said, there is not necessarily more holiness, charity or grace in the world every time 100,000 names are added to the baptismal registers. Though we multiply the signs of grace we do not necessarily multiply grace. For a review and bibliography of the whole question of indiscriminate baptism see R. X. Redmond, 'Infant Baptism: History and Pastoral Problems' in *Theological Studies* 30 (1969), pp. 79–89.

make his response. This is simply not true in twentieth-century Britain, and the responsibility for providing such an environment is thrown back on the local Christian community, which is more often than not powerless to influence or help a child if the parents are uncommitted or uninterested.

It is in the light of this that we can understand the emphasis in the new rite on the role of the congregation, the parents and the godparents. To say that children are baptized in the 'faith of the Church' means that the community goes guarantor for them and accepts responsibility for providing the environment and support in which the children can grow to personal faith. Baptism is a sacrament of the Church, by which new members are incorporated into the community of believers. The whole Church, therefore, through the concrete local community, has an interest and a responsibility and should accordingly be involved in the action. It is for this reason that the public baptism of several infants at a time with the participation of a congregation is regarded as the norm in the new rite. But the principal agents of this responsibility of the local church towards the children will necessarily be the parents, family and godparents. So most of the rite is addressed to them, and it is *they* who must profess their faith and give guarantees. Godparents should not be just family friends to whom a couple feel obliged, much less ornaments from whom they anticipate generous gifts, but a second line of guarantors to back them up and if needs be help them in the discharge of their responsibilities.

Faith and the parents

It is difficult to see how the rite can be celebrated honestly unless the parents, or at the very least their families and the godparents, give some credible evidence of faith. It cannot be prudent or moral to accept commitments on behalf of a child from persons who make no attempt to honour them in their own lives, and so to celebrate a sacrament which one knows will never be completed. Of course, a priest will not be in a position to make such a judgement on the spot, but the rite requires him to have met the couple previously and to have instructed them in the meaning of baptism. Even then it is not really for him to decide or to refuse baptism; much better that he should firmly and clearly acquaint the parents with their responsibilities, with the nature of the sacrament and the demands of the rite, and leave them to decide whether they can in conscience and sincerity accept them publicly.[8] But an obvious measure of their sincerity would be their willingness to receive such instruction as is necessary. All this suggests a considerable delay between the time of birth and the date of baptism. In no circumstances may one simply baptize all comers at an open service or at a fixed time on Sundays. If every couple is to contact the priest, become acquainted with the rite and receive instruction, baptism must be by prior arrangement and a delay of up to a month would seem to be indicated in most cases, probably longer in the case of parents long out of contact with the Church.[9] During this time the priest can help the couple to clarify their motives, recognize their responsibilities and deepen their relationship with the community.

Even when parents feel unable to go through with the baptism, unable as yet to accept its commitments, they should never be sent away empty-handed. A brief informal service of blessing and thanksgiving for the child's birth and of prayer for it and its parents could be arranged, perhaps in the home. And the Church's continuing interest and concern for the child must be made evident and effective in the pastoral contact which the priest maintains with the family. There is growing support in many quarters for the spreading out over several stages of the rite of infant baptism, analogous to the rite for adults and the practice authorized in mission territories.[10] All babies, then, could be 'enrolled' for baptism in a rite of welcome and inscription, which would manifest God's universal invitation to salvation through the Church and the community's acceptance of responsibility for the children. But only when the parents

[8] This is the policy recommended by the French bishops in their Pastoral Directives of 1966 (*La Maison-Dieu* 88 (1966), pp. 43–56) and by the Church of England Commission on Christian Initiation in their report *Christian Initiation: Birth and Growth in Christian Society*, 1971.
[9] The Church never officially insisted on the 'quam primum' until the Council of Florence's Decree for the Jacobites (D.S. 1349). That the new rite envisages at least a month is suggested by the fact that baptism is not encouraged during Lent except in case of necessity.
[10] Cf the articles by P-M. Gy, 'Un document de la Congrégation pour la Doctrine de la Foi sur le baptême des petits enfants' and by B. Rey, 'Que penser d'un rite d'inscription?' in *La Maison-Dieu* 104 (1970).

174

were fully prepared would a child be brought back for baptism itself, which would be very soon for committed parents but perhaps several months or years later for the lapsed or luke-warm. But the child would all the while be in a real relation-ship to the Church, analogous to that of catechumen, a real pastoral link would be opened up and maintained with the family, and all the catechetical resources of the community would be at their disposal.

Preparing the parents

The very first pastoral priority in relation to infant baptism is to ensure the requisite instruction of parents both in the mean-ing and demands of the sacrament and in their subsequent responsibility in bringing up their children in the faith. Ideally this should begin with a home visit during the later stages of pregnancy, when the human significance of the coming birth and all its implications can be discussed on home ground. After the birth when the parents seek a date for baptism they will be invited to attend a short series of 'instructions' and to make a provisional booking for their child at the first service of baptism to follow their instruction, and given a copy of the rite to take home and peruse. The pattern of instruction will obviously depend on the numbers involved and their level of commitment. In a large and populous parish there could be a perpetual cycle of, say, four-weekly sessions throughout the year, culminating each month in a celebration of baptism. In smaller communities the instructions would have to be arranged on a more individual basis. The talks could cover the Christian life, the meaning of the sacraments, the rite of baptism, etc., and could include discussions, filmstrips, planning of ceremonies and the like. The priest will usually be able to judge whether an individual couple might need further help through private visits. He might also dispense couples from the more fundamental topics if they have been through it before with previous children, or other-wise have no need of them. But even they should be asked to come again for the sessions which are devoted to planning and rehearsing the liturgy. It has been found that these sessions can handsomely repay the effort put into them: pastoral contacts have been forged or resumed, people have returned to the sacraments, irregular marriages have been sorted out, and older children brought to complete their initiation.[11] It can even happen that a group which has come together for this purpose asks for further meetings and forms itself into an ongoing discussion group or family circle.

Organizing the celebration

Except for emergencies, baptism should normally be celebrated on Sundays, and it is not permitted to have more than one celebration on the same day. But it is neither necessary nor desirable to have baptisms every Sunday. Both the theology and liturgy of the sacrament demand the presence and active participation of a congregation. This, together with the necessity for adequate preparation of the parents and the preference for multiple rather than individual baptisms, suggests a celebration no more than once a month in a large parish, less frequently in a small one. Where possible we should aim to have a special baptismal service as an independent liturgy, but the difficulty in assembling a congregation for that purpose alone means that we will often have to settle for a celebration during Mass or the evening service, when a congregation is already to hand. But whereas celebration during Mass is the ideal and the norm for most sacraments, this is not the case for infant baptism, for the obvious reason that the subjects of baptism can take no meaningful part in the Mass and may not, in our present discipline, communicate;[12] and that even the parents themselves may not feel ready to communicate, and should not feel in any way pressured to do so. If baptisms are regularly celebrated during Sunday Mass, care should be taken that it is not always at the same Mass, both so that the regular congregation may not have their normal Sunday worship habitually distorted, and so that different congregations may have the opportunity of being involved.

As in the Mass, we should endeavour to organize the celebration in such a way as to achieve the maximum distribution of roles, readers, servers, choir, congregation and clergy all contributing their proper share. The parents and godparents

[11] Cf J. Collins, 'The New Rite of Infant Baptism: a Parish Priest's Experience', in *Clergy Review*, August 1970, pp. 587ff.
[12] It should be remembered that in the Eastern churches babies are given communion under the form of wine immediately after their baptism and confirmation, and that this practice survived in the West until the late middle ages.

have their own part to play. Other members of the families should also be drawn in – grandparents or elder children might share the bidding prayers and join the processions, young brothers and sisters should be brought to the font for a good view, and may be asked to hold towels or to pass items as needed. Rather than simply operating a rota, as many clergy as are available – including guests, too, perhaps – should take part, not only because the number of babies might be considerable but also for symbolic reasons, to make clear that this is a celebration of the entire community gathered to welcome new members.[13] The rite demands singing, and our new hymnals do contain a baptism section in addition to the repertoire of Easter hymns. One way of guaranteeing both an interested congregation and enthusiastic singing has been to involve the schools of the parish, even if this has meant a weekday celebration.

Conscientious implementation of the new liturgy may demand a reconsideration of the geography of many of our churches. A liturgy such as we have described cannot work if the baptistery is tucked away out of sight under the gallery stairs, if the congregation can neither see nor hear what is going on there, or if it can accommodate no more than the priest and two adults. Should this be the case, we should look for some place in the Church where it can be resituated permanently in the sight of the congregation, and in the meanwhile make use of a temporary font.

Whatever the circumstances, everything must be done to secure a festive atmosphere, a well-staged and thoroughly enjoyable celebration, so that people will have cause to remember the liturgy of baptism as they generally remember a wedding.

B. CONFIRMATION

In contrast to baptism, confirmation could fairly claim to be one of the least memorable of liturgies. Many of us probably have difficulty in remembering the date or circumstances of our own, others will have recollections of an anonymous ceremony not altogether unlike a mass-vaccination session. Once upon a time (and now once again for adults) it was a high point of an integrated and continuous liturgy of initiation. But once sep-

[13] The rubrics encourage bishops, too, to join in baptism where possible.

arated from this context it has become something of an orphan, ritually insignificant, pastorally unstable, theologically uncertain and seemingly superfluous.

A revised rite was issued in 1971, but it would not be ungracious to observe that it has brought no significant improvement to the malaise and that our whole experience and practice of confirmation will remain unsatisfactory until we achieve a clearer idea of what it means, what it does, and why it is necessary in the first place. The Second Vatican Council asked for the rite to be revised and for the connection which this sacrament has with the whole of Christian initiation to be more lucidly set forth (CL 71). But a secure theological consensus has yet to emerge, and the rite and its introduction inevitably reflect the uncertainties and inconsistencies of the present situation.

Among all the competing theologies of confirmation it is still difficult to discern its true relation either to baptism or to the eucharist, but what is beyond dispute is that from earliest times the gift of the Spirit was given to all, adults and children, along with baptism and the eucharist in the same rite; that outside the case of clinical baptism and the reconciliation of heretics and schismatics no one ever dreamed of interrupting or altering the sequence of the sacraments of initiation; and that the gift of the Spirit was especially associated with the bishop who presided at the initiation. This unity only broke down when the number of candidates multiplied out of all proportion to the number of bishops, so that a bishop could not be present at every initiation. From that time the Eastern churches preserved the unity and sequence of initiation by permitting priests to confirm in a unitary celebration of baptism, confirmation and first communion; the West chose rather to preserve the episcopal prerogative by separating baptism and confirmation, and celebrating the latter only when a bishop was available. What must be stressed is that this separation of the sacraments in the West owed nothing to theological considerations, and that 'theologies' were only subsequently elaborated to explain an established pastoral practice.

In the West from quite early times theologians had attempted to distinguish the effects of the various stages of the initiation rites, many seeing the effect of water-baptism as the remission of sin and rebirth in the Spirit, while the laying-on of hands or anointing symbolized a further gift of the Spirit. This tendency was inevitably given great impetus by the separation of the rites. In the middle ages, some theories interpreted confirmation as a gift of the Spirit for the interior growth of the individual in the personal struggles of the spiritual life; others stressed the needs of the Church and regarded confirmation as a gift of the Spirit for witness. Perhaps the most popular theory in recent times, taking something from each of these, was that confirmation was the sacrament of Christian maturity, consecrating the commitment of the individual to the faith professed on his behalf at baptism. Confirmation came to be regarded as a sort of 'puberty rite' and, in more recent years, as a commissioning for the lay apostolate. Of these theories one can only say that there is no historical or internal evidence that confirmation was ever intended as a puberty rite; that baptism, which incorporates us into the priestly people of God, is already a commissioning for witness; and that theories based on commitment and personal acceptance of baptismal promises are entirely child-centred and leave the sacrament virtually meaningless when celebrated after adult baptism. Other more reticent theories have been content to regard confirmation as a 'completion' of baptism, an increase in the Spirit already given, resulting in a closer conformity to Christ and a fuller membership of the Church, the worshipping community.

Relation to baptism and the eucharist

The Council asked that the relationship of confirmation to the whole of initiation be made clear. But the trouble with most of the theologies of confirmation is that they have nothing to say about its relation to the eucharist, and what they say about confirmation and baptism fails to make clear either what is the precise link between them or what is the precise difference. The Council's own most specific statement asserts that 'Bound *more* intimately to the Church by the sacrament of confirmation, they are endowed by the Holy Spirit with *special* strength. Hence they are *more* strictly obliged to spread and defend the faith both by word and by deed as true witnesses of Christ' (Church 11. My italics). But like the theories which talk of an 'increase' of baptismal grace, a 'strengthening' of baptism, a 'special' gift of the Spirit, a 'more perfect' link with the Church, it explains confirmation in terms of some 'plus-value', over and above baptism, but refrains from suggesting what exactly it is or why it should be necessary. On the other hand, the theories which do attempt to identify the plus-value, the special effect of confirmation – whether it be spiritual struggle, growth, maturity, commitment or witness – seem too partial and unsupported by the liturgical and historical evidence.

It is clear that more serious attention must be given both to the liturgical and historical evidence and to pastoral facts, and to the way both of these should influence and limit theological speculation. The texts and prayers of the liturgy as they have come down to us from the early Church, the understanding of the rite at the time of its formation, the equally venerable texts and traditions of the Eastern churches are one series of indispensable controls. Equally, the fact of adult confirmation requires us to eliminate all theories which are entirely child-centred, and the fact of infant confirmation in the West as well as the East brings into question most theories based on maturity and commitment. On the other hand pastoral needs, however sharply felt, may not be allowed to determine or alter the essential meaning of a sacrament. To present confirmation as a sacrament of puberty or the lay apostolate, with whatever good intentions or pastoral concern, is to misunderstand its nature and the place of sacraments in the life of the Church, by diverting it from its proper end to serve as a psychological challenge or to assist in a particular crisis. It may well be that we have to invent some other liturgy for that, but what we may not do is manipulate a sacrament, or redefine its meaning, to solve a current pastoral problem.

Relation to the Church

The starting point for all speculation must be tradition. And an inescapable fact of tradition is that the sequence of baptism, confirmation and eucharist was almost without exception[14] regarded as intrinsic to the nature of the initiation process and to its intelligibility. This is the sequence which survived in the West until the middle ages and even until this century, which

---

[14] It is thought that in the Syrian church before the fourth century, the only anointing took place before the water-baptism. They seem not to have distinguished between the different moments and effects of the one liturgy of initiation.

survives in the East to this day, which is still presumed in
canon law (CJC 786, 788), in the documents of Vatican II
(CL 71; Church 11; *Ad Gentes* 14, 36, etc.) and in the text of
the new rite itself. The intrinsic significance of this sequence
would seem to be that baptism is completed by the acceptance
of the neophytes into the Spirit-filled community of the Church,
which is both manifested and made real most clearly and
characteristically in the celebration of the eucharist.[15] Classi-
cally confirmation was at once the conclusion of baptism and,
through the intervention of the bishop, the public acceptance
of the newly baptized into the worshipping community assembled to celebrate the Easter eucharist. It is the Holy Spirit
who assembles and gives life to the Church and makes the
eucharist possible. Before they could appropriately participate
in the eucharist, new members had to appreciate that they were
being initiated into the life of a body in which the Spirit is
present and active as the vital principle, the source of mission
and the bond of unity. This integration of the individual into
the Church community was expressed and achieved sacra-
mentally through the special intervention of the bishop or his
delegate, as the sacramental minister of unity, and the laying-
on of hands, the sacramental symbol of integration.

The rite of confirmation

The revised rite of confirmation (1971) is perhaps the most
disappointing product of the whole liturgical reform. Four
forms are provided: for celebration within Mass, outside Mass,
by a minister who is not a bishop, and in danger of death. There
is no appreciable difference between them, and we need only
consider confirmation during Mass, which is presented as the
norm. After the gospel the parish priest or an assistant presents
the candidates to the bishop. As far as possible each is called
by name and takes his place in the sanctuary. The bishop then
gives a short homily explaining the mystery of confirmation
and its meaning, first to the congregation then to the candidates
themselves. The candidates are then invited, by way of response,
to profess their faith in a formula closely related to that made
by their parents and godparents at their baptism. This is mis-

[15] Cf. A. Kavanagh, 'Initiation: Baptism and Confirmation' in *Worship* 46 (1972),
pp. 262ff.

leadingly called a 'renewal' of their baptismal promises. As we have seen, the parents and godparents at baptism profess their own faith. The candidate for confirmation cannot 'renew' that profession, which was not his; he can only endorse it for himself. However, the link with baptism could perhaps be highlighted ritually by relating this profession of faith to the font and to the Paschal Candle. Water could be sprinkled, as in the 'renewal' of baptismal promises at the Easter Vigil, and the individual candles of each candidate could be relighted from the Paschal Candle. The bishop next invites all present to a moment of silent prayer and then, together with any priests who happen to be confirming with him, he extends his hands over all the candidates collectively, and proceeds alone to recite the prayer for the sevenfold gift of the Spirit, which has been traditional in the Roman rite since well before the seventh century. The candidates then come forward one by one; their sponsor or parent with a hand on their shoulder presents each by name to the bishop, who anoints them on the forehead with chrism in the sign of the cross, pronouncing the sacramental formula: 'Receive the seal of the gift of the Holy Spirit' or 'Be sealed with the Holy Spirit, the gift of the Father', which is not the ancient Roman form but one borrowed from the Byzantine tradition. As at communion, the candidate himself answers 'Amen'. Again one would plead for something richer than the attenuated symbolism of a moist thumb. If the oil does not impregnate and does not carry a rich perfume it will not express the pouring out of the Spirit or conformity to Christ, and will be worthless as a symbol. To conclude, the bishop exchanges the peace with each candidate.[16] The newly confirmed then return to their places, and Mass resumes with the bidding prayers. Since confirmation admits to full liturgical participation, it is unthinkable that candidates should not receive communion in both kinds, though the rubrics do not seem to envisage this except in the case of adults. If children are not thought ready for it, one must question seriously not only their preparation and suitability for confirmation but also for communion of any sort.

[16] Incomprehensibly, the bishops of England and Wales have chosen to retain the mediaeval tap on the cheek. Surely our fathers in God could bring themselves to greet their children with more affection than a vestigial slap in the face?

Understanding the rite

The Second Vatican Council demanded that the words and rites of the revised liturgy should express clearly what they signify so that the people can easily understand them, without much explanation (CL 21, 34). The revised rite of confirmation has not only failed to achieve this, but in some ways makes matters rather worse than they were.

First it manages to heighten the confusion of symbols. There is no question that what we now identify as the sacrament of confirmation was originally conferred by the laying-on of hands and prayer. It is equally undeniable that in the course of the centuries, in both East and West, an anointing became the central feature of the rite, as in the Old Testament, giving visible symbolic expression to the operation of the Spirit. The Apostolic Constitution which accompanies the new rite asserts clearly that only the anointing is necessary for validity, but that the laying-on of hands is a biblical gesture which recalls the gift of the Holy Spirit in a way most suited to the people's understanding. It is therefore necessary for the 'integrity' of the sacrament: 'Confirmation is conferred by an anointing with chrism on the forehead, which is accomplished by the laying-on of the hand.' It is not impossible to regard the contact of thumb with forehead as a sort of laying-on of hands, but this is hardly an authentic symbol: no one would for one moment guess that that is what is being done or is what the scriptures understand as the laying-on of hands. Yet the preceding collective imposition of hands is given heightened ritual expression in a way which would normally express the gift of the Spirit. So a sacramental gesture which elsewhere in the Roman rite signifies the gift of the Spirit does not have that meaning in this rite, whereas anointing, which elsewhere in the Roman rite is an explanatory symbol,[17] does, and is itself to be regarded as an imposition of hands! This can only be described as utterly confused and confusing, and a breakdown of liturgical intelligibility and authenticity. Until the rubrics can be rectified, it would seem desirable for the bishop and those confirming with him to lay hands on each individual immediately before anointing them. It should not be too exhausting, and would at

[17] Cf the rite of Ordination.

least bring us a little closer to doing, and being seen to be doing, what we say.

Secondly, though the connection between confirmation and baptism is brought out strongly (albeit inaccurately in the idea of 'renewing' baptismal promises), its link with the eucharist does not emerge at all. It is affirmed in the Apostolic Constitution but ignored in the rite itself. The Praenotanda (13) do explain that confirmation should normally take place during Mass so that initiation may reach its culmination in the communion, but that if candidates are not yet ready to be admitted to communion, confirmation should be celebrated outside Mass. This would seem to favour the traditional sequence with first communion following confirmation immediately or after an interval, but it plainly evades the far more relevant question of what meaning one can give to confirmation when initiation has *already* culminated in communion long previously. And this is our normal situation. Admission to the eucharist before confirmation manages to obscure entirely a large part of its meaning. And then to require, as we do, the sacrament of penance as a precondition for confirmation makes the whole initiation process virtually unintelligible. To demand that young children be reconciled, restored, reintegrated into the Spirit-filled community before they have even celebrated their entry into it can only be described as perverse.

Organizing the celebration

It is unlikely that we shall see a restoration of infant confirmation and communion in the near future or a widespread expansion of adult baptism overnight, both of which would restore the sequence and the unity of the sacraments of initiation. The best we can hope for immediately is that a modicum of intrinsic intelligibility might be restored by a rearrangement of our present egregious sequence which neither accords with tradition or right reason, nor is of any pastoral advantage whatever to the candidates. The best immediately practicable pattern to be hoped for would seem to be: (a) baptism in infancy; (b) confirmation at about the age of seven (as recommended by the new rite), immediately before (c) first communion, followed when individual development suggests it by (d) first confession; (e) such rites of commitment, profession of faith, etc. as seem desirable in adolescence. Such a solution would remove at a stroke three anomalies facing us at the moment: How can the non-confirmed be considered suitable for communion? How can a person be ready for confession and communion but not for confirmation? Once communion is received, what further initiation or integration is possible?

Obviously, bishops in the present circumstances could not be present at everyone's first communion (though they could be there every third year or so). Parish clergy would have to be given more general authorization to confirm, if sacramental intelligibility and pastoral needs are not to be subject to and frustrated by the availability and convenience of bishops. Some would object to this proposal on the grounds that it would weaken, if not obliterate, the traditional association of the sacrament with the bishop. This is an undeniable danger (though the Eastern churches have lived with it for most of their history), but until we have many more bishops and they are freed from administration to devote much more time to the sacramental and pastoral ministry it seems a lesser evil than allowing the whole of sacramental initiation to continue in its present confusion.

Meanwhile, even with the rite and pastoral organization we have, much could be done to improve our celebrations. First, in regard to catechesis, the introduction to the revised rite states that 'It is the responsibility of the people of God to prepare candidates for confirmation. Catechists, sponsors and members of the local church should participate . . . (though) the initiation of children is for the most part the responsibility and concern of Christian parents' (3). As with baptism, catechesis is an integral part of the liturgy and should be taken as seriously as the rite itself. If we continue to reserve this sacrament to the age of discretion and to ask for a 'renewal' of, or personal commitment to, baptismal promises, then nothing can justify regimentation, pressure, or an 'assembly-line' approach. Like first confession and first communion, confirmation should be the result of a personal decision, fostered and assisted certainly by parents and community, but free from group pressures. Schoolchildren should have to opt in rather than opt out. This might suggest that it would be better to remove the preparation for confirmation from the classroom altogether and into smaller groups, where greater respect can be shown for the individual personality and its spiritual development.

Secondly, the sponsors are to take a more active role than the honorary function they fulfilled in the old order. There should be a sponsor for each candidate, and to underline the continuity between baptism and confirmation it is appropriate that the godparents at baptism should continue their role of sponsorship at confirmation. Even parents themselves may present their children for confirmation. In any event, sponsors should not be designated automatically from among the elders and worthies of the parish. The choice should not be in the gift of the clergy at all. Each child should be free to choose (with his parents) either a godparent or some other practising Catholic, possibly quite young, with whom he can identify and to whom he can look for inspiration and example. Only if the child or family cannot find such a person should the parish suggest one, and they should seriously consider young-marrieds or even committed teenagers, who are more likely to be of help and inspiration to children than the local J.P. or president of the Legion of Mary.

Thirdly, like baptism again, confirmation must be a community celebration.

'Attention should be paid to the festive and solemn character of the liturgy, especially if all the candidates are assembled for a common celebration. The whole people of God, represented by the families and friends of the candidates and by members of the local community will be invited to take part in the celebration, and will express its faith in the fruits of the Holy Spirit' (Introduction 4).

If this is to be more than a pious wish, the celebration will have to take place at a time when the community can assemble – a weekday evening or a Sunday – and in the candidates' own parish church where their full membership, witness and worship will be exercised.

The admission of the validly baptized into full communion
A particularly clear example of confirmation as the sacrament of entry into the Spirit-filled community of the Church is provided by the new rite for the 'reception of converts'. The old

manner of receiving converts showed little appreciation that the grace of reception could be given appropriate expression only in a celebration of the eucharist. The new rite is called the 'admission into full communion', which suggests at once both ecclesial and eucharistic fellowship. The rite must be seen as a celebration of the Church reaching its climax in eucharistic communion, and so is normally to be celebrated during Mass.[18] But on no account should the celebration appear triumphalist. Not only are no abjurations required, but neither is a large congregation. Due regard must be paid both to ecumenical considerations and to the real relationship of the convert to the parish community. Both suggest a more intimate and low-key celebration with a few relatives and friends and representatives of the community.

If the reception takes place on a Sunday or a major feast, the Mass of the day is celebrated, otherwise one may use the Mass for Christian Unity. After the homily the candidate is invited to come forward with his sponsor to profess his faith with the whole community. All together then recite the Nicene Creed, and the candidate adds his own solemn endorsement. The priest then places his hand on the candidate's head and proceeds immediately with the rite of confirmation, after which he welcomes the newly-received by taking his hands within his own. After the bidding prayers the rest of the congregation may likewise welcome the convert. It is recommended that the newly-received, his sponsors and catechists and, if possible, the whole congregation receive communion in both kinds.

FURTHER READING

J. D. Crichton, *Christian Celebration: the Sacraments* (on both baptism and confirmation), London, 1973.

Baptism
C. Davis, *The Making of a Christian*, London, 1964.
L. Brockett, *The Theology of Baptism*, Cork, 1971.
B. Moss (ed.), *Crisis for Baptism*, London, 1965.
Commission on Christian Initiation (C.of E.), *Christian Initiation: Birth and Growth in Christian Society*, London, 1971.

[18] If this is not possible, it is celebrated during a liturgy of the word, and the convert is urged to attend Mass and receive communion as soon as possible afterwards. Readings, psalms and model bidding prayers are provided.

C. Buchanan, *Baptismal Discipline*, Nottingham, 1972.

A. Bullen, *Parents, Children and God*, London, 1972.

D. Boureau, *L'Avenir du baptême*, Lyon, 1970.

The periodical literature is immense, but see especially

   Concilium, vol. 2, no. 3 (February 1967), a whole issue on adult Baptism

   Clergy Review, August 1970 and October 1973, whole issues on infant Baptism

   La Maison-Dieu, nos. 89 (1967), 98 (1969), 104 (1970) and 110 (1972).

Confirmation

A. P. Milner, *The Theology of Confirmation*, Cork, 1972.

M. Perry (ed.), *Crisis for Confirmation*, London, 1967.

J. P. Bouhot, *La confirmation: sacrament de la communion ecclésiale*, Lyon, 1968.

H. Bourgeois, *L'Avenir de la confirmation*, Lyon, 1972.

C.N.E.R.-C.N.P.L., *La confirmation: que dire? que faire?* Lyon, 1972.

La Maison-Dieu, no. 110 (1972).

13. Penance

Mark Searle OFM

A. THE LIFE OF CONVERSION

1. *The Church as community of conversion*

a. NEW TESTAMENT. In the NT penance is something which is primarily preached in view of the presence among men of the kingdom – or rule – of God (Mk 1:15). This preaching is fundamental to the gospel, which tends to speak, however, more of the divine offer of reconciliation than of the human response. Christ came to save, not to judge: nevertheless, the refusal to believe necessarily excludes reconciliation (Jn 3:17–21). The faith or conversion required is the acknowledgement of God as saviour and of our utter dependence upon him, expressed in a complete change of values from human self-sufficiency to total reliance upon God, turning to him with the heart of a child (Mt 11:25; 18:1–4). Such conversion to God results in the destruction of the reign of Satan and the healing of men (Mt 12:22–32). It is the occasion of great joy (Lk 15:7–10.32).

Jesus gave his Spirit to the Church to continue his work of reconciliation on earth (Jn 20:21–23) and he continues to create solidarity among those who submit to the rule of God, confronting unbelief and overthrowing the prince of this world (Jn 16:7–11). So the Church preaches a baptism for the forgiveness of sins (Acts 2:38). The 'saints' encourage and correct each other (1 Thess 5:11.14; Jude 22; Heb 3:13–14), avoid leading each other into sin (1 Cor 8:11–12), and pray for one another (James 5:16). The whole Church is responsible for the brethren (Mt 18:15–17), but the leaders of the Church have special responsibilities (Mt 18:18). They are entrusted with the power to bind and loose, which is the power whereby God takes over the world, releasing it from the dominion of Satan. The choice is now offered: to be converted and freed, or to refuse belief and remain enslaved. The Church is a community of 'converts', so that if a brother falls back into serious sin he may be excluded from the community, both for the good of the community (2 Thess 3:6.14; Titus 3:10), and for his own good (1 Tim 1:20; 1 Cor 5:3–5). Possibly there was a rite of reconciliation (1 Tim 5:20–22), but more place is given to the power of love to overcome sin in the community, a love which inspires fraternal correction (Gal 6:1–2), prayer (James 5:20; 1 Jn 5:16), patience (1 Thess 5:14), gentleness (Gal 6:1) and mercy (Jude 22).

b. HISTORY OF PENANCE. Since the first Christian sermon (Acts 2:38), the Church has ceaselessly called men from sin to conversion and manifested the victory of Christ over sin in the celebration of penance. The call to conversion and its sacramental celebration are both of the essence of the Church, but they have enjoyed different emphasis and different expression over the centuries.

The first six centuries maintained the loose distinction, already found in the NT, between daily sins of weakness and more serious sins. The former were combated by a constant striving for conversion which affected the whole Christian life and was expressed particularly in prayer, fasting and almsgiving. Even fairly serious sins were subject to nothing more than this. Grave sins, especially sins of a public character, were subject to the rigour of canonical penance, which lasted several years and culminated in public reconciliation with God and with his Church. In this period confession was made privately to the bishop simply to enable him to determine the need for public penance and its length. The most important part of the sacrament of reconciliation was considered to be the carrying out of the penance, a long and painful process in which the penitents were assisted by the whole local community, who encouraged them by prayer and example.

The *Middle Ages* saw profound changes in the penitential life of the Church. 'Private penance' done by the individual after confession to a priest, and without any reference to the community, led to private absolution, which was sought and obtained even for less serious sins and could be granted to a penitent several times in his lifetime. In the twelfth and thirteenth centuries, the emphasis in theology and practice moved from the penance performed by the penitent to the absolution granted by the priest. Penances imposed became gradually lighter and were eventually left to be performed after absolution had been conferred.

Emphasis on the importance of priestly absolution and on the judicial role of the confessor made it important that the penitent confess his sins in detail, that they might be 'judged'. This was the perspective of the *Council of Trent*[1] and has prevailed until our own days, largely determining the form penitential practice has taken. The sacrament of penance has been considered almost the exclusive means of obtaining forgiveness of sins in practice. It has been administered without reference to the community of the Church and has been seen largely in terms of submitting an accurate and detailed list of sins to the absolution of the priest.

2. *Christian life as life of conversion*

a. THE LIFE OF PENANCE. i. *The purpose of penance.* The final meaning of human history was revealed by God when he made known 'the mystery of his purpose, the plan he so kindly made in Christ from the beginning . . . that he would bring everything together under Christ as head' (Eph 1:9–10), 'because God wanted all things to be reconciled through him and for him . . . when he made peace by his blood on the cross' (Col 1:19–20). In the realization of that plan, God completely respects man's freedom: man can cooperate, or he can reject God's love and repudiate its ambition. To hear the word of God is to be drawn into the unfolding of God's purposes. It means renouncing egocentric independence and no longer standing apart from the divine economy. To refuse the word, on the other hand, is to rebel against the plan of God and to cut oneself off from meaningful existence.

The primary sacrament of reconciliation is 'baptism for the forgiveness of sins', while the eucharist, which proclaims the death of the Lord as being 'so that sins may be forgiven', is the celebration of reconciliation already won and the pledge of final unity. The sacrament of penance is primarily for those who, having once been caught up into the mystery of God's purpose – 'having been enlightened and tasted of the heavenly

[1] Sess. XIV, de sacr. penit., cap. 5. DS 1679.

gift' (Heb 6:4) – then fall away and by serious sin find themselves in the position of again having to be reconciled to God and to his people. Secondly and secondarily, but also most importantly, the sacrament represents an opportunity for Christians to deepen their involvement in this mystery of reconciliation by being confronted again with the word of God, acknowledging the truth of their situation, and surrendering more completely to God's merciful will-to-reconciliation. Frequent 'confession of devotion' is therefore recommended by the Church to all Christians in their struggle to grow more like Christ and more submissive to the action of his Spirit (Rite of Penance 7b – hereafter referred to as RP).

ii. *Ways of forgiveness*. In the early Church, the sacrament of penance could only be approached once in a lifetime. For most of their lives, therefore, Christians had to experience the mystery of divine forgiveness in other ways which were not strictly sacramental: common prayer, penitential rites, good works, seeking and granting fraternal reconciliation, and also by receiving the eucharist. In other words, the lack of frequent sacramental forgiveness was balanced by a profound sense of Christian life as being a constant striving for conversion.[2] Corresponding to the multiplicity of the relationships which make up our human lives, and to the varying degrees of personal commitment involved in different moral actions, there was a multiplicity of ways of striving to respond to the Good News of reconciliation and to shuffle off the sins that mar the Christian life. This was nothing less than an earnest effort to live out baptismal commitment to Christ and renunciation of Satan in all areas and levels of existence. This insight has never really been forgotten in the Church, but it has taken on new life in the light of developments in the theology of the Church and the sacraments.

The whole of human life, both individual and corporate, is the place of God's involvement with men and the context of man's acceptance or refusal of God's call to reconciliation. In Jesus himself, the sacred and the secular are fully integrated, so that all is grace (the self-communication of God) and all is

---

[2] A. Ramos-Regidor, 'Reconciliation in the Primitive Church', in *Concilium*, vol. 1, n. 7, pp. 81–2.

worship (the human expression of his love for the Father and of his submission to his plan). It is to this integration of faith and life that we are all called (CMW 43). The sacramental celebrations of the Church do not stand over against secular life,[3] but are celebrations and manifestations of what is ultimately at stake and at work in man's life and history: viz., the furthering or hindering of God's plan to reconcile all things to himself in Christ, establishing peace with men and among men. Thus the absolution which the penitent receives in the sacrament cannot be dissociated from the total effort towards reconciliation at every level in his life and in the society of which he is a part.

The sacrament of penance is no longer seen as an isolated and exclusive means of obtaining forgiveness of one's sins, but as the source and summit of a whole Christian life of conversion, where the one grace of forgiveness, won and mediated by Christ, and operative at many levels, emerges in a clear and manifest way in the celebration of the Church. So-called 'non-sacramental' celebrations of penance should be viewed in this context: although they are not at present recognized by the Church as sacramental in the strict sense, they are celebrations of the Church and they do offer Christ's grace of reconciliation to all who are contrite.

For the same reasons, it is important that the renewal of the sacrament of penance be rooted in a renewal of penitential life and in a serious effort by local churches to deepen the life of conversion. Paul VI has reminded Christians that the primary form of asceticism is fidelity to one's duties and responsibilities and patience in the face of life's demands.[4] He also underlines the contribution of those who suffer sickness, poverty and injustice in union with Christ. Moreover the traditional trilogy of non-sacramental means of forgiveness – prayer, fasting and almsgiving – have been constantly re-interpreted in the history of the Church and their meaning needs to be rediscovered for our own day: prayer as a serious striving to draw closer to God; fasting as the assertion of spiritual values in the face of materialistic and pleasure-oriented society; almsgiving as the

---

[3] K. Rahner, 'Secular Life and the Sacraments', in *The Tablet*, 6 March 1971, 236–8, 13 March 1971, 267–8.
[4] *Poenitemini*, III. Full text in *L'Osservatore Romano*, 18 February 1973.

devotion of one's time, talents and possessions to the service of one's neighbour.[5]

iii. *Penance and growth.* Human life and human history are a process in which the past conditions the present and the present contains the possibility of creating the future. This awareness of the historicity of man's existence is crucial for the life of penance. At the individual level, it means (a) being aware that a man's relationship with God is neither built nor broken by a single isolated human act; and (b) that specific acts of good or evil are manifestations of a person's attitudes and outlook. It will, in short, underline the importance of conversion as a change of heart, rather than just the repudiation of isolated acts, and as a growing appreciation of the true dimensions of sin and grace in a man's personal life.[6]

Human life is not only historical, but shared: of its nature, it is co-existence. This, too, has its implications for sin and grace. The good and evil that men do affect not only their personal future, but that of the society in which they live. Conversely, it will be appreciated that a man's present situation is very much affected by the sin and evil in the society in which he lives. Conversion, likewise, is not a purely interior experience, but is influenced by, and in its turn influences, other people. The early Church recognized very clearly the social dimensions of sin and conversion, and the revival of penitential services in our own time undoubtedly owes something to modern social consciousness and orientation towards the future – two characteristics shared by the early Church. Personal conversion needs to contribute to, and be supported by, community conversion, which may well express itself in Christian communities becoming aware of their collective responsibilities for Christ's work of reconciliation in the face of class divisions, poverty, racial discrimination, the moral degradation of our society, and so on. Thus the renewal of penance in the Church must lead to local communities, such as parishes, becoming aware of their collective guilt and, through communal celebrations of penance, being continually converted to a more serious collective commitment to the mystery of reconciliation. Thus parishes will

[5] See, for example, Cassian's *Conferences*, XIX, c. 8; or, for a modern example V. Solovyev, *God, Man and the Church*, tr. D. Attwater (London, n.d.), 35–90.
[6] Mary Holloway in *Penance: Virtue and Sacrament*, pp. 18–19.

seek to establish among their members a clearer sense of identity vis-à-vis the evil in the society in which they live, and a deeper conviction concerning their collective responsibilities towards that society.

b. THE ACTS OF THE PENITENT. i. *Contrition*. The authenticity of the sacrament of penance depends upon the sinner being genuinely contrite. This means that he accepts his fault as his own, not attempting to evade responsibility for it, and at the same time repudiates it as morally unacceptable and ultimately meaningless because incompatible with the unfolding mystery of God's purpose. Being contrite means repudiating one's God-less past as a basis for future action, opting instead to make God one's future. True contrition thus differs from the kindred sentiments of remorse and regret in that it is (a) forward-looking rather than backward-looking, and (b) more concerned with the other, God, than with oneself and one's feelings.

Christian repentance has little in common with infantile fear of being punished for transgressions, or with neurotic guilt and feelings of uncleanness. Christ came to free men from such fears, to set them free to serve the living God who offers a new future to all who will turn to him. Hence genuine contrition includes not only the negative resolution not to sin again, but a positive adherence to God and to his plan of reconciliation. Explanations of penance which suggest that imperfect con-trition (i.e. motives which do not include this positive turning to God) is sufficient for the sacrament of penance do the whole process of conversion a grave disservice by pretending that God can forgive those who do not turn to him in love. They also gravely compromise the self-revelation of God by suggesting that the conditions for forgiveness are imposed by him quite arbitrarily, instead of being in the very nature of things, given that penance is an encounter between God who mercifully calls and man who freely responds. Yet such a quasi-magical understanding of both sin and forgiveness is fairly widespread among Christian people.

ii. *Confession*. The Council of Trent teaches that all grave sins committed after baptism must be confessed in virtue of Christ's institution (DS 1679). This should be understood, not in the sense of an explicit directive ordering the confession of all such sins in species and number, but as implicit in the very nature of the sacrament as a celebration of repentance. Since the grace of reconciliation won by Christ is now mediated through the Church, the request for reconciliation must be made to the Church – a process that inevitably involves the generic admission, at least, that one is a sinner and needs reconciliation. More than that, sin is an offence against the Church (Church 11; RP 5), as well as against God, for the sinfulness of her members weakens the bond of the Spirit which constituted the unity of the Church, and compromises her mission to be a sign to the world of the presence among them of the kingdom of grace. Consequently, the sinner must seek the forgiveness of the Church for his sins by making at least a general confession of sin. The history of penance shows that the confession of specific sins is not quite so indispensable, but the discipline of the Western Church which upholds this practice does have a basis in the nature of the sacrament. Such is the nature of man as a body-spirit composite that the spiritual life of man is not fully his until it is embodied or expressed in word or action. What is internal to a man only takes on an objective, irrevocable existence when he 'utters' it: then he is committed to it and is held responsible for it. Thus, until a man expresses aloud, as it were, his guilt and his desire for forgiveness, he has not really committed himself. Now mortal sins are precisely those which affect his being most profoundly, radically destroying the orientation of his life towards God. It is then, even humanly speaking, of the utmost importance that he commit himself, in words spoken aloud to the representative of the Church, to a specific repudiation of that which he has loved too much and to a new acceptance of the merciful offer of divine reconciliation.

In any case, the insistence on auricular confession should not be regarded as an unnecessary and arbitrary imposition by the Church as part of the punishment for sin, but rather as a matter of the Church remaining faithful to her God-given mission to bring Christ's grace of forgiveness to the penitent in a way which is personal to each and takes account of his particular situation and its needs.

iii. *Satisfaction.* The term 'satisfaction' should be avoided as far as possible when speaking of penance, for it carries with it misleading overtones of paying off a debt incurred through infringement of a law. Any idea of 'satisfying' a God who sits on a remote throne, impartially and impassively administering the world, is to be avoided. 'Doing penance', on the contrary, means throwing oneself more wholeheartedly into the life from which one has broken or drifted away by sin. It means working, under God, to restore the divine order weakened or destroyed by sin. It is not compensation for the past so much as a positive contribution to the future: a struggle to undo the evil brought about by one's sins and the sins of others, and to affirm and strengthen the reign of God. Doing penance is the responsibility of the whole Church, but it is the particular responsibility of sinners who seek reconciliation, being the natural and indispensable expression of true conversion. Seen in this light, it is clear that the penance imposed on a sinner must take account of his condition and of the sins he has confessed. To reduce 'doing penance' to three Hail Mary's for all and sundry is absurd. A penance should help the sinner to turn his life in the direction it needs to go, and to exercise the virtues which have previously failed him (cf pp. 204–5 below).

B. THE MINISTRY OF RECONCILIATION

1. *The Christian community as context of conversion*

In the early Church, the *ordo poenitentium* served as a visible reminder to the whole community of the need for continual conversion, while the community, for its part, sustained those doing penance by their prayers and by voluntarily sharing the discipline of public penance during Lent. In our own time we need to acknowledge that 'the life and death of each of us has its influence on others' (Rom 14:7), that we have the power to build each other up as well as to drag each other down. And we need to think seriously about the concrete application of this principle. Parish priests will work to create an atmosphere in a parish where the Christian life is taken seriously and where there really is, and is seen to be, constant striving after conversion. This will mean proposing a realistic and demanding version of the gospel, discovering its implications for the parish and working in direct and practical ways to further reconciliation among men. Experience suggests that this is best achieved by small groups within the parish, where sharing the gospel life and mutual encouragement to conversion can be more easily expressed and experienced, but care must be taken that they remain open and alive to the wider community.

There is no single way of turning a parish into a community of conversion. It will involve the provision of every opportunity and encouragement for confessions, spiritual direction and counselling; the regular celebration of realistic and down-to-earth penitential services; engendering a common sense of concern for the moral and social welfare of the wider community. The overall aim will be to establish a strong sense of identity and vocation in the local community and an awareness of the need for both the community and its members to 'pursue incessantly the path of penance and renewal' (Church 8).

2. *The role of the priest*
The work of developing and fostering this sense of identity and mission will devolve largely upon the priest as *leader of the community*. In exercising his leadership, he will be concerned to uphold the primacy of spiritual values, respect for the dignity of the person, and the proper use of material goods.

He will encourage the community and individuals to further Christ's work of reconciliation through the social life of the parish and the operation of such groups as the SVP, CWL, Justice and Peace, and by projects going beyond the parish boundaries, such as adoption of a foreign mission. The importance of the seasons of Advent and Lent, of Fridays and other penitential days will also be brought home to the parish.

The priest must also *preach the Good News* of divine reconciliation and the need for men to repent and accept that reconciliation. This can be done in special sermons, but the urgency of the message should lead to its pervading all forms of communication of the word in the parish: parish newsletter, work with confraternities, preparation for the sacraments, parish visiting. In this way, Christians will become more aware of the place of penance as the basis of Christian life.

Acting in dependence upon the bishop as *minister of the sacrament* of reconciliation, the priest should remember that the judgement of God was given in the revelation of his love and mercy. The role of the priest as judge has little in common, therefore, with a criminal trial. It has more in common with a doctor giving a prognosis: the prognosis in this case being the Good News of the irreversible will-to-reconciliation of God and the presence of his saving grace to all who will accept it. But grace is not given in the abstract, so the minister of penance must help the penitent to recognize the saving action of God in his life and move him to a lively faith and confidence in God. This calls for discernment of spirits, which is the intimate knowledge of the workings of God in the hearts of men (RP 10), and means taking each person seriously, listening to him carefully, and respecting his dignity as a person. Clearly, the confessor's task will be easier if the penitent is already known to him, or if the penitent reveals something of his situation (RP 16). Penitents are increasingly asking for a face-to-face meeting with the confessor precisely for this reason.

3. *Sin and reconciliation*

Sin is essentially man's self-estrangement from God and from the mystery of his purpose (cf p. 196 above). It affects both the individual and the whole society of man, so that the race is implicated in the revolt of the individual and the individual in the estrangement of the race. Sin is not, therefore, simply an unfortunate infringement, but the source and expression of a tragic alienation and disorientation affecting the whole human community. The role of the Church is to be the sacrament of healing and forgiveness in a world torn and twisted by sin and its consequences. Consequently, the celebration of penance must not be trivialized as a mechanism for the ablution of peccadilloes. It is a confrontation of the believer with the tragedy of human history, and with his own part in it, and at the same time it is his opportunity to break through to a new future with Christ.

If forgiveness is seen as 'an unconditional willingness to re-build or to continue building a relationship', then God's justice and fidelity mean that this offer is always and everywhere available. If reconciliation takes place, it is because man turns and avails himself of God's permanent offer and not because God changes. Reconciliation, then, is impossible without a change in the sinner. This change, and the re-opening of the relationship, make the sinner in his turn once more part of the whole mystery of reconciliation, since it means submitting to the plan that God has made, not only for the sinner himself, but for all men. So reconciliation with God makes possible, and necessary, reconciliation with one's fellow men (Mt 18:21–35) which overflows into family, social and even political life.

An awareness both of the dimensions of sin and of the fact that being reconciled with God means being caught up in God's work of reconciling all men with himself and with each other is of primary importance if penitential services are ever to become authentic experiences. Such considerations will also influence the kind of penance imposed upon the repentant sinner and the repentant community.

C. CELEBRATION OF RECONCILIATION

1. *Elements of the rite*

a. THE PENITENTS. Throughout the new *Ordo Paenitentiae*, the emphasis is on adapting the rite to the condition of the penitent or the penitential assembly. The personal element is to be given a large place because it is of the nature of this rite that it is a personal encounter between the sinner and Christ present in the person of the priest and in the reconciling community. More than in any other sacrament, perhaps, the believer has to play an active role in the celebration. What he does is not a purely private act for, even as a penitent, he acts as a member of the Church and his contribution is part of the sacramental celebration of the Church, to be completed by absolution. Confessor and penitent *together* celebrate the sacrament of penance: they are concelebrants. In this the sacramental action reflects and expresses the economy of salvation, for the penitent not only receives from the Church, but by his conversion makes a real contribution to the building up of the Church (RP 11). This personal element will be expressed in the *individual celebration* of penance if the penitent chooses his own reading from scripture, and if the confession takes the form of a fraternal colloquy, rather than an anonymous encounter. For this reason the faithful are to be advised of the value of going to a confessor who knows them, but in any case, the penitent is encouraged to speak freely to the priest about himself, his situation in life, and any special problems he may have (RP 16).

The personal element will come across in *communal celebrations* if everything is done to choose texts and draw up a rite with a particular congregation in mind. In this, the priest should readily seek the help of others, including laypeople, in preparing the celebration: in the first place, obviously, those for whom it is intended (RP 40b). In short, the texts of the ritual are not to be regarded as ready-made rites, but as material to be used in the community's celebration of its own liturgy of penance.

b. TIME AND PLACE. The *time* for hearing confessions is whenever someone wants to confess. Besides announcing fixed times for the hearing of confessions, priests should make themselves available at any time and let people know that this is the case. The only time explicitly excluded is while another liturgical celebration is being held in the same church: confessions should not be heard during Mass (RP 13). Communal celebrations should be held from time to time, the seasons of Advent and Lent and Fridays throughout the year being particularly suitable, as also days preceding major feasts, days of recollection, parish missions, retreats, etc.

It is left to Episcopal Conferences to make what stipulations they see fit regarding the place for hearing confessions, and it is to be hoped that, in this country at any rate, those penitents who wish to make a face-to-face confession will be encouraged to do so. Some existing confessionals could be adapted as confessional rooms, where priest and penitent could face each other and talk together easily. As a concelebrant with the priest, and as the party most personally concerned, the penitent should, as far as possible, be able to choose the confessional box or confessional room, whichever will allow him to confess more easily and fruitfully (RP 17). Ultimately, considerations of place are secondary to considerations of opportuneness.[7]

c. STRUCTURE OF THE RITE. The structure of both individual and communal celebrations of penance is basically identical: that of a dialogue between God and the penitent, reflecting the dialogue which has taken place in salvation history, of which indeed the celebration of penance is a part. First, there is a

---

[7] The discrimination against women, consequent upon the insistence on the grille (CJC, c. 909–10), is not maintained in the rubrics of the new rite.

proclamation of the divine promise of forgiveness, included in which is a call to repentance. The penitent accepts the word of God personally in a contrite *confession*. The immediate divine response to this is a proclamation of the mystery of reconciliation as a present and effective reality for the penitent himself (*absolution*), to which the penitent and priest respond together in an act of *thanksgiving*. In communal celebrations, this outline inevitably becomes more formal and elaborate, with chants, homily, several readings, etc., but it is important to establish the pattern of the rite as a whole and to give each part its due place within the context of the total rite.

d. PRAYER. The celebration of penance is a sacramental dialogue: not counselling, but encounter with Christ. Priest and penitent stand together in his presence and act as his instruments, to the glory of God the Father. For this reason, prayer is important in the celebration of penance. Opportunities for prayer might include the beginning of the rite, after the readings, before the absolution and at the end, before the dismissal. The rite for reconciling individual penitents suggests simply the prayer before absolution as a prayer for forgiveness, but the other rites are a little more imaginative. The ritual itself provides a large number of prayers, and even spontaneous prayer would not be out of place. For the prayer before absolution, the rite for reconciling individual penitents suggests 'a prayer composed from scripture', while the other rites order the 'Our Father' to be said. This is understandable, given the high value attached to this prayer by the Christian tradition precisely as a prayer for forgiveness. The repentant sinner returns, like the prodigal son, to his Father and once again submits to his authority and gives himself over to working for the coming of the kingdom by doing the Father's will. There is also in this prayer the explicit link between the forgiveness sought from God and the reconciliation offered to one's fellow men, as well as the request for deliverance from temptation and from the Evil One. The priest could join with the penitent in careful recitation of this prayer, thereby showing that he is a fellow-penitent and brother in Christ to the sinner.

e. THE WORD OF GOD. The RP says it is fitting for the celebration of the sacrament of penance to begin with the reading of the word of God (RP 24) and suggests that this should happen even in the rite of individual reconciliation (RP 17). This is because the sacrament is always an act of submitting oneself to the judgement of God's Word. This means seeing Christian life as a total response to the message of God, and not simply as conformity to a set of arbitrary rules. If priests and penitents will make the effort to choose a suitable reading and explore its message for their lives, this will surely lead to a real enrichment and deepening of the life of faith, hope, and love. People will be able gradually to break away from the 'laundry-list' and begin to recognize the presence, action and call of God in their lives. On the positive side, this will mean a joyous and grateful acknowledgement of all that is good in human life; on the negative side, it would go a long way towards helping people to bring their moral consciousness into line with the areas of their real responsibility in life, so reducing the gap between daily living and the life of faith.

The purpose of the readings is primarily to arouse faith and hope in God's power to save. Consequently, all that follows – and not simply the confession of sin – should be inspired by, and be a response to, the Word of God: the prayers, the exhortation and encouragement, the final thanksgiving.

Even where, for practical reasons, the reading of scripture has to be omitted, the priest should try to arouse a lively faith and hope in the penitent. This is the primary purpose of the homily. Although it must lead the faithful to examine their consciences and return to God, it is not itself meant to be an examination of the congregation's conscience. It should seek to make the faithful aware of four truths: (a) that the mercy of God is more far-reaching than any of our sins; (b) that the mercy of God is available to all who will accept it by interior conversion, expressed in willingness to make good the evil that one has done; (c) that sin and grace have a social dimension, so that we have the potential to save or to destroy each other; (d) that the work of penance demands, besides carrying out a specific penance, real love of God and one's neighbour (RP 25).

In communal celebrations it will usually be found helpful to have a period of silence or at most a piece of instrumental music to follow the proclamation of the word in the readings and homily. This is to give people a chance to take the word to heart and examine their own consciences. Sometimes it will be helpful, especially for congregations who are not used to penance services or who need guidance, to use a penitential litany or a guided examination of conscience based on the text of scripture (RP 26).

f. CONFESSION. The reasons for confession have already been discussed (pp. 195–7). In penitential services there is always a common confession of sin, followed on occasion by individual confession of specific sins to a priest. In making a private confession, the penitent may, if he so wishes, preface the confession of personal sins with a general act of confession, but this is in no way necessary. The priest should help the penitent as and when required, even to the point of turning the confession itself from a monologue into a conversation: but here so much depends upon whether the priest is a listener and has the discretion and sympathy to know when to speak and when to be silent. It has been found valuable for the penitent to 'confess' the good as well as the evil in his life, so that he acknowledges the saving power of God and sees his sin as a failure to respond to the grace of his presence and his call. This again is something which the priest, exercising discernment of spirits, will be able to help the penitent with.

g. SATISFACTION. Since contrition is essentially forward looking, the penance imposed on those who sin must also be concerned more with directing their future than with punishing their past. The penance must be something in which a person can 'incarnate' his conversion. Prayer will often be suitable, but the self-discipline of some form of fasting, and particularly charitable works which benefit those who have been sinned against, or counteract the sinful tendencies of the sinner, should also be considered. Such practical penances might include the following: helping out a poor person; visiting the sick; making a deliberate effort to understand and sympathize with the person against whom one has sinned; taking positive steps to remedy a situation which is conducive to sin; scripture reading; prayers to be said daily over a period of time; renunciation of specific luxuries for a prescribed period; using time and money for some charitable purpose. In communal celebrations, where general absolution is given, a common penance is imposed (RP 35a). Again, this may take the form of prayer, but some of the suggestions given above might be useful. Even in penitential services where there is no sacramental absolution, a collection could be taken up for a specific charity, or the penitential liturgy could be associated with the launching of some new community enterprise, such as a parochial effort to aid a foreign mission or to work for better community relations in the area. One form of 'penance' which has been found particularly suitable for such occasions is a bread-and-cheese supper following the service, for which participants are encouraged to pay far more than the cost of the food provided in order to raise funds for helping the poor. Here again there is a good opportunity for the priest to consult the penitents themselves as to what penance they would consider suitable.

h. ABSOLUTION. The new text runs as follows:

> 'God, the Father of mercies,
> through the death and resurrection of his Son
> has reconciled the world to himself
> and sent the Holy Spirit among us
> for the forgiveness of sins;
> through the ministry of the Church
> may God give you pardon and peace,
> and I absolve you from your sins
> in the name of the Father, and of the Son,
> and of the Holy Spirit.'

It is accompanied by the laying on of hands, or at least by the priest stretching his right hand out over the penitent. This is the gesture used in the NT to indicate healing, exorcism of evil spirits, and the giving of the Holy Spirit. The penitent will express his submission to this gesture of reconciliation by kneeling or bowing.

The words and gesture of the absolution constitute a clear proclamation and manifestation of God's merciful love for the sinner, which takes the initiative and draws him back into the historical unfolding of God's plan for mankind. They proclaim a sort of divine break-through into the closed circle of man's frailty and folly, whereby a man is caught up into Christ's own movement from this world to the Father and becomes part of the historical incarnation of the divine love of the Father for the Son and of the Son for the Father, of which the Church, gathered and bound by the one Spirit, is the visible sacrament.

j. THANKSGIVING. Joy and gratitude are characteristic of man's response to the healing and forgiveness of Christ (Lk 10:17; 13:17; 15:7.10.32; 19:6; Acts 3:8). For individual celebration, the opening verse of Ps 135 is suggested as versicle and response. In communal celebrations, a hymn may be sung, followed by a prayer of praise and thanksgiving. (The prayer is omitted in a service of general absolution.)

The formula of dismissal, 'The Lord has freed you from sins . . . Go in peace' echoes several gospel texts: Mt 9:22; Mk 2:5; Lk 7:48.50. This both indicates the continuity of Christ's work in the gospel and in the sacrament, and it also underlines the true nature of the sacrament of penance as a sacrament of faith and not an act of legal or ritual purification. Moreover, the official dismissal constitutes a sacramental expression of the fact that the penitent is being commissioned afresh by God to do the works of God. For this reason it is never to be omitted (RP 21). Alternative forms combine the note of joy with the formula of dismissal (RP 93).

2. *The rites of reconciliation*

a. INDIVIDUAL CELEBRATION OF PENANCE. After the initial informal greeting, the penitent makes the sign of the cross and the priest offers a brief encouragement to faith and trust in God. A text from scripture is then read by priest or penitent, in the light of which the penitent can recognize his own sinfulness and God's merciful call to conversion and to trust in him. The priest may perhaps help the penitent to understand the implications of what he has read, and then the penitent goes on to make his confession. Again the priest may offer a few words of encouragement and give the penitent a suitable penance. The penitent then prays for forgiveness and is granted absolution. After a brief prayer of thanksgiving, the penitent is dismissed.

The immediate reaction of many priests to this new rite is that it is all very well, but that it won't work in their parish on a Saturday night, and that in any case their people will not adopt it lightly. Others perhaps, will find in it just the sort of thing that they themselves and many devout Catholics in a crisis about the sacrament of penance have been looking for. In either case, it should not be forgotten that the rite for the reconciliation of a single penitent is published by Rome in the context of a whole effort to renew the spirit and practice of penance at both the individual and the communal level. While there will still need to be fixed times for confession, during which people may be queuing up and the time available for each penitent consequently limited, the new rite does provide a framework which is sufficiently flexible to be adapted to different situations while still encouraging a more personal penitential experience, and it would be disastrous if the whole renewal of penance was reduced to using the new texts in a formalistic, anonymous and routine manner.

The emphasis has moved away from the presentation of a list of sins towards exploring the implications of the word of God for the life of the believer. In this context, the priest will try to help the penitent see why he commits the sins he has confessed, appreciate the true moral character of his actions, and really put his trust in God's mercy and power. The scripture text should be used to help the penitent recognize in the sacrament of penance a real encounter with the living Christ who assuages the anguish of the penitent by re-affirming God's promises; who renews the call of God to one who has previously turned away from it; who reaches out with love to one who has refused that love; who brings his peace and consolation to one who has isolated himself and disrupted his life by sin; who offers the warmth and strength of his Spirit to one who, in his weakness, has drifted out into the cold. The importance of this personal dimension can be brought home to the penitent if the confessor asks him, for example, which of his sins would seem to him the worst if he were suddenly to find himself face-to-face with Christ; or by making him see the good things in his life as gifts of God and signs of the Spirit's presence, and then asking him how he has used them.

b. PENITENTIAL SERVICES WITH INDIVIDUAL CON-
FESSION AND ABSOLUTION. These have proved popular in
France in recent years and they would seem to combine the
advantages of communal celebrations with the pastoral and
theological securities of individual confession and absolution.
After the liturgy of the word and a homily, there is a period of
silence for examination of conscience. Then there is a general
confession, followed by a hymn or litany, the Our Father said
together and a collect. Confessors then go to their appointed
posts to hear confessions, and they impose a suitable penance
before giving absolution to each penitent. Meanwhile, the rest
of the congregation occupies itself with prayers, readings, hymns
or instrumental music. After all confessions have been heard,
the confessors return to the *presbyterium* and the service concludes with a common act of thanksgiving, blessing, and dismissal. Whatever the theoretical advantages of this form of
penitential celebration, it does demand either a very small group
of people or else a large number of confessors. Unless there is a
high ratio of confessors to penitents, the length of time people
are kept waiting can assume absurd proportions. Paradoxically,
the more successful the service, the more problematic it becomes, because if the word of God really strikes home penitents
will hardly be content with a perfunctory confession of a list
of sins and a hasty absolution. The one occasion when this form
of penance can work is at an all-night vigil, when time is not
important.

C. PENITENTIAL SERVICES WITH GENERAL ABSOL-
UTION. Apart from cases where there is imminent danger of
death, general sacramental absolution may be given after only
generic confession of sin whenever there is a grave necessity:
i.e. when the number of penitents is such that there are insufficient confessors to hear the confessions of all the penitents
within an appropriate time, with the result that, through no
fault of their own, they would be deprived of sacramental grace
or holy communion for a long time. This can often happen in
mission territories, but it may sometimes happen elsewhere. It
is not lawful, however, to grant general absolution in this way
simply because of a great number of penitents coming together,
as may happen, for example, on a pilgrimage (RP 31).

The judgement as to whether such conditions are verified is left with the local ordinary, in consultation with other members of the episcopal conference (RP 32). Should the need for general sacramental absolution arise in a case not provided for by the local ordinary, the priest must have recourse to the Ordinary concerned; and if this is not possible, he is to inform him as soon as possible afterwards of the fact that general absolution was granted and the circumstances which made it necessary (RP 32).

Penitents must be properly prepared and disposed for general absolution: each must truly repent of his sins, must intend to make good any scandal or loss caused, and must intend to confess in due time each serious sin that he is at present unable to confess. The priest is to bring these conditions to the notice of the people during the rite (RP 33).

The obligation to make confession of any major sins, even though they are forgiven by general absolution, should be noted. Unless prevented by a just cause, penitents guilty of grave sin are bound to make auricular confession of such sins before receiving absolution in this form again, and are strictly obliged in any case to confess their sins within a year, unless prevented by moral impossibility (RP 34). With this ruling, the history of penance enters another stage, the order of procedure now being absolution, penance, confession – the exact reverse of the original order! The reasons for this insistence on subsequent confession (absolution is not repeated) are the same as those which make confession of sin necessary under normal circumstances (cf pp. 195–7 above).

The structure of the rite is the same as for other communal celebrations of penance. Those wishing to receive absolution must give some sign (e.g. kneeling down or standing with bowed head). One and the same penance is imposed on everyone, but individuals can add to this for themselves (RP 35). The absolution takes on a more solemn and imposing form by being located within an extended address to the penitents which invokes the forgiveness of the Father and the outpouring by Father and Son of their Spirit, for the remission of sins and the gift of new life. This longer form is designed to impress upon the penitents the seriousness and importance of what is happening to them, in case the whole rite should appear to be nothing more than the dispensing of 'cheap grace'. The formula provided for the reconciliation of an individual penitent may be used as an alternative.

Theologians have recently been arguing that, whatever Trent did or did not say concerning the necessity of confessing specific grave sins, general absolution could be given on a much wider scale than has hitherto been permitted because the average faithful Catholic who would come to such penance services would rarely, if ever, commit such a sin. For the time being, however, a rite for general absolution has been provided, but no change made in the discipline of the Church concerning occasions when it would be lawful to use it – although there is no suggestion that unlawful giving of general absolution would invalidate that absolution.

d. PENITENTIAL CELEBRATIONS WITHOUT SACRAMENTAL ABSOLUTION. People may question the value of penitential services without absolution: for this reason it is important to situate such services in the context of what has already been said concerning different ways of forgiveness (pp. 192–4 above). But, aside from their intrinsic value as grace-filled celebrations of the Church, experience has already shown that they do help people prepare for a more fruitful celebration of the sacrament. On the one hand, they can arouse genuine contrition and deeper awareness of the demands of the gospel; while, at the same time, they help the sinner to situate himself as a member of a sinful community – an awareness which may be very valuable for certain types of penitent who tend to get wrapped up in themselves and isolated from their fellows by an obsessive sense of guilt and uncleanness which makes the acceptance of God's merciful forgiveness psychologically problematic.

One very important consideration concerning these celebrations is that they are the sort of liturgy which can be celebrated without a priest. They can therefore be adapted and used by private families, communities of religious women, and so on. If they were taken up in this way, these services could have a very important contribution to make to the renewal of penance in the Church and to the spread of the awareness that it is communities and families as such, and not simply individuals, who are called to holiness and hence to conversion.

The RP presents a mass of material for such services and some models of the kind of thing that might be done. It should be realized, however, that these are only models and that the greatest freedom is left to the community to use music, songs, and non-scriptural readings. The structure of the rite, however, should reflect the structure of the economy of salvation (cf pp. 201–2 above), and consequently will be modelled, at least loosely, on the liturgy of the word at Mass. If there is a problem with these celebrations, it lies in the lack of any obvious climax. The climax, in fact, will be the confession of sin and prayer for forgiveness, but these need to be expressed in some kind of gesture or celebration of repentance, mutual forgiveness, fraternal reconciliation, or purpose of amendment. This might involve nothing more than kneeling for the confession and standing for the thanksgiving; or it might take the form of exchanging the sign of peace. With some imagination and careful preparation, small groups will find their own symbolic gestures: burning the list of sins used in the examination of conscience in the flame of the paschal candle; each individual presenting a written purpose of amendment at the altar. The search for appropriate gestures and symbols needs to go on.

3. *Special groups*

Penitential celebrations should always take account of the special circumstances of the people who celebrate them, together with their way of thinking and speaking and their general level of ability (RP App. II, 2). Experience suggests that, while parochial celebrations certainly have their place, there are advantages in having celebrations for more homogeneous groups, such as young children, teenagers, married people, the elderly, working men, and so on. This enables the celebration to focus more exactly on the life-experience of those involved and to speak more accurately to their situation. Two groups in particular are in need of this kind of special provision:

a. CHILDREN. Christianity is primarily an adult religion and the NT demands of faith and conversion are addressed to adults, and to children only insofar as they are capable of responding in accordance with their age and the stage of their development towards adulthood. It is consequently very important that the initiation of children to the practice of penance and to its sacramental celebration take account of their status and give them a proper perspective on such fundaments of the faith as the plan of God for the world, the social character of life in the Spirit, the true nature of sin as repudiation of the covenant. The best way of doing this, as evidenced by both modern and patristic experience, is not by instruction only, but by gradual and reflective initiation into sacramental practice such as could be provided by the new penitential services,[8] which are already grace-filled, liturgical celebrations, similar in structure and identical in purpose with the full sacramental rite (cf RP 35–36). This would surely go a long way towards meeting the demand of the Roman Declaration of May 1973, that children be introduced to the sacrament of penance before approaching the table of the Lord.[9]

b. RELIGIOUS WOMEN. Many religious women are suffering a crisis of confidence where the sacrament of penance is concerned. Some of them, it must be admitted, are hardly helped by the traditional convent confessional routine which, when coupled with inadequate instruction and lack of opportunity for proper spiritual direction, has not infrequently resulted in positive harm: perpetuation of scruples, of an infantile spirituality, morbid preoccupation with self, and so on. More perhaps than any other group in the Church, religious women stand to profit by a diversification of penitential practice. It would seem advisable to introduce penitential services into convents to broaden the outlook and deepen the religious understanding of the sisters, while at the same time providing better opportunity for more personal, if less frequent, individual confession and absolution. It must be admitted that convents are not always well served by the clergy responsible for them, who frequently lack any real appreciation of religious community life. In such circumstances, there is no reason why the sisters should not take matters into their own hands and celebrate their own penitential services, which 'are most useful, are very helpful in promoting conversion of life and purification of heart . . . (they)

---

[8] Cf. *The Sower*, 259 (April 1971), esp. art. by M. Hooker, pp. 52–5.
[9] Text in *The Tablet*, 21 July 1973, p. 690. Cf statement of Canadian Bishops in *The Clergy Review*, LIX (1974) 10, p. 690.

help the faithful to prepare for confession which can be made individually later at a convenient time ..... they offer help in reaching that perfect contrition which comes from charity and enable the faithful to attain to God's grace through a desire for the sacrament of penance' (RP 37).

CONCLUSION

It should be clear from what has been said, that the renewal of the celebration of penance can only take place within the context of an overall renewal of the life of penance, and this presents an immense pastoral challenge. Dissatisfaction with prevailing confessional practice cannot be met simply by preaching theological explanations: the rites have to be changed so that they express what they really mean. On the other hand, the simple administrative imposition of new rites, as we have already learnt to our cost, is no guarantee of a resurgence of sacramental life. What is needed is a broad-fronted approach to renewing and deepening the spiritual life of our parishes, in which the principles underlying the rites themselves – serious sense of conversion, community involvement, wider sense of responsibility towards the world – are carried over and applied to the rest of parochial life. In short, 'In order that this sacrament of healing may truly achieve its purpose among Christ's faithful, it must take root in their whole lives and move them to more fervent service of God and neighbour' (RP 7b).

FURTHER READING

P. Anciaux, *The Sacrament of Penance*, 1962.

P. Fannon, The Sacrament of Reconciliation, in *Clergy Review*, LVI (1971) 9, 651–64.

J. Fitzsimons, (ed.), *Penance: Virtue and Sacrament*, 1969.

F. Heggen, *Confession and the Service of Penance*, 1967.

Sr Laurence SND Murray, *Confession: Outmoded Sacrament?*, 1972.

B. Newns, 'Penance, Virtue and Sacrament', in *Clergy Review*, LIII (1969), 780–6.

B. Poschmann, *Penance and the Anointing of the Sick*, 1964.

K. Rahner, 'Problems Concerning Confession', in *Theological Investigations*, III (1967), 190-206.

See also articles in *Concilium*, vol. 4, no. 3 (April 1967), and vol. 1, no. 7 (January 1971).

14. The Anointing and Pastoral Care of the Sick

Brian Newns

As the title implies, this chapter will cover not only the anointing of the sick, but also other liturgical rites involved in the pastoral care of the sick, such as communion, viaticum and the commendation of the dying. But before proceeding with this, it is useful to look at illness as a human phenomenon, and in the context of our Christian faith.

The enigma of illness

Among the many evils of our world, warfare, poverty, crime, unemployment, homelessness and so on, illness and pain in particular defeat our understanding. As the Introduction to the Rite of Anointing (RA 1) says, 'Sickness and pain have always been a heavy burden to man and an enigma to his understanding.' We cannot understand why we or those we love should have to suffer. It seems pointless. Moreover illness rarely comes unaccompanied. With it go fear, unhappiness, depression and anxiety. Illness is not only an evil in itself, it presages the greater evil of death. It reminds us that we are mortal, that man is for most of his life a dying animal.

Another problem with illness is that frequently it isolates us from our family, friends, workmates, and from society in general. There is the psychological isolation of the illness itself, in that we suffer alone, and others, however sympathetic, do not share our sufferings. But there is often also physical isolation and loneliness. The sick person usually cannot work or join in his usual recreations. He is withdrawn from the society of family and friends to the isolation of the sick room or the hospital ward. Hence the feeling that he is redundant and unnecessary, perhaps unwanted, a nuisance. He feels the world can manage without him. Sickness can therefore bring us face to face with the limitations of our own being. It calls us to face the ultimate questions of our own existence, and that at a time when we are least equal to doing so.

Illness and the Christian

All that has been said about illness applies to the sick Christian. For him illness may well be accompanied by temptation to despair. Yet for the Christian who believes, it is possible to see some significance in his sufferings. As the Introduction says, 'Christians suffer sickness and pain as do all other men; yet their faith helps them to understand better the mystery of suffering and to bear their pain more bravely' (RA 1).

Illness is closely related to man's sinful condition, but it cannot be considered a punishment which man suffers for his personal sins (RA 2). Jesus makes this clear in what he says about the man born blind (Jn 9:3). He himself suffered, though sinless. Illness, like death itself, is a sign of the evil Christ has conquered, not only by his miracles of healing but by his death and resurrection. To quote from the Introduction again, 'he bore all the sufferings of his passion and understood human sorrow' (RA 2).

The Christian is baptized into the death and resurrection of Christ, so for him illness not only involves loneliness and the temptation to despair, it is a summons for him to fight in his own flesh the conflict with evil which Christ fought and won in the Garden of Gethsemane and on the cross. In a sense 'Christ still suffers and is tormented in his followers whenever we suffer' (RA 2). 'We should always be prepared to fill up what is wanting in Christ's sufferings for the salvation of the world' (RA 3). Illness is a sharing in Christ's cross, one way in which we ratify our baptism, our eucharist, sharing by our own life and death in Christ's death and resurrection.

In the sick, therefore, Christ continues his redemptive work, giving them a share in his passion, willing that they contribute to the salvation of the world. This view of illness can only be understood in the context of the doctrine of the Mystical Body, and bearing in mind the union of Christ the head and his Body the Church. Seen in this way the sufferings of the sick are part of the messianic tribulations which prepare us and the world for eternal life in glory, and we can look forward to the setting free of creation in the glory of the sons of God.

None of this means that we should submit passively to sickness. 'It is part of the plan laid down by God's providence that we should struggle against all sickness and carefully seek the blessings of good health, so that we can fulfil our role in human society and in the Church' (RA 3). Again 'Not only the sick person should fight against illness; doctors and all who are dedicated to helping the sick should consider it their duty to do whatever they judge will help the sick both physically and spiritually. In doing so they fulfil the command of Christ to visit the sick, for Christ implied that they should be concerned for the whole man and offer both physical relief and spiritual comfort' (RA 4). And so 'Every scientific effort to prolong life and every act of heartfelt love for the sick may be considered a preparation for the gospel and a participation in Christ's healing ministry' (RA 32).

The Church stresses, then, that we should fight against the evil of illness, and she encourages the work of all who do this, particularly doctors and nurses. But it is worth pointing out that the advances of modern medicine have in some ways made the problem of illness more acute. Formerly those who were seriously ill were likely to die fairly soon. Nowadays a person with, for example, cancer or a heart ailment may be able to live a fairly active life for some considerable time. Illness therefore becomes something to be understood and lived with, and not merely the harbinger of death. This greatly affects the Church's pastoral care of the sick, to which we must now turn.

The pastoral care of the sick

We need only open the gospels to see Christ's concern for the sick. We know 'that Christ loved the sick and that during his life he often looked upon the sick and healed them' (RA 1). Moreover, as we have already seen 'Christ himself was sinless, yet he fulfilled what was written in Isaiah: he bore all the sufferings of his passion and understood human sorrow' (RA 2). The Church has always imitated her Master in caring for the sick. Her concern for the sick found and still finds expression in the medical field, in hospitals, nursing and medicine, all of which the Church did so much to pioneer, and which she still encourages and supports, seeing in them a sharing in the healing ministry of Christ. But the Church's particular concern is with the pastoral care of the sick, in which the Church seeks to bring solace and encouragement and spiritual healing.

The pastoral care of the sick seeks to remedy the loneliness brought about by the physical and psychological isolation of illness, the 'No one knows how I feel' which can accompany suffering. On the physical level the Church encourages the visiting of the sick by relatives, friends, neighbours and the priest. At least one organization has been formed to link permanent invalids to each other by telephone. In these and other ways it is possible to make the sick aware that they are part of a community which cares about them. The isolation of the sick is diminished still further when they become aware of their union with the suffering Christ.

This leads to an awareness that the plight of the sick is not senseless and cruel suffering, but rather a trial which God permits them to endure, willing that from it they should grow in maturity as followers of our crucified Lord, and by imitating him in his passion grow in holiness and become saints, sharing in the glory of the sons of God. Through this the sick come to realize that they are not useless and redundant, but that they play a crucial role in the Church. Through their sufferings they fill up what is wanting in the sufferings of Christ, to use St Paul's phrase (cf Col 1:24), and so by sharing in Christ's cross contribute to the salvation of the world and the well-being of the Church.

The living witness of those who suffer is of immense value and encouragement to other Christians and to human beings generally; the sick show other men and women that man's mortal life is redeemed by Christ's passion, death and resurrection, and we are reminded by the sick of the importance of life, death and salvation, compared with the trivial things which so often concern us. In a sense the risen Christ still suffers in his Mystical Body the Church, and notably in those who are sick. If the sick need the Church it is no less true that the Church needs the sick.

The pastoral care of the sick can be considered at a number of levels. The bishop of each diocese, surrounded by his priests, blesses the oil of the sick at the Mass of Chrism on Holy Thursday. This should not merely be a rubrical fact of life, but should rather symbolize the concern of the bishop for the sick of his diocese. This concern can find practical expression in a number of ways, for instance by the bishop visiting the sick in hospitals and in their homes when he comes to the parishes, by gatherings of the sick of the diocese in the cathedral for the celebration of the Anointing of the Sick, and perhaps best of all by the diocesan pilgrimage to Lourdes.

In the parish it is traditional to read out the names of the sick at the Sunday Mass. Nowadays they can be prayed for in the Bidding Prayers every Sunday. But the concern of the parish should not stop there. As the Introduction says, 'If one member suffers in the Body of Christ, which is the Church, all members suffer with him. For this reason, kindness shown toward the sick and works of charity and mutual help for the relief of every kind of human want should be held in special honour' (RA 32). Parish societies such as the Society of St Vincent de Paul and the Legion of Mary will give a lead here in visiting the sick, but this is something any parishioner should be prepared to do, particularly where sick neighbours and old people are involved. Young people are often prepared to give generously of their time and attention to the sick and elderly, once they are made aware of the problem. The first chapter – 'Visitation and Communion of the Sick' – of the Rite of Anointing says: 'All Christians should share in the care and love of Christ and the Church for the sick and should show their concern for them, as much as each one is able, by visiting them and comforting them in the Lord, offering them fraternal help in their need' (RA 42).

The same point is made in the Introduction: 'It is thus fitting that all baptized Christians share in this ministry of mutual charity within the Body of Christ: by fighting against disease, by love shown to the sick, and by celebrating the sacraments of the sick. Like the other sacraments, these too have a communal aspect, which should be brought out as much as possible when they are celebrated' (RA 33). This common concern of all Christians for the sick should therefore find liturgical expression in the communal celebration of communion of the sick in the homes of the sick, with relatives and friends present and communicating, and in the communal celebration of the anointing of the sick in the parish church from time to time.

Obviously the family and friends of the sick person have special obligations towards him. 'The family and friends of the sick and those who take care of them have a special share in this ministry of comfort. It is their task to strengthen the sick with words of faith and by praying with them, to commend them to the Lord who suffered and is glorified, and to urge the sick to unite themselves willingly with the passion and death of Christ for the good of God's people' (RA 34). Moreover the priest will rely upon the relatives to inform him of the sick person's illness. 'If the sickness grows worse, the family and friends of the sick and those who take care of them have the responsibility to inform the pastor and by their kind words prudently to dispose the sick person for the reception of the sacraments at the proper time' (ibid).

The leader of the parish in caring for the sick as in all else is the priest. He will visit the sick and 'offer them words of faith and explain the significance of human suffering in the mystery of salvation'. (RA 43). He will also 'urge the sick to realize that through their faith they are also united with Christ's suffering and that with prayer they can sanctify their sickness and draw strength to bear their suffering' (RA 43). When visiting the sick the priest will pray with them and read the scriptures to them, bless them and lay his hands upon them (cf RA 45).

In particular the priest will celebrate the sacraments with the sick, penance, communion, anointing and viaticum, as each is appropriate. In doing so he will stir up the hope of those present and strengthen their faith in Christ who suffered and is glorified. By expressing the Church's love and the consolation of faith he will comfort those who believe and raise the minds of others to God. The Introduction assumes that the priest will plan the rites of the sacraments, taking into account the condition of the sick person and as far as possible consulting him and his family (RA 37). This can well be done as part of the explanation of the meaning of the sacraments which the priest will normally give, as he prepares the sick person to celebrate them.

Besides concerning himself with the care of individual sick people, the priest will need to think of the parish as a whole. He will want to make his parishioners aware of the sick among them, and encourage them to feel some responsibility towards them. He will wish to make the sick aware that they are not alone, especially the permanently sick, and besides seeing that they are visited he may be able to bring them into contact with each other, even if this is only by telephone. From time to time he may be able to arrange services, such as the anointing of the sick, in the parish church, for those who can be taken to church.

Finally the priest will be anxious to teach the meaning of suffering in Christ's revelation to his people. Often when people are ill there is a limit to the amount of instruction they can absorb; this makes it all the more important to convey this teaching to people when they are well. This can be done in the Sunday homily, in the parish bulletin and perhaps best of all by involving parishioners in the care of the sick, and in the communal celebration of the sacraments of the sick, either with their sick relatives and friends or in the parish church or the cathedral.

We must turn now to the sacraments themselves and their celebration with and for the sick.

Communion of the sick

The importance of communion of the sick is self-evident. If we see frequent communion as desirable for the laity in general this must apply with special force to the sick. In their situation the consoling and strengthening union with Christ which communion is must be seen as particularly vital. Furthermore, in communion we are united with other members of the Body of Christ, with the Church and in particular with the Church in this particular place. Consequently communion for the sick person should unite him with the Christians of the locality and diminish the feelings of loneliness and isolation which may afflict him.

It is therefore important that the sick and aged should be able to receive communion frequently. The introductory rubrics to the new rite of communion of the sick (RA 46) maintain that 'Pastors should see to it that the sick and aged, even if not seriously sick or in imminent danger of death, be given every opportunity to receive the eucharist frequently and even daily, if possible, especially during the Easter season.' They may receive communion at any time and the Instruction *Immensae Caritatis*, which is dated 29 January 1973, reduces the fast for the sick and aged to *about* a quarter of an hour. Moreover those caring for the sick and relatives can receive communion with them, fasting for the same amount of time if they cannot conveniently observe the normal fast of one hour. This encouragement of frequent communion for the sick is obviously appropriate for those accustomed to communicate frequently when well. One has heard from the sick themselves the deprivation they feel when, lying in bed, they hear others on their way to daily Mass, to which they were once accustomed to go. In their illness they feel the need for frequent reception of Christ in communion still more, and this need should be met.

But what about those who were not accustomed to frequent communion when well? It would seem wrong to assume that a pattern of infrequent reception of communion, established when the person was in good health, should necessarily be perpetuated when the person falls ill. Priests should seek to encourage everyone to progress towards daily communion, and this applies all the more strongly to the sick. If their illness becomes for them a time of spiritual growth, which is what the pastoral care of the sick is all about, then it would seem normal that their desire to receive our Lord in communion more frequently should grow and should be met. We need to remember also that illness can be a time of temptation; the suffering and inactivity involved in illness can lead people for the first time in their lives to undergo temptations against faith. In these cases the need for frequent communion is evident.

It must however be recognized that most priests are too busy to take communion to the sick as often as they would wish. For this reason we must welcome the permission, given in *Immensae Caritatis*, the Roman Instruction mentioned above, for lay people to be designated as extraordinary ministers of communion, so that where a priest, deacon or acolyte is either not available or is prevented from taking communion out by some other pastoral ministry, communion can be taken to the sick by approved lay persons.

One consequence of this development which we may hope for is that communion may be taken to the sick and aged on Sunday, the day when the local Church assembles to celebrate the presence of its risen Lord. This is a day when the link of the sick with the rest of the Christians of the locality should be underlined. Already we read out the names of the sick and, one hopes, pray for them in the Bidding Prayers. But it should henceforth be possible for a lay person to take communion to the sick from the Sunday Mass, and in the course of the communion service read one or other of the Sunday readings and give the gist of the priest's homily. Afterwards the news of the parish could be given in friendly conversation. Perhaps a member of the sick person's own family could be deputed to bring him communion. In this way not only could the sick receive communion more often, but also their sense of isolation could be diminished and their links with the parish strengthened.

The rite of communion of the sick is simple and adaptable to the condition of the sick person. On entering the priest greets the sick person and places the Blessed Sacrament on the table provided. He may then sprinkle the sick person and the room with holy water. If desired he then hears the sick person's confession; otherwise one of the penitential rites from the Mass is used. A short reading from scripture may then follow, briefly explained by the priest. Then the Lord's Prayer is said and communion is given. A period of silence may follow, which ends with the concluding prayer and the blessing.

A shorter rite of communion of the sick is provided for use in hospitals and similar places, where communion is given in several rooms of the same building. This begins with the antiphon *O sacrum convivium* or an alternative in the chapel or first ward. Then the priest says 'This is the Lamb of God . . .' either to all the communicants or to each individually. The communicants reply 'Lord I am not worthy . . .' and then communion is given in the usual way. A concluding prayer is said in the chapel or the last ward to be visited. This brief rite can if desired be expanded with the inclusion of elements from the longer one.

Anointing of the sick
The Anointing of the Sick is seen by the Council of Trent as one of the seven sacraments, instituted by Christ and promulgated by St James in his Epistle where he says: 'If one of you is ill, he should send for the elders of the Church, and they must anoint him with oil in the name of the Lord and pray over him. The prayer of faith will save the sick man and the Lord will raise him up again; and if he has committed any sins he will be forgiven' (5:14–15).

A number of things are worth noting in this text. Firstly, the sacrament is for the sick, although the forgiveness of sins may also be involved. Secondly, it is the elders of the Church who confer the sacrament, by anointing the sick person with oil in the name of the Lord and praying over him the prayer of faith. Thirdly, the word 'save' can refer either to bodily health being recovered or to the salvation of the sick person's soul, or indeed to both.

Throughout the history of this sacrament there have been two basic questions: firstly, is this sacrament for the sick or for the dying? Secondly, is this sacrament for healing or for forgiveness? During the first eight centuries the whole emphasis was on physical healing. Christians used oil blessed by bishops and priests for themselves and for others when they were ill.

During the scholastic period, however, the emphasis was on forgiveness of the sins of the dying. The administration of the sacrament was restricted to priests and it was given only to those on the point of death. In the first centuries it had been customary to anoint the part of the body where the pain was greatest or where the malady was, but now it became the practice to anoint the five senses, with formulas stressing the forgiveness of sins committed through the senses.

The Council of Trent's view of the sacrament was more moderate than either of the two opposed and extreme views we have outlined. On the effect of the sacrament it said, 'This reality is in fact the grace of the Holy Spirit, whose anointing takes away sins, if any still remain to be taken away, and the remnants of sin; it also relieves and strengthens the soul of the sick person, arousing in him a great confidence in the divine mercy; thus sustained, he may more easily bear the trials and hardships of his sickness, more easily resist the temptations of the devil "lying in wait" (Genesis 3:15), and sometimes regain bodily health if this is expedient for the health of the soul.'[1] The Council of Trent also taught that the Anointing was to be administered to the sick, 'especially those who are in such a condition as to appear to have reached the end of their life, whence it is also called the sacrament of the dying'.

The Second Vatican Council, in its Constitution on the Sacred Liturgy, preferred the name 'anointing of the sick' to 'extreme unction', pointing out that it was not a sacrament solely

[1] This and the following quotation from the Tridentine teaching on the anointing of the sick are both taken from the Apostolic Constitution *Sacram Unctionem*, which heads the *Ordo Unctionis Infirmorum Eorumque Pastoralis Curae*.

for those at the point of death. The time for its reception has certainly arrived, according to the Council, when someone begins to be in danger of death through sickness or old age. Subsequently, in the Constitution on the Church, the Council speaks of the sacrament in terms of the sick pure and simple:

> 'By the sacred anointing of the sick, and the prayer of her priests, the whole Church commends those who are ill to the suffering and glorified Lord, asking that he may lighten their sufferings and save them. She exhorts them moreover to contribute to the welfare of the whole People of God by associating themselves freely with the passion and death of Christ' (Church 11).

The Introduction to the Rite of Anointing summarizes the effects of the sacrament in these words:

> 'This sacrament provides the sick person with the grace of the Holy Spirit by which the whole man is brought to health, trust in God is encouraged, and strength is given to resist the temptations of the Evil One and anxiety about death. Thus the sick person is able not only to bear his suffering bravely, but also to fight against it. A return to physical health may even follow the reception of this sacrament if it will be beneficial to the sick person's salvation. If necessary, the sacrament also provides the sick person with the forgiveness of sins and the completion of Christian penance' (RA 6).

What then are we to conclude with regard to the effects of the sacrament and those for whom it is indicated? It would be mistaken to see the anointing of the sick as purely medical, as an attempt by the Church to compete with the doctor. But it would be equally extreme to see it as the forgiveness of the sins of the dying, pure and simple. Rather we should see it as addressed to the whole man, body, mind and spirit, offering him salvation from the evil which besets him on each of these levels, in the form of illness, temptation and perhaps sin. This salvation is hidden and spiritual to some extent, but its psychological impact is frequently evident, and at times it may result in physical recovery.

This view of the anointing as directed to and saving the whole man is not only true to the scriptural view of man and salvation, it is also in accord with modern medicine, which is

more reluctant than it formerly was to deal with man's physical
ills in isolation from those of his mind and spirit. It also finds
expression in the prayers of the rite, notably in the prayer for
the blessing of oil:

> Lord God, loving Father,
> you bring healing to the sick
> through your Son Jesus Christ.
> Hear us as we pray to you in faith,
> and send the Holy Spirit, man's Helper and Friend,
> upon this oil, which nature has provided
> to serve the needs of men.
> May your blessing
> come upon all who are anointed with this oil,
> that they may be freed from pain and illness
> and made well again in body, mind and soul.
> Father, may this oil be blessed for our use
> in the name of our Lord Jesus Christ
> who lives and reigns with you for ever and ever.

The conclusion we reach with regard to the effects of the
sacrament inevitably affects the conclusion we reach with
regard to who may be anointed. As we have already seen, the
recent Council stated that: 'as soon as any one of the faithful
begins to be in danger of death from sickness or old age, the
appropriate time for him to receive this sacrament has certainly
already arrived' (CL 73). The Introduction to the Rite states:
'The Letter of James states that the anointing should be given
to the sick to raise them up and save them. There should be
special care and concern that those who are dangerously ill
due to sickness or old age receive this sacrament' (RA 8). These
texts make it clear that people beginning to be in danger of
death through sickness and old age should be anointed, but they
are so expressed as to allow the view that the requirement for
anointing is simply serious illness. Such a view seems in accordance with the statements of the Magisterium and with the
prayers of the rite, with their plea for recovery. It is for the
priest to determine whether the illness is serious enough to
warrant anointing, in other words whether it is serious enough
to represent a threat to the person's physical, mental and
spiritual health and salvation, and danger of death is one

criterion, although doctors make clear that many illnesses nowadays could be said to involve danger of death and yet are usually followed by recovery. But in any case, as the Introduction says, 'A prudent or probable judgement about the seriousness of the sickness is sufficient; in such a case there is no reason for scruples, but if necessary a doctor may be consulted' (RA 8).

The sacrament may be repeated during the same illness if the patient gets worse, and it may be given before surgery, when this is caused by a dangerous illness. Old people may be anointed if they are weak, even if there is no dangerous illness present, and children may be anointed if they have enough understanding to be comforted by this sacrament. The unconscious sick may be anointed if they would have asked for the sacrament when conscious, as Christian believers. The dead should be prayed for, not anointed, but if it is doubtful whether a person is dead he may be anointed conditionally. (On all this cf RA 9–15.)

The new Order nowhere discusses the plight of the physically and mentally handicapped. Yet these can be in a situation where evil threatens their salvation, where their faith risks becoming weaker and where they undergo temptation. The question of anointing such people must at least be considered, as it is in a positive way with regard to the physically handicapped by Claude Ortemann in his article 'La pastorale des sacrements auprès des malades', in *La Maison-Dieu* 113.

The rite of anointing is relatively simple and straightforward. The priest greets the sick person and those present, and may then sprinkle them and the room with holy water. After some words of introduction or an introductory prayer, both of which recall the text from St James' Epistle quoted above, the penitential rite follows, unless the sick person then makes his confession. There is then a short scripture reading, which the priest may explain to those present.

A short litany of intercession may be said, or it may follow the anointing, or be said at some other time in the service. After this the priest lays his hands on the head of the sick person in silence, a gesture which recalls Christ's acts of healing. The oil of the sick is normally blessed on Holy Thursday, but if necessary it may be blessed at this point of the rite. If the oil is already blessed a responsorial prayer of thanksgiving is said over it.

Then the sick person is anointed on the forehead and the hands, the priest saying:

> Through this holy anointing
> may the Lord in his love and mercy help you
> with the grace of the Holy Spirit. R/Amen.
> May the Lord who frees you from sin
> save you and raise you up. R/Amen.

After the anointing a prayer is said, chosen according to the sick person's condition. The rite ends with the Lord's Prayer and the blessing. If the sick person is to receive communion this follows the Lord's Prayer.

This rite can be celebrated during Mass, in which case it follows the homily and can precede the Bidding Prayers, unless the litany is said immediately after the homily. When celebrated during Mass therefore the rite begins after the homily with the litany or the laying-on of hands, followed by the prayer of thanksgiving over the oil, the anointing itself and then the Bidding Prayers, unless the litany has already been said. The Biddings end with the prayer after anointing, after which Mass continues. The sick person and all present may receive communion under both kinds. Provision is also made in the Order for the celebration of the sacrament in the context of a pilgrimage or other large gathering, inside or outside Mass. Given the presence of several priests they can each lay hands on some of the sick and anoint them, using the sacramental form, the principal celebrant reciting the prayers. This form of celebration has become familiar on pilgrimages to Lourdes.

From this it is evident that there are a number of options open to the Church in her celebration of this sacrament. One can anoint the sick in their homes or in hospital, alone or in the presence of their family and those who care for them, inside or outside Mass. From time to time it is possible, if the sick can be brought to church, to have a celebration of the Anointing of the Sick in the parish or deanery church in the presence of parishioners, inside or outside Mass. The pastoral value of such celebrations needs no emphasis. Similar celebrations on a diocesan scale can and have taken place in the cathedral, and as we have already remarked they have become a normal feature of pilgrimages to Lourdes.

Preparation and catechesis are of course essential. Many elements in the rite are optional, with texts to be selected, included or omitted, according to the state of the sick person. It is therefore necessary to take account of this, and indeed as far as possible to prepare the rite with the sick person and his family. Preliminary catechesis is important as we have already seen. This applies particularly to this sacrament, because as the Introduction says 'The anointing of the sick, which includes the prayer of faith (see James 5: 15), is a sacrament of faith. This faith is important for the minister and particularly for the one who receives it. The sick man will be saved by his faith and the faith of the Church which looks back to the death and resurrection of Christ, the source of the sacrament's power (see James 5: 15) and looks ahead to the future kingdom which is pledged in the sacraments' (RA 7).

Perhaps the principal danger to be guarded against in teaching people about the sacraments is the widespread conviction that this is the sacrament of the dying. To quote the Introduction again 'In public and private catechesis, the faithful should be encouraged to ask for the anointing and, as soon as the time for the anointing comes, to receive it with complete faith and devotion, not misusing the sacrament by putting it off. All who care for the sick should be taught the meaning and purpose of anointing' (RA 13).

The liturgy of the dying
Christian death is discussed elsewhere in this volume, but since viaticum and the rite for the commendation of the dying form part of this Order we shall say something about them here. We need first of all to appreciate the crucial significance of death, as our ultimate and most personal sharing in Christ's death and resurrection, presaged by our baptism and our sharing in the eucharist. In life and in death we are called to ratify and confirm the action of Christ in which we have shared in the liturgy.

The name *viaticum* means food for the journey. Before undertaking this last and most mysterious of all journies the dying person receives the eucharist, a promise that Christ will be with him on the journey and a pledge of the future resurrection: 'He who eats my flesh and drinks my blood has eternal life and I will raise him up on the last day' (Jn 6:54). All baptized

Christians in danger of death who can receive communion are obliged to receive viaticum and the Church throughout her history has always tried to ensure that no one should die without it.

If possible viaticum is to be given within Mass, to permit communion under both kinds. It is also appropriate because, as the Introduction says 'Communion received as viaticum should be considered as a special sign of participation in the mystery of the death of the Lord and his passage to the Father, the mystery which is celebrated in the eucharist' (RA 26).

If the condition of the sick person permits, a short homily is given after the gospel, explaining the meaning of viaticum. This is followed if possible by the dying person's renewal of his baptismal profession of faith, which he does by saying 'I believe' in response to the credal statements of the priest. The Bidding Prayers can be omitted if they would tire the dying person too much. Communion can be under both kinds for all present; when he gives viaticum to the dying person the priest adds 'May the Lord Jesus Christ protect you and lead you to eternal life' to the usual words of administration. Mass ends with the blessing and the priest may add the form for the plenary indulgence for the dying.

When given outside Mass the rite of viaticum begins with a greeting, an optional aspersion with holy water, words of introduction and the penitential rite, unless the dying person makes his confession. This may be followed by the plenary indulgence for the dying. It is appropriate then to have a short scripture reading, which the priest may explain briefly. This is followed by a renewal of the baptismal profession of faith and a short litany of intercession, if the condition of the dying person permits. After the Lord's Prayer viaticum is given, and after an optional period of silence the rite ends with the final prayer and blessing. The priest and those present may then give the dying person the sign of peace.

The Church also provides a special prayer book for the dying, the order of commendation of the dying. This word *commend* is the clue to the meaning of this rite. On the cross Christ said, quoting the fifth verse of Psalm 30, 'Into your hands I commend my spirit.' In Acts we find St Stephen praying in similar terms, 'Lord Jesus receive my spirit.' The use of the word 'commend' in the title and prayers of this rite therefore links the death of the Christian with that of Christ.

The rite consists of scriptural ejaculations, scriptural readings, prayers and a short litany, from all of which the priest can choose according to circumstances. These texts are designed to help the dying person, if he is conscious, to overcome his anxiety at dying by imitating Christ who suffered and died, so that he dies hoping for the heavenly life and resurrection Christ has gained for us. Even if the dying person is not conscious, the prayers and readings should help to console those present, teaching them the paschal meaning of Christian death. Priests are to try to be with people when they die to say these prayers with them. If this is impossible they should ensure that the laity present do this, and consequently they are to ensure that the laity have texts of these prayers.

Conclusion

We live in an age of doubt and unbelief, where people think in terms of power and strength. The weak, the sick and the aged are despised and forgotten. The concern is with those who are well, young, and able to work and to play. These are the people who count where politics, big business and leisure are concerned.

Against this modern view the Church sets her face, teaching us that the sick and the aged do matter. They matter in themselves, because they are at a crucial point in their development as followers of Christ and need support, but also because in their sickness or old age they have much to give the Church and world. We need them. Their prayers and sufferings, offered in union with Christ, benefit us all.

When death comes modern man tries to banish it to the hospital ward and the undertaker's parlour. But the Church celebrates death; what looks like man's ultimate defeat, sin's final victory, man's tragic destiny, is seen by the Church as the ultimate and complete sharing in Christ's death. Our whole lives are a preparation for death, from the day we are baptized into the death of Christ. As Christians we face death in the confidence our faith brings, assured by Christ that if we share in his death we shall share in his resurrection.

15. Celebrating Marriage

Patrick Byrne

Marriage is unique among the sacraments because it is the couple themselves who marry each other in Christ. The priest is the chief witness for the community of faith, representing the Church and asking God's blessing upon their wedded life; in many countries, the priest also represents the civil government as he witnesses the couple's vows.

Pastorally speaking, each marriage is an occasion for priest and parish to help the couple and their families grow in the knowledge and practice of their faith. The sacrament is a spiritual event of importance in the life of the parish community, as well as in the life of a young man and woman.

God's plan for his people
God uses the image of marriage to describe his benevolent love for us, and to emphasize the close union that exists between him and his people. St Paul describes Christ's love for his Church – the people of God – in similar terms. Each marriage is therefore an image of God's love, of how he showers love and life and gifts on us. Each couple coming to prepare for marriage will be a new and further sign and proof of the covenant that God makes with his people. How well their marriage will reflect his love depends greatly on the good will of the couple, but also to some extent on the way the priest and, where possible, the parish liturgy committee work with them during the time of preparation.

Christian marriage is part of the Father's larger plan for his glory and our salvation, for he chose us in Christ before he created the universe. He picked us out in love to become his family, his adopted sons and daughters, his Church, so that we would live holy and sinless lives in his presence. By the death and rising of the Lord Jesus, the Father has freed us from sin's power. He has showered his rich graces upon us, and leads us to praise his glory. As a splendid completion of his act of love, he has given us a vision of his great plan: to restore all creation to himself by bringing it under the control of Christ its head.

How does marriage fit into this plan? It is one of the most important ways in which God wishes to achieve his will, for it is the vocation of most people on earth. Through the marriage of each couple, he wishes to bless their lives as they live together in love, a unique, fresh image and reflection of his love for us. His creative power works with them to bring their children into the world, and they help their little ones to grow in wisdom, age and grace before God and man. By their lives, their love, their teaching and example, these parents lead another generation closer to God, and continue to let Christ rule their marriage. In the same way, they are working out their own salvation. This is God's plan; unfortunately, it is not always carried out by his people.

And so we begin to realize a little more the importance of marriage in the plan of salvation, and work to make it a reality in our parish community. The Church is deeply concerned about the way young people prepare for marriage, because their marriage is not just their private affair, but part of God's plan for creation and redemption.

Ideas for preparation and celebration, based on scripture and liturgy, are described below, but their success depends greatly on the faith and effort of the priest and liturgy team members who work together in this area, as well as on the faith and co-operation of the couple and their families.

A. GENERAL PREPARATION OF THE PARISH

Christian marriage preparation in the parish starts long before the couple comes to see the priest about their wedding. If there is to be any hope of improving prevailing standards, all the members of the parish have to be led to a more serious and more spiritual point of view. Priests and parish worship committee need to take a thorough look at the way weddings are being carried on at present, and at the preparation (or lack of it) for the celebration of the sacrament.

An overall programme of marriage preparation and celebration should be drawn up, including the points discussed in this chapter. These could form guidelines for good pastoral and liturgical preparation and celebration of the sacrament.

This plan should be discussed with all the people of the parish, and gradually become part of the thinking and acting of the community.

Whose standards?

One of the greatest obstacles facing any parish is the degree to which secular rather than Christian standards govern the minds of all involved. For too many, it is the whims of society and fashion that are more important than the will of Christ and his Church. Combating this secular mentality is not easy, but unless it is done, the whole institution of marriage is in danger of going beyond the control of Christ, and so will not bring about the kingdom of God.

In your area, by your efforts, your parish community can help restore marriage as God intends it to be. The priest and liturgy team have to analyse the situation in this particular parish and community, determine which situations are good, acceptable, or undesirable, and set out to establish Christian standards here.

How do we bring these truths to the members of the parish? An overall plan would include preaching (the homily should lead us into the eucharist, and the eucharist into life); religious education of adults; discussion with young families; use of the parish bulletin, information sheet or magazine as a means of educating people in the teaching of Jesus and his Church on marriage. Parish organizations, including the parish council and liturgy committee, need a better grasp of this aspect of Christian life, and would welcome the opportunity to go beyond their penny catechism knowledge of days gone by.

The teaching on marriage must be included as part of a larger picture: people need to realize they are God's chosen people with a responsible mission in this world. As a community of faith and love, their lives are to guide others to the Lord Jesus. Gifted with the Spirit, they have his strength and light to lead them on the way of Christ. The role of the sacraments in our spiritual life must also become familiar to them, with the eucharist as the centre of the life and work of each Christian and of the believing community.

The community needs to grasp the fact that all are responsible for marriage preparation. Young people understand marriage by the example and practice of their parents and of the other families in their community.

Marriage announcements

The way the parish community hears about marriages influences its attitude towards the sacrament. If only the legislation is preached, will people form a more Christian view of this sacrament and vocation?

Some parishes announce wedding banns in a warmer, less formal way, and ask people to pray for those about to marry, that God may bless them in their vocation. Others may include them in the prayer of the faithful, at least the Sunday before the wedding. Prayers for married couples and for those preparing for marriage can also be offered occasionally in the general intercessions.

The more that faith and Christian joy are reflected in sacramental announcements, the more people will be influenced to look on them with the mind of Christ.

Spiritual preparation of the couple

A couple wishing to celebrate a Christian wedding should meet with a priest a long time ahead, not only to set the date but also to discuss their vocation. Ideally, this is best done when they begin to realize that they want to marry each other.

With him they can discuss their maturity, their goals in life and their spiritual outlook. Such matters as age, education, job security are important, but fuller attention needs to be paid to spiritual maturity, prayer life, the way they have taken part in parish life or neglected it, and their role in the community after they marry. This means of course that the parish should be a community of prayer rather than a neighbourhood social club.

The Second Vatican Council calls on the priest to help his people to take part in the liturgy, with full understanding; by their active cooperation, they will be able to achieve the spiritual effects of their participation (CL 11, 14, 18, 19). Since such participation is the 'primary and indispensable source of the true Christian spirit' (St Pius X), a pastor (anyone involved in spiritual care of the people of God) is to work with zeal in everything he does to help his people participate in liturgy with this fervour. In other words, the spirit and power of the liturgy are to penetrate the priest, so that he is able to live the liturgical life and share it with all who believe.

It takes zeal and patience as he instructs his people in the spirit of the liturgy, and helps them to participate as well as possible, but this is one of his chief duties. By his personal example, he is to share the liturgical spirit with his people.

The marriage ritual emphasizes the priest's responsibility to strengthen and nourish the faith of couples preparing for marriage, since their life together must be based on faith (Introduction, no. 7). He will help them by instruction and in other ways described below.

REVIEWING THE FUNDAMENTALS OF OUR FAITH. Most adults need a fresh and mature perspective in which to appreciate their Christian faith. One way of helping them to achieve this would be by a careful, prayerful reading of Paul's letter to the Ephesians. Using appropriate sections of the epistle, the priest would lead the couple to discuss what they read in faith, and encourage them to practise what they believe:

Eph 1: meaning of our Christian vocation.

Eph 2-3: Christ our Lord, his death-resurrection, and our share in his paschal mystery.

Eph 4-5: living the new life in Christ.

Eph 5-6: family life in Christ.

Instructions should be given on the Church's teachings on marriage and the family, so that the couple will build their faith on a more solid base than the whims and fashions of the world and of the current generation.

These sessions should be enriched by insights into our faith from other scripture passages, Second Vatican Council documents, the marriage rite and its introduction (especially nos. 1–6). Readings from the marriage section of the Lectionary may serve to reinforce these teachings; the use of these texts during the period of preparation will help the couple when the time comes to choose the scripture readings for their marriage ceremony.

PRE-MARRIAGE COURSES. While he concentrates on their spiritual preparation, a wise priest will also encourage a couple to become involved in a marriage preparation course, to help them prepare for married life. Over a number of sessions, these courses help the couple to look at their wedded life from different angles (economic, legal, psychological, religious) and at their new roles as partners and parents. The sessions include ample time for discussing general and particular problems with experts, ordinary married couples, and young people like themselves who are preparing to marry.

In larger centres, these courses are available at various times of the year, and are often ecumenical. For those living in a small town or in a rural area, such courses may be available less frequently. Some courses may be taken by mail.

The priest helping the couple prepare for marriage should give them more information on these courses; if none is available in the area, perhaps priest, liturgy committee, and couples should work together to arrange a number of sessions for local couples who are preparing for marriage.

Marriage courses won't replace serious discussion by the couple of their personal attitudes towards marriage, working wives, children, education, religion, and many other considerations, but they will help them to discuss them openly, and to develop a mature and mutual understanding on many matters that could cause problems in their life as husband and wife. In some communities, young married couples are welcomed to these courses, especially if they did not have the opportunity of following one before their wedding.

A day of recollection, a retreat, or a day of prayer for engaged couples could be encouraged. Sometimes several parishes could combine to arrange such events.

Books about marriage continue to be issued each year. The priest and his liturgy committee should be familiar with what is available in their area, and recommend them to the couple. Some parish libraries will lend these books to couples during their time of preparation for marriage.

INVITATION TO PRAY. From the first time they come to see him, the priest should invite the couple to pray together as they prepare for their marriage, and should pray with them. They should pray for God's help in this time of preparation, and for a happy and holy life together. Prayer may be in their own words; at times they may prefer to use a formula such as the one given below.

PRAYER BEFORE MARRIAGE. The couple may wish to use this prayer, even daily, as they prepare for their marriage:

Together:

Lord Jesus,
bless us as we prepare for our wedding.
Look at our hearts,
and deepen our love for you and for each other.

Help us to become holier,
and make us more concerned for others.
Let us share your love and your ideals,
so that we will always be generous
in giving our time and talents to others.
Make us ready to help your friends
build a better world for all people.

Young man:

Lord, teach me to be a man of faith.
Help me to become a good husband and loving father,
the protector of our home
and teacher of our children in your ways.

Young woman:

Lord Jesus, help me to be a woman of faith,
a good wife, a loving mother.
Protect our family and bless our home throughout our lives.

Together:

Send your Spirit to bring us light and strength.
Keep us pure in our love,
and protect our lives from evil.
Lord Jesus, listen to our prayer,
and bless our lives in your service.

Holy Mary, pray for us,
and ask your Son to guide us.

St Joseph, pray for us.

CELEBRATING THE ENGAGEMENT. Some couples may wish to celebrate their engagement by a brief bible service in church, surrounded by their families and close friends. It need not be formal. A reading or two from scripture, some community prayers, a blessing of the engaged couple and of their rings could be followed by a happy family gathering. The liturgy committee could design a service with options so that the couple could use it if they do not wish to design their own. (The National Liturgical Commission of England and Wales has recently composed a betrothal rite on this pattern.)

Preparing the celebration
While it is true that a wedding is a special celebration for the couple and their family and friends, it is also a celebration of the people of God, especially of this believing community, the bride's parish: another Christian home, a little Church (church 11), is being founded. A fresh image of God's love is being planted in the community, and God's work is renewed and continued through their family life.

A wedding is not a private affair or happening. Every marriage is an act of liturgy, of public worship. Because a sacrament is being celebrated, the Church surrounds it with prayers and ceremonies to enhance its solemnity, to ask God's special blessing, and to help this couple and this community appreciate more fully its sacredness and importance. In the wedding Mass, the Church is celebrating God's creative love which he has shared with this couple. The prayers and readings of the Mass and marriage ritual teach Christ's attitude towards marriage and family life.

In arranging the details of their wedding celebration, the couple, their families and their friends could bear this in mind and consider inviting the whole parish to the liturgical celebration of their marriage.

CHOOSING THE PEOPLE. Everything about the wedding celebration should teach the Christian vision of marriage, and build up the faith of all who take part in the celebration.

Priest: The first choice should be a priest from the bride's parish, where the wedding normally takes place. The local priest shares the responsibility for the spiritual growth of all parishioners. Because each marriage celebration is another step forward in the development of this Christian community, he is interested and involved. Normally he – with his liturgy committee in more progressive parishes – will help the couple to prepare themselves spiritually, and will plan the celebration with them. While the couple may ask another priest (a relative or close friend, for example), other things being equal, it is preferable to have the local priest officiate at each wedding in the parish. The priest appointed to a parish belongs to that community, and is more directly concerned with the adequate preparation of the couple before their marriage, and, if they are to remain in the parish, with their life after their wedding day celebrations have become memories.

Attendants: The people who form the bridal party should obviously be Christians of good character, examples of the virtues and ideals proclaimed by the liturgical celebration. They should be men and women of faith, who understand the sacredness of the celebration and what it means.

PLANNING THE CELEBRATION. The wedding should be planned in accord with the mind of the Church: it is to be an act of public worship, a celebration of faith, in which all are able to participate fully. There are many areas which the couple should discuss with the priest and the liturgy committee:

Date and time: The Church does not forbid marriage during Advent and Lent, but does ask the couple and their families to respect the special nature of these liturgical seasons by refraining from too much pomp. A general programme of parish education would recommend that weddings be celebrated in the other forty-two weeks of the year.

In some countries, such as Canada, the Church strongly discourages weddings on Sundays, holy days of obligation and during Holy Week, because of the practical conflict between community and family interests.

The hour chosen for the wedding should not be too close to announced times for the sacrament of penance or other parochial services. If several weddings are scheduled for the same day, adequate time needs to be left for unhurried celebration and for the extra delays occasioned by photographs and friendly gatherings.

Invitations: Most couples let a printer prepare their invitations, using a book of standard, innocuously worded forms. A parish liturgy committee could do a great service for parishioners by preparing and suggesting a positive Christian wording for invitations, both to the wedding of two Catholics and to a mixed marriage. These forms would indicate clearly that the family is inviting the guests to take part in a sacred celebration of public worship.

Clothes and flowers: In too many human affairs, inconsequential things take first place, overshadowing what is more important or more urgent. This is certainly true in many weddings. While wedding gowns and flower arrangements are part of the whole celebration, they should not be allowed to eclipse the spiritual preparation of the couple.

A parish liturgy committee might wish to draw up suggestions for the correct use of flowers for the wedding liturgy. Usually a few flowers well arranged – with the rest kept at the bride's home and the wedding reception – will provide a good adjunct to the liturgical celebration.

Music: Since the wedding is a service of worship and a celebration of the Church's faith, all music used at it should contribute to the religious spirit. Both music and words should express and deepen the faith of the community. First consideration should be given to encouraging all to sing, and to providing them with suitable aids for participation. Singing by a soloist or choir to the constant exclusion of the congregation is against the spirit of the liturgy.

Parishes which wish to promote proper liturgical music at weddings will make sure that good hymn books are provided for everyone, and that suitable music is chosen from them. Many diocesan liturgical commissions provide specific guidelines for wedding music.

Banners and posters: The liturgy committee may wish to design a few and have them available for wedding celebrations. These should express ideas and phrases from the liturgical texts. If the couple and their friends wish to design some, care should be taken that they are in good taste. A tradition of designing a banner and presenting it to the parish church could be established in some communities.

Celebration: A good wedding celebration will be more like the best Sunday Mass than a weekday eucharist. It will build up faith by a careful choice of all its elements and by well chosen ministers who are thoroughly prepared. Full participation by the entire congregation will be encouraged, in order that everyone present will be led by the dignity and beauty of the liturgy to a deeper understanding of Christian marriage.

Specific suggestions for the wedding Mass are contained on pp. 242 ff, under the heading *Celebrating marriage*. Each of these points should be considered by the couple in the months before their wedding, and discussed with the priest.

Wedding rehearsal: In many communities, it is customary to hold a practice a night or two before the wedding. The priest can use this as a further opportunity for helping the couple and their families to keep the spiritual aspect of marriage foremost in their preparation. The actual wedding practice should be simple. Because of the excitement of the occasion and the emotional exhaustion of the couple, the priest is well advised to rehearse only the most evident parts of the ceremony. This would include the entrance procession and their arrival at the places where they will be during the celebration. It is usually simpler to have them stay in the same place throughout the Mass and the marriage ceremony; some priests, however, prefer to have the couple come to the altar for certain parts of the rite. As far as standing, sitting or kneeling is concerned, it is simpler for the priest or commentator to invite the entire congregation – including the bridal party – to do so at any given moment, rather than trying to cram a set of rubrics into their tired heads. After giving any specific instructions they will need for the celebration (such as communion under both kinds, or the procedure for signing the marriage register, where this is done), he shows them how to leave the sanctuary in the recessional.

Nervous tension will tend to make the participants in the rehearsal uncomfortable. This nervousness may tend to be shown by loud talking, inattention, or skittishness. Despite these natural obstacles, the priest should try to emphasize the spiritual aspects of the sacramental celebration for which they are all preparing.

The rehearsal may also provide an opportunity for celebrating the sacrament of penance with the bridal party, their families and their friends. This should be discussed during the period of instruction and again shortly before the actual date, so that all may prepare for it, and not complicate the celebration by arranging parties too soon after the rehearsal.

Some priests may wish to suggest the possibility of having another priest available to celebrate the sacrament of penance, so that all will feel perfectly free in seeking absolution.

SECULAR CELEBRATIONS. A serious problem in weddings today is that community pressures may thwart positive, Christian celebration of an important religious moment. The rushing and fuss of preparations – hiring halls and caterers, arranging menus and flowers, preparing decorations and invitation lists – usually leave the couple near emotional exhaustion: by the time their wedding day arrives, the hectic whirl has left them fatigued, with no time for spiritual preparation. The problem arises from the well-meaning but misguided actions and plans of friends and families who organize a continuous round of stag parties and gatherings, while forgetting the emotional drain on the couple at a time when they need time for prayer, meditation and peace.

B. CELEBRATING MARRIAGE

The celebration of the sacrament of marriage should be the high spiritual moment: everything else should lead up to or continue this celebration.

Some suggestions for a better celebration of the liturgy of the wedding Mass are described in this section. They should be discussed in detail with the couple during the time of preparation, in order that their wedding will be celebrated according to the mind of the Church as well as according to their own desires. By having such discussions early during the period of spiritual preparation, misunderstandings and disagreements can be avoided, and a worthy celebration prepared.

Marriage is normally celebrated during Mass. Special circumstances and problems are considered later.

NATIONAL ADAPTATIONS. The Roman Ritual permits national conferences to adapt formulas, to vary the order of the rites, and to add suitable local customs. These must be taken into consideration when preparing and celebrating the wedding Mass.

Introductory rites

The tone and spirit of the wedding liturgy is set by the introductory rites, which are intended to help those present become a worshipping assembly or community, and to prepare them to listen to the word of the Lord and to celebrate the eucharist.

Often a commentator will introduce the celebration by a few well-prepared sentences, emphasizing the sacred nature of the celebration.

ENTRANCE PROCESSION. The ritual provides two forms; others may be suggested by local traditions.

(1) The priest is vested for Mass, and goes with the servers to the main door of the Church. He greets the couple warmly, expressing the joy that the people of God share with them on this happy occasion. Then the servers lead the priest, the couple, and their two main witnesses to the altar. The reader, bearing the lectionary, goes before the priest as on Sunday. Others may join this group. As they come up through the church, a processional song is sung, preferably by the entire congregation. A hymn of praise and thanks to God for his blessings is fitting. This form of entrance procession promotes a good beginning to a better liturgy of marriage.

(2) The groom and his attendant are seated in a pew near the front. The bride arrives with her attendants, and comes up the aisle. At the front, the groom accepts her from her father, and the couple moves together to their place at the edge of the sanctuary, or inside it. There the celebrant greets them warmly in the name of the Church, which shares the joy of their wedding day. (One shortcoming of this form of entrance is the tendency it has to turn into a fashion show, with dawdling pace and widely spaced participants.) While an organ piece is usually played during this procession, a hymn sung by all would serve better to unite the congregation in prayer.

Only where no music or song is possible would one read the entrance antiphon.

Courtesy and consideration for others should lead all members of the wedding party to arrive at church in good time, so that the entrance procession may begin at the scheduled time.

PENITENTIAL RITE. The third penitential rite may be developed to reflect the day's celebration, without however losing the nature of repentance. The concluding Lord, have mercy may be sung by all.

If the entrance hymn and Lord, have mercy are sung, it may be better not to sing Glory to God, lest the introductory rites become overburdened.

OPENING PRAYER. Three distinct Masses are provided in the Missal, and while parts of one may be interchanged with others, it would seem better to follow one formula through Mass prayers, preface and nuptial blessing. The couple may wish to express their preference for a particular set of prayers.

Liturgy of the word

Many important decisions must be made by the couple with the priest about this part of the Mass, for it leads directly to the celebration of the sacrament of marriage and then into the liturgy of the eucharist.

INTRODUCTION. Those present for the celebration will benefit more from the reading of God's word if a brief introduction to the scripture texts is given before the readings begin, or before each reading. This may be done by the celebrant or by a commentator. After helping to choose the readings, the couple may cooperate in preparing these words of introduction.

READINGS. The liturgy of the word of God is to be adapted to the celebration of the sacrament of marriage. The word of God has power to instruct those who are present about the sacrament of matrimony and married life; it also reminds the couple of the Christian responsibilities they are undertaking.

A wide variety of readings from God's word is provided in the lectionary for weddings, but for good reasons the couple may choose other suitable scriptural texts. When three readings are used, the first is normally from the Old Testament. The most important reading chosen is the gospel text; the other readings should be chosen in the light of this selection. Couples should be involved in choosing these texts, and should not abandon this privilege to others. A concerned parish liturgy committee would see that a copy of these texts and of the entire marriage ritual is given to the couple so that they may become familiar with it during the months of preparation.

Non-scriptural readings – even from Christian sources – have no place in a eucharistic or sacramental celebration. While some communities tolerate such texts if read before the liturgical service begins, the happiest solution is to relegate them to the wedding banquet or reception.

READERS. If three scripture readings are proclaimed, it is preferred to have an individual reader for each of the first two readings, rather than the same reader for both.

SILENT PRAYER. The celebration of marriage has serious need of reflection. A little of this is provided by moments of silence for quiet meditation after each reading. After the first reading, the reader may introduce this moment of silent prayer by words such as these:

> We have heard the Lord speaking to us.
> Let us pause for a moment
> to think about what he has said,
> and to ask him to help us live for him.

RESPONDING TO GOD'S WORD. The Church wishes to encourage a positive, scriptural response to the word of God by the singing of the responsorial psalm and the gospel acclamation. The psalm is a response to the first reading, and normally reflects its message; the refrain is generally simple, and should be sung by all. The gospel acclamation is the community's greeting and welcome to the Lord Jesus, who speaks through the gospel text. Where possible, it is sung: the people sing the *alleluia* (or refrain during Lent), and the choir or cantor sings the verse; if this acclamation cannot be sung, it may be omitted.

GOSPEL. Where possible, the gospel text should be proclaimed by a deacon or another priest, while the celebrant presides at the liturgy of the word. Only when no one else is available should the celebrant proclaim the gospel reading.

HOMILY. The celebrant should base his homily on the scripture readings which have just been proclaimed. While speaking of Christian marriage, he is aware of the particular circumstances of the wedding being celebrated. The dignity of marriage between Christians, the graces which Christ offers in this sacrament, and the responsibilities undertaken by people who marry are part of his homily as he proclaims the teaching and leadership of the Lord Jesus. The ritual (no. 5) suggests that the priest should keep the principles of faith in mind during the homily.

Rite of marriage

The celebration of the sacrament is placed near the end of the liturgy of the word, just before the liturgy of the eucharist.

INTRODUCTION. The text given in the ritual is a model and example; while the celebrant may use it, he may prefer his own words – about the same in length and import – to introduce the rite of marriage.

FREEDOM is established in the premarital discussions and – preferably – by the priest's personal acquaintance with the couple. It is expressed publicly by the ritual questions.

CONSENT. Because they marry each other by the public exchange of their consent, the couple should be helped to appreciate the holiness of this moment.

Two forms for declaring consent are given in the marriage ritual: one in which the groom and then the bride declares full consent; the other in which the priest, as the official witness of the Church (and usually of the state) asks the couple to give public consent and declaration to their intention of marriage.

Except when dealing with very nervous persons, the priest can avoid the kindergarten parrotry of having each repeat phrases after him. Instead of 'I, John, take you, Mary,' '*I, John, take you, Mary,*' he may simply hold out his ritual containing the form, or a neatly typed card, and they read from it in turn. Depending on local law and custom, one name – but not a nickname – instead of the full John Joseph Smith, may be used.

RINGS. The Church blesses the rings as a lasting sign of the mutual love and trust of this couple. They might consider having a Christian symbol engraved on their rings.

When they present the rings to each other, they may use the words of the ritual, or may develop a similar form. The parish liturgy committee could prepare a few models to help them develop their own. As with the words of consent, the couple may read the words from the celebrant's book or from a typed card.

PRAYER OF THE FAITHFUL (general intercessions). Encouraging the couple to prepare the petitions for their wedding is one way of helping them make this Mass an experience in worship for all who take part. While following the general rule (prayers for the Church, for all mankind, for the oppressed, for the community), greater emphasis may be placed on the couple who are celebrating this sacrament. The liturgy committee could prepare several samples for their consideration.

The priest introduces the prayer briefly, and then someone else, such as the reader, makes the petitions; in some cases, the couple may wish to read one or more of them. All make the response, which may be sung. The celebrant closes the intercessions with a brief prayer.

Liturgy of the eucharist
The rest of the Mass follows the usual order, with a number of significant changes.

GIFTS. The newlyweds may bring the bread and wine to the priest at the altar. As a way of encouraging fuller participation, the liturgy committee could consider inviting the families to bake the bread and, where winemaking is common, to provide the wine. A suitable recipe and cooking instructions should be found and tested beforehand by the committee.

SINGING. A meditative hymn may be sung by the congregation or by the choir during the preparation of the gifts; a solo may be sung or a brief organ piece played.

PREFACE. The preface is chosen to harmonize with the Mass formula chosen.

ACCLAMATIONS. The three acclamations (at the end of the preface, after the words of institution, and at the end of the doxology) should be sung by all present.

NUPTIAL BLESSING. Each of the three Mass formulas has a distinct nuptial blessing, following the Our Father and replacing the prayer, 'Deliver us'. After a brief invitation to pray, the entire congregation pauses in silent prayer for the couple. Then the priest continues the blessing. Depending on circumstances, several phrases or lines may be omitted, but the time of silent prayer should never be hurried.

GREETING OF PEACE. Bride and groom may express the sign of peace by a kiss, and should offer a similar greeting to both sets of parents. This moment may be a little less subdued than at a Sunday celebration. A good introduction by the priest to the rite will keep its Christian significance before all.

COMMUNION UNDER BOTH KINDS. The right of the married couple to receive from the chalice is clearly indicated by the ritual; it cannot be refused by the celebrant or others. In some countries, such as Canada, this has been extended to all present. An explanation of its meaning and value should be part of the preparation for the celebration. A wise celebrant will also explain the rite briefly to all present before giving communion in this way. As it becomes more normal, less explanation will be needed. The parish liturgy committee needs to discuss ways of making this rite practical and dignified.

COMMUNION SONG. This contributes to the sense of community celebration, and is normally sung by all: a psalm is quite effective; depending on the number of communions, additional hymns may be sung by the congregation or choir, or an organ solo may be played.

Concluding rites

The usual greeting, simple blessing and dismissal are expanded in a wedding Mass.

MARRIAGE REGISTER. In some countries, the civil or ecclesiastical marriage register, and official marriage documents, are signed by the couple, the two witnesses and the priest. Sometimes this is done in the sanctuary before the concluding rites, or before the recessional. The celebrant or commentator may wish to introduce it in these or similar words:

> Because the home and family life are the foundation of our nation, the setting up of a new home by marriage is of importance to both the Church and the civil government. They protect marriage and family life by their laws.
> The bridal party will now sign the public register of marriages, that all may know that their home is blessed by God.

Any necessary documents are signed by all concerned. In England, the 'marriage lines' are customarily presented to the bride. A small table placed in front of the couple will simplify the signing.

SOLEMN BLESSING. The Church provides three solemn blessings for the couple. When they are explained by a brief sentence beforehand, the congregation will be more ready to respond with a hearty 'Amen!' after each blessing.

RECESSIONAL. The entire congregation may sing a rousing song of joy, praise or thanks as the newlywed couple goes in procession through the church to the main entrance. This is more desirable liturgically than an organ solo.

Areas of choice and preparation

The couple and their immediate families may work together with the priest to choose and prepare the following parts of the celebration:

ENTRANCE RITE

(1) Form of procession.

(2) Entrance song: A hymn sung by all is better than an organ solo.

(3) Penitential rite: One of three forms may be chosen; the third rite may be developed by priest and couple; Lord, have mercy may be sung.

(4) Mass formula: They may choose the Mass formula and nuptial blessing they prefer.

LITURGY OF THE WORD

(5) Readings: Three or two scripture readings may be chosen from the lectionary; the couple should be involved in making this choice.

(6) Introduction: A brief introduction to each reading or to all may be given by celebrant or minister; the couple may help prepare these words of introduction.

(7) Readers may be chosen from among the persons who normally proclaim God's word in this community, in which case the couple should be free to ask for particular readers from the parish roster of readers.

(8) Response to God's word: Plans should be made to include the singing of the responsorial psalm as a normal response to God's word, and the gospel acclamation as a preparation for meeting Jesus in the gospel and homily.

RITE OF MARRIAGE

(9) Introduction: Though the introductory remarks are primarily the responsibility of the celebrant, the couple may wish to suggest a direction they may follow.

(10) Consent: In some countries the couple may choose the form they wish to use.

(11) Rings: The couple may wish to prepare their own wording for exchanging rings, and may consider having a Christian symbol engraved on their rings.

(12) Prayer of the faithful: Petitions may be prepared by the couple; some examples prepared by the liturgy committee would be useful.

LITURGY OF THE EUCHARIST

(13) Gifts: The couple may bring the gifts to the altar; their families may wish to prepare the bread and even the wine for the celebration.

(14) Music: A choice should be made of a hymn to be sung by all, the choir or by a soloist, or of a brief organ piece at the preparation of the gifts. Every effort should be made to sing the three acclamations during the eucharistic prayer, the Our Father, Lamb of God, and a communion psalm or hymn.

(15) Greeting of peace: The priest and couple should discuss the form this will take.

(16) Communion under both forms: Considering local circumstances, they discuss who will receive this besides the bride and groom.

CONCLUDING RITES

(17) Marriage register: The priest and couple may wish to discuss various methods of signing any official documents.

(18) Solemn blessing: The text of the blessing may be chosen by the couple.

C. SPECIAL CIRCUMSTANCES

Lax Catholics

There are many people who do not practise their faith, and who feel no need of spiritual preparation for marriage; others just want to be married in church with no fuss. Parish liturgy committees and priests may wish to help them to a more serious view of religion, but will generally find that a last-minute effort to revive their faith is not successful.

In such cases, should the parish refuse to have the marriage celebrated? Or should the eucharist be omitted, since it now has little part in their lives? Should the parish take a firm stand, and suggest that they really are not Catholics? Can people with little or no faith celebrate sacraments of faith?

These questions are difficult to answer, and may not be solved quickly, but priests and liturgy committees need to be asking them, as noted under 'General preparation of the parish' above.

Teenage marriages

Responsible people everywhere have a growing concern as they come to realize that too many teenage marriages are ending in failure. Most of the time this results because the partners are not mature enough to cope with adult problems: they have been catapulted from school desk to parenthood with no time in between for growing up.

Gradually both civil and ecclesiastical authorities are recognizing the gravity and frequency of these cases, and are working to make sure that young people who enter marriage are truly ready for a lifelong commitment to each other. Some of the trends in recent legislation are longer waiting periods (six months before the wedding date, to avoid last-minute haste), and serious interviews with the couple and their parents.

Because such marriages are often accepted on the occasion of pregnancy, serious and balanced counselling is needed; sometimes, when the two people are not ready to enter a lifetime marriage, they are encouraged not to marry each other, at least not for some time, until they have become mature enough to make a realistic choice.

Shot-gun marriages

It has been known to happen that a young couple find a child is on the way; in a reaction of panic, parents and families try to 'get them married' as soon as possible.

Some basic questions need to be answered very quickly before rash decisions are made:

If the couple had been planning to marry in the near future, plans may easily be advanced. Provided that the couple still wishes to marry, they may make adequate preparations, and the marriage is celebrated as usual.

If the couple had no plans for marriage, or at least not for some years, then plans for their marriage should not be made too hastily.

What is best for this couple? for the child? Should they or should they not marry, at least at this time? All these questions have to be given very serious consideration.

Civil marriage

Some countries require a civil ceremony to take place before the religious ceremony. People should be encouraged to take part in this with due respect, and where necessary, helped to understand that the religious celebration is the more important.

D. HAPPILY EVER AFTER

The celebration of the sacrament of matrimony does not end on a couple's wedding day. This is the beginning of a lifelong promise of help from the Lord Jesus in the work of spreading the kingdom. He is always ready to listen to them and to give them his strength and courage through his Spirit.

As well as helping a couple prepare for and celebrate their marriage, a parish community should continue to assist them to grow in holiness in their vocation of Christian marriage. The priest and the parish liturgy team should consider some of the opportunities open to them in order to continue and develop the foundation laid in the preparation and celebration of the sacrament. Some of these would include:

PRAYER. The prayer life of the community is an important part of the liturgy committee's responsibility. This may be done by promoting family prayer, by helping couples to deepen their ways of prayer, by encouraging others to pray with them and for them. Parents and their families should be remembered often in the general intercessions.

CHRISTIAN EDUCATION. Since a full sharing in the liturgy is the primary and indispensable source of the true Christian spirit (CL 14), the liturgy committee should be ready to assist catechists and teachers in the parish programme of religious education. Proper preparation for the sacraments is part of this concern.

SPIRITUAL ASSISTANCE. Many parishes seem to be child-centred, almost forgetting about married couples. A community which is concerned for all its members will see that days of recollection and prayer, retreats, positive programmes such as the Christian Family Movement, and other spiritual helps are provided for couples.

WEDDING ANNIVERSARIES. Couples and families should be encouraged to celebrate wedding anniversaries each year in a spiritual way: a Mass of thanksgiving could be an important part of the family celebration. On major anniversaries, such as the twenty-fifth and fiftieth, the jubilee Mass should be the most important part of the celebration.

On each anniversary the couple should pause and ask: How well are we doing? Some special moments of prayer together and time to reflect on the image of the Church and of Christ that the world finds in their marriage should lead them to renew their promises of love and trust in each other.

A CHRISTIAN COMMUNITY. The first task of the parish is to be a Christian community which carries on the work of the Lord Jesus by praising God and helping to sanctify his people. Entertainment, social teas and sports are not the main work of God's people; where such parish activities absorb the energy of clergy and parishioners to the detriment of their principal vocation, an honest and probing examination of conscience is urgently needed.

It is one of the major responsibilities of priests, parish councils and their committees to give strong leadership in spiritual affairs, so that the Christian faith may permeate and inspire the witness of each believer, and lead to a strong presence in the parish and civic community. Such developments, however, depend on how seriously the parish is letting the spirit of Christ's gospel penetrate and guide every one of its activities and projects.

The influence of families and parish is mutual: the quality of the parish liturgy and apostolic efforts influences the lives of all in the community, while each family's sincerity and zeal in Christian living builds up the body of Christ in that parish. Blessed indeed is the parish whose priests are zealous in celebrating the Christian life in liturgy and in action, whose people are eager for good deeds in the service of the Lord (Titus 2:14).

Marriage is the vocation God has chosen for most of his people. It is the way by which he wants to lead them through this life to eternal salvation.

The sacrament of marriage is one of the ways in which Christ and his Church work to advance the coming of the kingdom of heaven among men. Parish communities, led by their priests and their liturgy teams, can help to deepen the quality of Christian family living by working with the couple to prepare for marriage, and by positive efforts to help more people to have the mind of Christ on married life. As better wedding celebrations take place, a stronger influence on community attitudes will develop. By continuing serious efforts to help parents and families grow in Christian family living, parishes will be promoting the peace, holiness and joy of the kingdom of Christ.

16. A Note on 'Mixed Marriages'

Harold Winstone

In spite of the restrictive marriage regulations that various tribal laws and traditions, national governments and religious bodies have established in the past and continue to urge for the good of the particular community and the protection of its members, the natural right of all men and women to marry the person of their choice is rapidly finding universal acceptance.

Catholic legislation on mixed marriage which was considered perfectly normal and natural in past centuries is in many respects no longer acceptable to a people who are learning to abhor every kind of discrimination on racial and religious grounds and every attempt to interfere with the consciences and rights of individuals. In England, for quite a long time now, dispensations for Catholics to marry other Christians or even non-Christians have been very easy to obtain, and since Vatican II the non-Catholic partner has not been asked to make any signed undertaking regarding the upbringing of the children. All that is required is that the Catholic sign an assurance that he will keep the faith and do his best to see that the children of the marriage are baptized and brought up as Catholics. The non-Catholic partner has to be informed that the Catholic has given these assurances, but need not make any personal declaration. It is left to the couple to sort out the practical problems for themselves.

For the priest this is a matter of some consequence since probably seventy per cent of all marriages celebrated in Catholic Churches in England and Wales are 'mixed'.

We are concerned in this chapter not so much with the theological and canonical aspects of this situation as with the way in which the priest handles it.

The couples who knock on the presbytery door to see the priest about getting married can be grouped for the sake of convenience into four categories:

(1) a nominal Catholic and a non-Christian or a purely nominal Christian of some other Church;
(2) a nominal Catholic and a committed Christian of another Church;
(3) a good Catholic and a non- or nominal Christian;
(4) a good Catholic and a committed Christian of another Church.

When we speak of non-Christians we are not necessarily thinking about people with no clearly defined religious views. The non-Christian may be a good Jew or Moslem or some other person of high principles and religious convictions. In this case the priest needs to bring out in the course of conversation the good and positive elements that form the core of that person's religious beliefs and to show how closely they correspond to and even complement the faith of the Catholic partner. On this shared basis of faith it may be possible to build a spiritual relationship where each respects and values the religious insights of the other and finds enrichment for his or her own spiritual life. The difficulties which will inevitably arise in a marriage of this kind cannot obviously be brushed aside, but they can best be met and overcome in the light of this mutual respect and understanding. Having said this, let us consider the above categories in turn.

1. *The marriage of a purely nominal Catholic and a non- or nominal Christian*
If these people come to the priest at all it is presumably because, for one reason or another, they want a 'church wedding' and not just a registry office marriage. The priest must welcome them with cordiality because it is only on a basis of friendship that he will be able to give them any help they need. If he rebuffs them at the outset and tells them that the sacraments are only for the committed, he will be throwing away the one golden opportunity he has of influencing them for good.

His first care must be to find out what they really think about life in general and then about married life, family life and the Church. He must encourage them to talk to him and not put them off by flatly contradicting them or preaching to them too early in the relationship. If they find the priest a nice person to talk to, they will not mind coming again as often as he likes.

It may be that he will eventually have to decide reluctantly that a church wedding is just not on in their case as it would be an abuse of a sacrament. But if so, this fact should emerge from the realization of the couple themselves who have come to understand what is involved in the celebration of the sacrament. Though they may not have the faith, most young people are fundamentally honest with themselves and they soon come to realize the hypocrisy of going through a religious ceremony that they do not believe in. Even so, much positive good can accrue to them from their talks with a priest, and this may bear fruit in later years.

But often the couple have not really lost their faith. They have merely given up going to church for various reasons, often because their understanding of the faith has not advanced beyond a fairly infantile stage. With patience and understanding the priest can often help them quite a lot, praying all the time that the Holy Spirit will give them light.

The best place to start is not with the duties and obligations of a Catholic, tempting as it must be to do so. This is precisely where they have a block – a guilt complex, if you like. They will feel uneasy and on their guard, and in consequence will not be very receptive or very communicative. The best place to start will normally be on the topic which interests them most at the present time: love and marriage. A question like 'Have you ever read what the bible has to say about love and marriage?' may at least arouse their curiosity. From then on it is up to the priest so to present the bible message on this subject that they find it interesting to start with and gradually absorbing. One could start with the Canticle of Canticles, if this is not thought a trifle too 'heady'. Whatever starting-point is chosen, it is a good idea to let the couple borrow a bible and to talk about the subject bible in hand, not just from selected texts. Before long many of them may want to buy a bible of their own. An added advantage of this approach is that when the time comes for them to choose readings for their wedding celebration they will have some background knowledge and know what they are choosing and why.

Once it has been established that they really want a church wedding and that it makes sense in their case, the question of a nuptial Mass can be discussed. Sometimes the couple want it for some extraneous reason, such as 'Mother wants it' or they would like an impressive ceremony. Needless to say, none of these reasons should carry any weight. If during the preparation period the Catholic party, at least, starts coming to Mass again of his or her own volition, then a nuptial Mass may make sense. Otherwise, it will probably be better to settle for a simple wedding ceremony which they can understand and take part in wholeheartedly. In any event part of the priest's aim in preparing the Catholic spiritually for the marriage should be to encourage the making of a good confession before the wedding.

All that has been said so far assumes that the couple have approached the priest a considerable time before the wedding. Unfortunately this is not always the case. They may come to him and tell him that they want to get married in two or three weeks' time, and for many reasons he may not be able to persuade them to defer the date. In that case all that the priest can normally hope to do, apart from completing the forms, applying for the appropriate dispensation and taking them through the details of the ceremony, is to try to establish a friendly relationship with them with a view to being able to continue helping them after the marriage. This again may not always be possible. They may go to live miles away from the parish, even abroad. Nevertheless the priest should know their address, inform their new parish priest of their whereabouts and circumstances and, if he cannot visit them in person, write to them from time to time to show that he values their friendship. To this suggestion a priest might object that he could not possibly keep up a correspondence with all the couples he has married in the course of a busy ministry. The answer is that he will not need to in most instances, but to a busy man an extra letter now and again is not much of a hardship to write and it may do untold good.

2. *The marriage of a nominal Catholic with a committed Christian of another Church*
Other things being equal, the committed Christian will probably want to marry in the church where he or she usually worships. On the other hand there will be pressures on the Catholic party to marry in a Catholic church. The parents

may even say that they will not attend the wedding if it is in a non-Catholic church. Hence a difficult situation arises and one which will require very delicate handling.

But first one must make the most of the opportunity which presents itself. A nominal Catholic is fortunate enough to have fallen in love with someone for whom the Christian faith is alive and meaningful. The committed Christian may or may not be willing to consider the claims of the Catholic Church; one thing is certain: the person who stands most in need of a conversion is the nominal Catholic. This is the situation, and the priest has to realize its potential. He has an ally in the committed Christian, and one whose influence is bound in the very nature of the case to be more effective than his own.

The fact that the couple have come to him in the first instance and not by-passed him altogether in favour of the committed Christian's minister is probably due to pressures from the Catholic's family. The non-Catholic may only have agreed to come under protest, and the priest should not be surprised if the atmosphere is a bit strained at first. He should re-assure them at the outset that they are perfectly free to marry in the church of their choice, whatever anybody says, and do his best to win their confidence and their friendship so that they will want to see him again even though they may eventually decide to marry in another church.

In practice it normally works out that the wedding will be in the church of the bride. If she is the committed Christian she will want anyway to marry in her own church. If he is the committed Christian he will probably defer to her parents' wishes and marry her in the Catholic church. Such is the etiquette inherent in the situation. In any event the priest should be in touch with the minister of the other church, offering his own co-operation in the preparation of the couple or enlisting the co-operation of the other minister.

It is hardly to be expected that the nominal, non-practising Catholic will be converted at once as a result of a few pre-marital talks with the priest. The priest can only do his best by prayer and study to be a channel of grace. He cannot force grace upon anyone, and he must realize that in God's plan he may be nothing more than the first sower of the seed. He may never live to see the fruits of his labours.

But he must nevertheless have confidence that what he is trying to do is in God's plan for the salvation of this person. All is not lost if the Catholic does not return to the practice of the faith before the marriage. Nor will it be a disaster if the still purely nominal Catholic marries in a non-Catholic church without a dispensation. It could however be disastrous if the Catholic were given the impression that by marrying in a non-Catholic church he was cutting himself off for ever from the Catholic Church and it was no longer interested in him.

The question of getting a dispensation to marry in a non-Catholic church will only arise if the Catholic returns to the faith. There is obviously no point in applying for a dispensation for one who is a Catholic only in name. It would not be granted, if only for the reason that a nominal Catholic in these circumstances could not honestly undertake to bring up the children in the Catholic faith. They would in any event be better off in the care of the committed and practising Christian – unless one really believes that it is better to be a bad Catholic than a good Protestant!

Whether or not a dispensation is obtained, the priest should visit the parents of the Catholic and talk over the whole matter with them. Very often they are not as intransigent as at first appeared. Their opposition was conditioned by their fear that the Church would condemn the wedding and that they would somehow be involved in the disgrace.

3. *The marriage of a good Catholic with a nominal Christian of another Church*
In this case there will not normally be a difficulty about the church in which the ceremony is to be held, and any hesitations which the non-committed Christian may have about the upbringing of the children can often be overcome with a little patience and persuasion.

What must be realized is that this meeting with the priest is probably the first personal encounter the non-Catholic has had with the official Church, and the impression that it makes is going to be long-lived. It could be the first step in a process of conversion or the final confirmation of an already deeply rooted suspicion.

In the Catholic's whole attitude to prayer and worship, to

life and marriage, the non-Catholic will see the faith in action and this discovery will be better than any sermon. In the course of his conversations with the couple the priest may discern areas in the Catholic's life, or his attitude to life, where the image is tarnished. It will be in these areas that he will have to exercise his pastoral concern.

Every care must be taken to avoid giving the non-Catholic the impression that he or she is being brought to the priest to be instructed in the faith. They have both come to prepare for their marriage together. But for the non-Catholic, beside the adventure of being in love, there is the added thrill of discovering in the beloved a quality of life and a spiritual dimension never before experienced. This is the situation of which the priest must be acutely aware and which he must know how to handle and turn to good.

4. *The marriage of a good Catholic and a committed Christian of another Church*
This is a truly ecumenical situation. The way in which it is handled is an indication of whether or not we have the courage to put into practice the principles to which we pay lip service in all our encounters with other Christian bodies.

If we begin from the fear-inspired premise that the faith of the Catholic must be preserved from all possible danger and from any watering down of doctrine, then it is unlikely that any positive good will be achieved. If on the other hand we begin by making an act of faith in the goodwill of both parties, assuming that both are concerned about truth and will enrich each other spiritually, then there is every chance that the cause of Christian unity will be advanced at the all-important grass-roots level.

The foundations of Christian unity are love and truth. In the marriage of two Christians of different Churches we can assume the former. Their love for each other should be complete; that is to say, it should overcome every kind of barrier which exists between them. To insist on preserving an insurmountable religious barrier would be little short of criminal. It would certainly be disastrous from the point of view of the spiritual fulfilment of the marriage. On the other hand, an honest concern for truth as each of the parties apprehends it might make it impossible for one of the partners to accept wholeheartedly the religious allegiance of the other. Each must be prepared to grow in the knowledge and understanding of the truth, and must be given every help and encouragement to do so.

The quest is no easy one. There are bound to be very real problems and difficulties, because the couple have inherited a deplorable situation of Christian disunity. The only permanent solution to their difficulties would be the achievement of unity between the Churches, a goal which may still be far-distant. But no situation in this life is ever perfect. Every good has to be striven for, and there is adventure and exhilaration in the actual striving for something that is so eminently worthwhile. They are not the sole contestants in this struggle. By their Christian life together they are actually furthering the cause of Christian unity and bringing its realization nearer. Nor are they without special divine assistance, for by their baptism and their marriage they share the Holy Spirit who makes them one in Christ and who is continually working in them for the perfection of this bond of unity.

All this is what the priest has somehow to bring to their awareness. Clearly, the first practical problem is going to be a decision regarding the church in which they are going to celebrate their marriage. It is probable that the choice will fall on the church of the bride, and if she is the non-Catholic Christian a dispensation from canonical form will have to be applied for.

The rite will presumably be that of the Church in which the wedding takes place. It is appropriate that the priest or deacon who has been preparing the couple for marriage should be present at the wedding and, if invited to do so, take part in the non-eucharistic part of the ceremony. It is forbidden to have the simultaneous performance of different rites or the addition of any second rite which includes the giving or renewal of matrimonial consent. However, a second service of blessing and thanksgiving in the Church of the other party, provided it does not include the giving or renewal of consent, is positively recommended, as it provides this other party with the opportunity of giving witness to his new responsibilities before the Christian community to which he belongs.

There are legal difficulties with regard to a Catholic priest officiating at marriages in Anglican churches, but this is not the case regarding other churches. If the couple would like him to officiate in one of these churches he may do so with the permission of his local Ordinary and of the minister and trustees of the non-Catholic church in question. He would also need written delegation from the Catholic priest in whose parish the non-Catholic church of the wedding is situated, or from the local Ordinary. Usually this delegation is included in the rescript granting permission for the marriage to take place in the non-Catholic church.

The next difficulty concerns the signing of the promises. In England a dispensation will not normally be given for a mixed marriage unless the Catholic is prepared to sign a statement to the effect that he will do his best to see that the children of the marriage are baptized in the Catholic Church and brought up as Catholics. The universality of baptism can be explained to the couple, but in fact more than this is involved. There is the whole question of allegiance to a particular Church. The committed non-Catholic might very well object to being 'put upon' in this way, even indirectly, and the Catholic, though truly committed to the faith, might be unwilling at the very outset of their marriage relationship to make a unilateral decision about an issue which concerns his partner just as much as himself. In this case the priest can only present the matter to the bishop in the most favourable possible light and leave it to his decision. It may sometimes be helpful if an appointment can be made for the bishop to interview the couple and weigh up the situation for himself.

Since both are committed Christians the preparation for the marriage should be on a frankly spiritual level. The priest should be principally concerned with laying the foundations of a shared life of prayer which will continue on into their married life and bring about a true union of minds and spirits in the one Lord, Jesus Christ. From this will flow all kinds of blessings for themselves and their children in their future life together and a solution to most of their practical problems.

17. Religious Profession

Philip Gleeson OP

The religious life, with its public profession of poverty, chastity and obedience, is a special way of dedicating oneself to the service of God and the good of mankind. It is a way of deriving more abundant fruit from the grace of baptism, a way of answering the call to holiness which Christ addresses to all his followers. Of course it is not the only way of following Christ; the grace of baptism yields abundant fruit outside the religious life.

Vatican II devoted a chapter of the Constitution on the Church (ch. 6) to the religious life, and was sufficiently concerned about the need for renewal to issue a decree on the subject, *Perfectae Caritatis*. Besides this, to the surprise of many religious, the Constitution on the Liturgy prescribed that,

> 'A rite of religious profession and renewal of vows shall be drawn up, in order to achieve greater unity, sobriety and dignity. Apart from exceptions in particular law, this rite should be adopted by those who make their profession or renewal of vows within the Mass. It would be praiseworthy for religious profession to be made during Mass' (CL 80).

As profession ceremonies were traditionally the concern of the various religious communities, some thought it strange to see a move towards centralization at a time when the general trend seemed to be away from uniformity. However, the new Rite of Religious Profession duly appeared in 1970. Some communities adopted it almost as it stood, while others showed more interest in the clause, 'apart from exceptions in particular law', than in the details of the typical edition.

The new ritual, in comparison with many existing ceremonies, is indeed sober and dignified. It has provided religious with the opportunity of dropping any unsuitable rites with which they may have been burdened. It is also something of a call to unity, an indication that the Church feels that all religious have much in common; perhaps this unity needs to be stressed in contrast to a tendency to emphasize the special character of each institute in a way which is harmfully divisive. At the same time, the ritual does not impose rigid uniformity. Those who follow it are expected to make adaptations which reflect the spirit of their own institute; and there is also room for exceptions in particular law.

One of the principal aims of the new ritual is to provide rites which are appropriate to the different steps which lead to final profession in the religious life. We are familiar with the way in which these steps are carefully distinguished from a juridical point of view. However, the ceremonies which accompanied the steps did not correspond to the nature of the steps; for example, most reception ceremonies had an air of finality which did not correspond to the nature of the novitiate. The history of how this came to pass is too complex to summarize.

In the following pages we shall comment on the typical edition as it stands, but it must be remembered that different communities adapt the rite to fit in with their history and way of life, and that some are governed by particular law. The contents of the Rite of Religious Profession include: a general introduction; the rite of profession of religious men (dealt with in five chapters which give the rites of reception into the novitiate, temporary profession, final profession, renewal of profession, and various texts); the rite of profession of religious women (with the same arrangement of chapters); the rite of the promise which in some institutes follows the novitiate.

Reception into the novitiate

Reception into the novitiate, which in many instances used to be a rather dramatic affair, is now a simple ceremony. It is reserved to the religious community, and if possible takes place somewhere not too public, in a chapter room, for example. It is inserted, not in the Mass, but in a liturgy of the word which expresses the spirit of the particular community. The simplification of reception ceremonies is something which was badly needed. There was often a very real clash between the ceremony and the juridical and psychological aspects of entry into a novitiate, which does not imply a definitive commitment on the part of the novice or the community.

The new ritual does not envisage the giving of the habit at this stage. This reflects the assumption, expressed in Vatican II and in the Rite of Religious Profession, that the habit is a sign of consecration, and so should not be given before profession. It must be admitted, however, that attitudes to the religious habit vary. For many it is indeed a sign of consecration. But for others it is just a part of the life which is led within the religious house; it is what the religious wears 'at home'; as such it is one of the things which the novice should try out during the novitiate. Whatever about this, there is certainly no room for the ostentatious change from secular to religious clothing which was the highlight of so many reception ceremonies. If in a particular institute the novices do wear the habit, it should be given discreetly, maybe without ceremony. Exaggerated attention should not be given to the question of the habit, and there should be tolerance of different usages.

The reception of novices, while it is reserved to the religious community, is of interest to the Christian community at large. People do ask if any novices have been received recently, sometimes perhaps out of idle or morbid curiosity, but more often out of real concern for the vitality of the religious community. It is good to let people know about the novices, and to ask for prayers. Incidentally, any such request for prayers should respect the freedom of the novices – sometimes one hears a mention of 'perseverance' which might be seen as implying that leaving the novitiate is a desertion, a loss of vocation.

Temporary vows

At the end of the novitiate, if the novice has decided to stay and the community is happy to have him, he commits himself to the life of the community for a certain length of time, either by making temporary vows or by a promise. The ritual accepts the existence of both forms of commitment, and tries to provide suitable ceremonies for each.

Temporary vows may be made during Mass, but special solemnity should be avoided – this first profession should not look too much like final profession. Besides the actual profession of poverty, chastity and obedience, the rite may introduce certain signs of profession; for example, the habit may be given, and perhaps the book of the rule and constitutions. In the case of women religious, if it is at this stage that the clothing takes place, the habit is given on the eve of profession and the veil is given during the profession ceremony itself. One notices that while the ritual calls the habit a sign of consecration it does not demand that it be kept back until final profession, although the word, 'consecration', traditionally involves the idea of perpetuity. But, as has already been said, in many communities the habit is just one element of religious life. It is usually best not to draw too much attention to this somewhat debatable sign. Common sense and awareness of the reality of the situation are indispensable guides in this matter. It would be unwise to speak glowingly of the habit as a sign of consecration if in fact the religious do not wear it outside the house.

In some communities the novitiate is followed not by temporary vows but by a promise. The ritual provides a simple ceremony for this promise, which may be made during a liturgy of the word or during the divine office. For special reasons, it may be made during Mass, but the ritual concedes this in a rather guarded way. A non-eucharistic celebration is regarded as more suitable, less liable to make the promise look like a vow or a consecration.

Final profession

Final profession itself is to be given all due importance. In making final profession, the religious enters into a commitment for life. A major concern of the new ritual is to bring out the seriousness and uniqueness of the step. Because of the custom of making a big thing out of reception and first profession, the special nature of final profession became obscured. This is certainly true from the liturgical point of view. It may also be true in other respects. Religious sometimes ask themselves why it is that the 'bonds' of religious life, whether temporary or perpetual, seem so easy to loose. Comparisons, unflattering to the religious, can be made with the permanence of Christian 'marriage vows'. On the other hand, there are those who feel it is inhuman to stress the permanence of any commitment. These are serious problems, but the new ritual has no hesitation in trying to create an atmosphere of lasting dedication, of permanent and full commitment.

It is most fitting that the rite of final profession should take place during Mass, so that the self-offering of the religious is associated with the mystery of Christ's self-offering. Sunday is suggested as a suitable day, or perhaps a feast of the Blessed Virgin or some other feast which has a special meaning for the community.

Final profession may be made in a church attached to the institute, in a parish church, or even in the cathedral. The rite is meant to be public in a very real sense. The ritual even thinks of mentioning that the faithful should be told the day and the time, so that they can be present in good numbers. In other words, the religious is regarded as part of the Church, part of the larger Christian community; final profession is more than a purely internal affair of the religious community.

In this respect, some remarks must be made about one of the suggestions found in the new ritual. It suggests that sometimes a number of religious institutes might make profession during the same ceremony, in the presence of the bishop. This would certainly emphasize the ecclesial dimension of religious life, and it would show that besides their differences the various institutes have certain basic values in common. Of course, such a 'massed' profession ceremony can be successful only if the religious are happy about it. To many it might be as unappealing as the idea of massed marriage ceremonies would be to most couples. The element of commitment to a particular community might be submerged in such a ceremony, even though everything would be taken care of juridically, with each religious making profession to his own superior. Needless to say, it would be invidious if non-clerical institutes were pressurized into making profession together merely for reasons of convenience. When these reservations have been made, it remains true that such a combined celebration has possibilities which should not be ignored.

Profession is made after the gospel of the Mass, unless particular usages put it elsewhere. Those making profession may be called by name, or they may present themselves without being called; there is no question here of a solemn call as at the beginning of the ordination rite; it is simply a question of showing that those making profession are not anonymous units but men and women who have made a personal decision and are being accepted as individuals. There is a homily which expounds whatever readings have been chosen and speaks about the religious life. Then follows an interrogation which helps to bring out the nature of final profession. The interrogations, which naturally tend to focus attention on the decision being made by the religious, are followed by a litany which expresses an awareness that without God's love and help there can be no religious life, without Christ's invitation there can be no response.

The actual formula of profession is, according to the ritual, read by the religious. It may be written in his own hand, and may perhaps be laid on the altar after being read. Some practical steps may need to be taken to make sure that the congregation hears the religious making profession. It is a little frustrating if this important part of the rite is inaudible.

When all have made their profession of poverty, chastity and obedience according to the rule of the institute, there is a prayer of blessing or consecration, which thanks God for his benefits and prays for the religious. This is another part of the rite which emphasizes the grace of God and prevents profession from being seen as nothing more than an individual's decision and a juridical acceptance by his superior. It is a richly composed prayer, and can be a valuable addition to the celebration. A minor objection which may be raised is that it tends to be a doublet of the eucharistic prayer, which has a special preface and special memories of those who have made profession. After the prayer of consecration, the religious may be given some sign of final profession – the ritual explicitly mentions the ring in the case of women religious.

The religious superior may then say a few words indicating that the religious is welcome in the community, and there may be a kiss of peace or some other expression of community. Many religious, in looking through the new ritual, have felt that the element of community occupies a rather secondary place. Here at least there is some opportunity of putting matters right, and one must presume that the homily will have mentioned community. It would be disastrous if religious were presented as juxtaposed individuals who make promises to God, or as a collection of people with similar religious status, whereas they are a community whose life reflects the reality of God's love and fidelity. When the religious makes his vows, he must be assured that the community will be faithful to him. There must be a mutual expression of fidelity.

Mass continues with the preparation of the gifts, and the religious who have made profession should normally associate themselves with this eucharist by bringing forward the gifts of bread and wine.

Renewal of profession
The new ritual gives a rite for renewal of profession. This is the renewal, having juridical effect, which may precede final profession. There is also mention of the fact that there may be renewal for reasons of devotion, for example on the silver or golden jubilee of profession, but this should not be made confusingly like a real profession ceremony.

Consecration of virgins
Besides asking for a new rite of religious profession, Vatican II stated that, 'The rite for the consecration of virgins which is currently found in the Roman Pontifical is to be revised' (Constitution on the Liturgy, 80). Whereas in the case of religious profession there was no existing Roman rite to be revised, here it was indeed a matter of revision. The old ceremony, which seems to be cognate with the nuptial blessing, had moved far from its original simplicity, partly because of unfortunate assimilation to the rites of marriage and ordination. The revised rite for Consecration to a Life of Virginity appeared in 1970, and it is undoubtedly an improvement, being much simpler and clearer than the previous rite.

Nuns who use this rite may either combine it with their monastic profession or perhaps have it as a separate ceremony on a different day. Reactions to the rite vary. Some feel it adds nothing to the rite of monastic profession, but others feel it emphasizes in a very special way the idea of God's grace and invitation. Some feel it is unwise to single out chastity for special attention, especially as this is not done in the case of men religious. (One notices how the nuptial blessing has had to be revised to include the man as well as the woman.) But on the other hand it seems quite natural to some women to make the consecration of virginity the starting-point and in a sense the focus of a life dedicated to the following of Christ.

The rite for the consecration of virgins is open not only to nuns who make monastic profession but also to women 'living in the world'. It is good to see an attempt being made to uphold the positive value of a life of consecrated virginity. But it is by no means sure that the present rite will ever become widespread. Apart from anything else, it has a kind of solemnity which would seem to make it unsuitable in the case of women living in the world.

One thing is clear about the rite for the consecration of virgins. For all its solemnity, it is not a pretentiously triumphant assertion of virginity. It is more in the nature of a beginning, an expression of trust and love which will develop into a life of complete consecration to Jesus Christ.

In speaking about all the rites which mark entry into the religious life, it is easy to be lost in details. While it is important to try and have the details right, the success of a profession ceremony depends on broader considerations. The important thing is that the Church is conscious of the value of religious life, that there are men and women willing to make profession, and communities ready to welcome them into a life which gives its own witness to the faithful love of God which has been revealed in Christ Jesus.

FURTHER READING

Pierre Raffin, 'Liturgie de l'engagement religieux: le nouveau rituel de la profession religieuse', in *La Maison-Dieu*, 104 (1970), pp. 151–66.

I. M. Calabuig, 'La profession religieuse', in *Dans vos assemblées* (ed. Gelineau), II, pp. 511–31.

René Metz, 'Le nouveau rituel de consecration des vierges. Sa place dans l'histoire', in *La Maison-Dieu*, 110 (1972), pp. 88–115.

Marguerite-Marie Croiset, 'Virginité et vie chrétienne au regard du rituel de la consecration des vierges', in *La Maison-Dieu*, 110 (1972), pp. 116–28. This is an account of how different nuns have reacted to the rite.

As aids to reflection on the nature of religious life, mention may be made of:

Jacques Colette and others, *Engagement et fidélité, problèmes de vie religieuse*, Cerf, 1970. On the meaning of commitment 'until death'.

Jerome Murphy-O'Connor, 'What is religious life? – Ask the scriptures', in *Supplement to Doctrine and Life*, 45 (1973, Dublin). On the centrality of community in religious life.

18. Funerals

Clifford Howell SJ

The Christian attitude to death

The funeral liturgy is a product of the many periods of history
and the various cultures through which the Church has lived
since her foundation, and scholars can now tell us the prov-
enance and period of almost every item. They observe that
the earliest strata of the liturgy are instinct with joy in Christ's
victory, with wonder at his glory and with longing for his
return. The usual title for Christ was *Kyrios*, or *Dominus* – 'the
Lord'. Early prayers end with the word *Maranatha* ('Come,
Lord Jesus') almost as frequently as with the other Hebrew
word *Amen*. 'Lord Jesus Christ . . . Lord God, Son of the
Father . . . seated at the right hand of the Father . . . the Most
High . . . in the glory of God the Father'; 'Through Our Lord
Jesus Christ your Son, who is living and reigning . . .' 'He
ascended into heaven, where he is seated at the right hand of
the Father. He will come again in glory . . .' – all these familiar
phrases go back to the fourth century or even earlier. The
oriental liturgies express the same outlook even more insistently.

Early Christian art displays the same outlook – joy in
Christ's victory and longing for his return. There still exist
quite a number of very ancient churches built in the fifth
century or even before that. In nearly all of them a conspicuous
feature of their decoration is the mosaic in the apse above the
bishop's throne (behind the altar). Its usual subject is Christ
in glory. Our Lord is depicted as seated on a throne, surrounded
by angels and saints. He is dressed in magnificent garments of
royal purple, ornamented with gold; in one hand he holds a
great book (the Gospels? the Book of Life?) or else the orb of
the world; with the other hand he gives a blessing or wields the
sceptre of authority; on his head is a golden crown scintillating
with jewels, and his countenance wears an aspect of majesty
and power. Details, of course, vary, but the subject is the same
– Christ in glory. This picture is known in the east as *Christos*

Pantokrator (Christ the Ruler of All), and in the west as *Majestas Domini* (The Lord in Majesty). It was the typical way in which Christians thought of Christ.

Obviously the first and most important preparation for death is the living of a good Christian life! But the acquisition of the devotional attitude common among early Christians is a very great help. If we can accustom ourselves habitually to think as they did about Christ, keeping the other ways, the 'memories' in which we imagine him at some stage of his human life – a baby in a crib, preaching in Palestine, hanging on the cross – for particular seasons and occasions, then we shall foster in ourselves that longing for the Second Coming of Christ which is an essential ingredient of balanced Christian piety. This enables us to see death as it really is – the greatest personal event of our existence. In death we meet our triumphant Saviour whose glory we are to share. Death is our personal individual Passover – a Pasch which completes and fulfils the Exodus we began in our baptism. We see our earthly years as resembling the desert wanderings of the Jews after their passage through the waters of the Red Sea. During their sojourn they were fed with manna; as the walls of Jericho – the last obstacle – collapsed, they entered into their promised homeland. Just so we began our journey by passing through the waters of baptism; on our way we are fed with the true Bread of Heaven; as the walls of our flesh dissolve we enter into our everlasting home. During our whole Christian life, from baptism to happy death, we 'wait in joyful hope for the Coming of our Saviour, Jesus Christ'; death which brings him to us is a Passover with and in our glorious Lord. If that is the way we look at death we are well prepared to meet it.

Why revision of the funeral rite was necessary

Just as the Church celebrates the Passover of Christ, so also she celebrates the Passover of Christians in her liturgy surrounding Christian death and burial. Until recently this has been done according to the rite found in the *Rituale Romanum* of 1614, but the Council ordered that it should be revised. Why so?

Because that rite had many shortcomings. It did not have the appearance of a celebration, laid emphasis on the depressing aspects of death, was exclusively clerical and unintelligible to the people. It had been put together by selection from an enormous variety of Latin prayers, hymns and responsories which had long been in use in different countries of Europe. Some of them dated from the sixth and seventh centuries, a time when Catholic doctrine about particular judgement and purgatory was hardly developed, and when the New Testament teachings about resurrection from the dead and the general judgement had crystallized into somewhat imaginative ideas about a journey to be made by the soul from earth to heaven: all along the way it was menaced by devils but protected by angels.

A strong influence in the formation of that rite was the reaction of the West, especially in the ninth and tenth centuries, against Arianism which had been brought over from the East during the invasions by the Visigoths. Arianism amounted to a *denial* of Christ's divinity. The Church, of course, reacted by emphasizing the divinity. The truth that Christ was God was hammered into the people in every possible way. Of course his humanity was never denied, but it received comparatively little attention because the heretics had not denied it. So the people were constantly being reminded of what separated them from Christ: his Godhead and the infinite distance between creator and creature – rather than of what united them with Christ: his human nature. The early Christian attitude of longing for the Second Coming died out and was replaced by fear of Christ, the terrifying divine Judge whom it would be impossible to deceive; he would come in majesty to judge sinful man and send him to hell unless he had expiated his sins and amassed merits by prayer, fasting and alms-deeds such as giving money to have Masses celebrated. There was a hypertrophic growth of 'reverential awe'; preachers spoke of the 'awful mysteries', the 'terrible moment when Christ came down on the altar', the utter purity and sinlessness which men must have if they are to approach the dreadful presence of God in holy communion. People became intent primarily on avoiding sin and escaping hell.

This attitude of fear and sin-consciousness was expressed in many of the prayers and hymns of those days, some of which found their way into the funeral services. The *Dies Irae*, the *Non intres in judicium* and the *Libera me* were among those retained in the 1614 Rituale. Though hope in the resurrection and the joys of heaven are not excluded from mention, these themes are very much overshadowed by the far more extensive development of themes concerning guilt, punishment, judgement, fear of hell and the need for intercession, with the result that the 1614 rite, taken as a whole, was somewhat grim.

Moreover it was entirely and explicitly clerical; the faithful did not take any part beyond being present and joining their intentions to the prayers and responsories sung on their behalf in an unknown tongue by the clerics. For, at the time of the Tridentine reforms, that was the concept of liturgy then in vogue – it was something done by clerics and their trained assistants in the name of the Church for the benefit of the faithful who, however, were not agents in its performance but only spectators and beneficiaries.

These are some of the reasons why the Second Vatican Council, in the Constitution on the Liturgy (n. 81), decreed that 'The rite for the burial of the dead should express more clearly the paschal character of Christian death, and should correspond more closely to the circumstances and traditions found among the people in different parts of the world.' A subcommittee of the *Consilium* was set up to collect information about what was actually happening in various countries, and to revise the funeral rites accordingly. As a result they produced a three-part service designed to be very flexible, so that it could be used in one way or another in almost every funeral, no matter where it might take place.

The new rite

Part I is preliminary, and may be in the home of the deceased or in the church. Part II is the Mass followed by the rite of Committal or Farewell. The Mass, of course, is celebrated in the church or mortuary chapel of the cemetery if there is one. This is the usual place for the Committal, but if there is any good reason for doing so the Committal or Commendation may be transferred to the cemetery. This is the place for Part III – the actual burial.

The first draft of the new rite came out in 1965, was used *ad experimentum* in several countries for two years, after which reports were sent in to the Subcommittee which examined them thoroughly. These reports showed that in all countries the *sensus fidelium* had given an overwhelming approval to the general tone of the new rite, on account of the prominence it gave to the paschal character of Christian death, the note of hope, and the explicit insistence on faith in the resurrection. These things had eliminated the lugubrious and excessively sin-conscious tone of the former rite. The provision made in the new rite for active involvement of the people was also highly appreciated.

The subcommittee now revised their first draft; they in-corporated many things that had been suggested and eliminated others which had called forth criticism; their revised version was approved by the bishops of the *Consilium* in October 1968; next month it received the approval of the Pope who ordered its promulgation, and this took place in 1969.

Now let us consider *Part I, the Preliminary Rite*. This can take place any time between the death and the funeral Mass, and is envisaged as an intimate or semi-private celebration concerning the family and close friends of the deceased. The priest is meant to comfort them in their loss, to lead them in a psalm, and then to say a prayer for the dead person followed by a prayer for the mourners. Several alternative prayers are pro-vided; they are simple, direct, free from superfluous verbiage and from undue preoccupation with sin and its punishment. Ideally this is done in the home, around the deathbed. But it may well be that circumstances prevent this from being done – the body may have been removed by the undertaker soon after death, and the first time the priest will meet it will be when it is brought to the church. In that case the Preliminary Rite would take the form of a short bible service, in home or church, *absente corpore*, on the night before the funeral. But perhaps the body is being brought to the church that night – in which case it would be received there with a service of similar character, built up on a reading taken from the Lectionary, a hymn or psalm, a brief homily and some prayers.

Part II is the *Celebration of the Funeral Mass*. Why have a Mass at all? What has the Mass got to do with death? There are several answers.

Firstly, a Christian's death is his Passover, and the Mass is a celebration of Christ's Passover – a showing forth of his death until he comes again. By death the Christian fulfils the paschal mystery into which he was plunged at his baptism; he passes from death to life with and in Christ, realizing in himself the paschal mystery of Christ made present and active in the Mass.

Secondly, the death of a Christian does not concern himself alone. He was a member of the Church, baptized, confirmed and nourished by the eucharist in the bosom of the Church. His merits enriched the Church just as his sins and faults harmed it. Wherefore it is very right and fitting that the local community, by assembling to celebrate Mass for him, should render the Church present and active in his regard.

Thirdly, death – even though conquered by Christ – remains nevertheless an evil, a penalty for man's disobedience. Except for our Lord and his holy Mother all men are sinners; all need the mercy of God. In the celebration of Mass the propitiatory power of Christ's paschal mystery is applied to the deceased, that he may be loosed from his sins.

Fourthly, his relatives and friends have suffered a grievous loss by his passover; they are plunged in sorrow, oppressed by grief. They stand in need of human sympathy from all the community. They will be comforted by the prayers of their brethren, especially by the offering of the holy sacrifice; they will be sustained by the faith and hope of the others who gather with them before the altar. It is remarkable that the 1614 rite contained no prayer whatever for the mourners. It is only by local custom that a prayer in this sense was usually added at the graveside. The recasting of the rite has remedied this defect: instead of the depressing and gloomy 'Absolutions' so redolent of sin-consciousness and fear, we now have the very human and tender ceremony of *Commendation* which normally follows the Mass. It has the nature of a farewell to the dead person. A great variety of prayers is offered for this occasion. The body is sprinkled with holy water and incensed. After the prayer by the priest all say or sing the *Subvenite*:

'Saints of God, come to his aid!
Come to meet him, angels of the Lord!
Receive his soul and present him to God the Most High.'

Another prayer, and the body is carried out of the church while all sing or say one or more of three antiphons, such as:

> 'I am the resurrection and the life.
> The man who believes in me will live
> even if he dies,
> and every living person
> who puts his faith in me
> will never suffer eternal death.'

This farewell by the community really belongs at the end of the Mass, but the rite expressly provides that it may be done at the graveside instead, whenever the body has had to be taken directly from home to cemetery. This does happen sometimes for one reason or another.

Now we look at *Part III* – what happens *at the graveside*.

If the grave has not been blessed beforehand, the priest blesses it now with a new prayer filled with hope:

> 'Lord Jesus Christ . . .
> give our brother peaceful rest in this grave,
> until that day when you,
> the resurrection and the life
> will raise him up in glory.'

Instead of the *Benedictus*, there is a new prayer to be said as the body is lowered into the grave:

> 'Since almighty God has called our brother N.
> from this life to himself,
> we commit his body
> to the earth from which it was made.
>
> Christ was the first to rise from the dead,
> and we know that he will raise up our mortal bodies
> to be like his in glory.
>
> We commend our brother to the Lord:
> may the Lord receive him into his peace
> and raise up his body on the last day.'

There follow some Bidding Prayers in the usual form; all the petitions are very apt to the occasion, but it is lawful to substitute others or to add to them. It is recommended that the whole rite be brought to a conclusion by some suitable hymn.

A few words now about the readings, prayers and songs in general. There is a great variety of these, and it would be a serious impoverishment always to use the first one that is given. Priests should therefore become familiar with all the possibilities and then make a careful selection beforehand of those best suited to the occasion, bearing in mind the personality and status of the deceased, whether man or woman, boy or girl, and so forth. He should think also of the kind of congregation likely to be present – wholly Catholic or mixed, fervent or containing the weak in faith, well instructed or rather ignorant. In making the choice it may be possible for the priest to consult some member of the bereaved family. If he can, he should do this, but not infrequently he will have to do the choosing by himself.

The readings are contained in the Lectionary and there is an abundance of them – eight from the Old Testament, eighteen from the writings of the Apostles, and seventeen Gospels. From these should be chosen one for the Preliminary Rite; and for the Mass one Old Testament reading, an apostolic extract, and a gospel. The homily at Mass should, of course, be based on the readings chosen, and should not as a whole have the character of a panegyric. Some brief reference to the deceased would, of course, be admissible provided the context suggests it.

As regards the prayers, these ought to manifest the connection between Christian death and the paschal mystery, and when they plead that the soul of the deceased should be purified from sin (and thereby imply the Catholic doctrine of purgatory) they should not do it in terms of some mythical journey which the soul must undertake after death (for this is not a Catholic doctrine). Also due importance should be given to consoling the bereaved – an aspect which was missing from the 1614 rite now happily superseded.

Singing offers difficulties for lack of vernacular hymns of the required type, or of music for the responsories for which texts are provided in the rite. We must hope that poets will write hymns and composers will produce tunes in order that this very beautiful and satisfying liturgy for Christian Burial may, in due course, be carried out with impressive solemnity.

A Note on Contributors

MGR JOSEPH C. BUCKLEY. Parish priest of Westbury-on-Trym, Somerset, and director of the Newman Centre. Extensively engaged in liturgical renewal and ecumenical dialogue.

REV. PATRICK BYRNE. Assistant director of Canada's National Liturgical Office. Ordained priest in 1956. Has been curate and pastor in a number of parishes, as well as serving as a member of diocesan and regional tribunals. He edits the National Bulletin on Liturgy, Guidelines for Pastoral Liturgy (annual liturgical calendar), and other liturgical books in Canada.

FRANCES COLLINS. Senior lecturer in movement and philosophy of education at Coloma College of Education, West Wickham, Kent.

REV. J. D. CRICHTON. Parish priest of Pershore, Worcestershire. Author of *The Church's Worship, Christian Celebration: Vol. I: The Mass, Vol. II: The Sacraments,* and many other books and articles.

REV. PHILIP GLEESON OP. Teaches liturgy in St Mary's College, Tallaght, and in Mt St Anne's Liturgy Centre, Portarlington, Ireland. He studies in Tallaght, Fribourg and Paris. Has contributed articles on liturgy to many journals.

MARTIN HALL. Director of music at Our Lady of the Angels, Erith, Kent. Member of the music subcommission of the Southwark Liturgical Commission. A director of Boosey and Hawkes, music publishers.

REV. CLIFFORD HOWELL SJ. Ordained 1934. Army chaplain 1939–47. After demobilization became active as preacher and lecturer on liturgical subjects. Has written several books, among which *The Work of our Redemption* (Fowler Wright) and *Preparing for Easter* (Geoffrey Chapman) are the best known. Contributed numerous articles to periodicals at home and abroad. Lecture tours in USA, Canada, Australia, New Zealand, Malta, Africa; *peritus in liturgia* at the Second Vatican Council.

REV. A. J. MCCALLEN. A diocesan priest attached to a parish on

Humberside. Has had varied experience of working with young people and with the mentally and physically handicapped. The second edition of his book of biblical readings for junior children (*Listen!*) will be published by Collins in 1976. A member of the National Liturgical Commission of England and Wales.

REV. EDWARD MATTHEWS. Lecturer in liturgy at St Edmund's College, Corpus Christi College of Catechetics, and St Thomas More Centre for Pastoral Liturgy, London. Chaplain at Finchley High School. A member of the Commission which produced the *Directory for Masses with Children*. His book, *Celebrating Mass with Children*, is published by Collins (1975).

REV. BRIAN NEWNS. Teaches liturgy at Upholland College, Lancashire. A member of the Rites and Pastoral Liturgy Department of the National Liturgical Commission for England and Wales. Chairman of the Liverpool Diocesan Liturgical Commission. Has contributed to books and periodicals, in particular *The Clergy Review*.

PATRICK REYNTIENS. Designer of stained glass windows at Coventry Cathedral. Founder of the Reyntiens Trust, a charitable company to encourage education in the arts and to promote courses and exhibitions at Burleighfield House Studios and Gallery.

REV. MARK SEARLE OFM. Born in Bristol. Entered the Friars Minor in 1958. Ordained 1965, studied in Rome and Trier. Has been teaching liturgy since 1969 and is currently engaged at the Franciscan Study Centre, Canterbury.

REV. CHRISTOPHER J. WALSH. A priest of the Shrewsbury diocese. Lectures in liturgy at Ushaw College and at Durham University. Was editor of *Life and Worship* and is now liturgical consultant to the review *Music and Liturgy*. Studied liturgy in Paris, and has experience of parish work in France, Germany and USA.

AUSTIN WINKLEY AA DIPL., RIBA. Architect of St Margaret's Church, Twickenham, and St Elphege, Wallington. Reconstructed St John's Cathedral, Portsmouth and Campion House Chapel, Osterley. A contributor to the Architect's journal, *Church Design Guide*.

REV. HAROLD WINSTONE. Director of the St Thomas More Centre for Pastoral Liturgy, and parish priest in a north London parish. Has a wide pastoral experience. Lectures in liturgy at various London colleges.

Index

absolution, 190, 202, 205-6, 208, 209

adaptation, for children 107-12, 116, 124, 131
  of initiation rite, 166ff

admission, of baptised adults, 186-7

adult liturgy, 106, 211

adults, Christian formation of, 32ff, 35, 122, 136-7, 162-3, 167-8, 175-6, 177, 232-5, 257-8, 275
  at Mass, 102, 103-4, 146
  see also assembly, baptism, confirmation, initiation

Agnus Dei, 62, 130

altar, at children's Mass 124-5, 128
  for communion of the sick, 149

altar bread, 125

Amen, 130

anglican liturgy, 89

anointing, in rites of initiation, 165n, 168, 170-1, 182, 183

anointing of the sick, new rite of, 15, 148, 214-30
  celebration of rite, 227-8
  theology of, 219, 222-6

apostolate, *see* Church, modern world

architecture, 45-54, 76
  arrangement of sanctuary, 35, 50-3, 120
  audibility, 91
  lighting, 53-4
  multipurpose space, 45-6
  place of font, 53, 164-5, 176
  seating plan, 46-9, 143, 155

art, 73-80, 274-5
  with children, 122, 143-4

assembly (community) and funerals, 280
  and penance, 191, 194, 197-8, 200-1, 202
  and religious profession, 269
  and rites of initiation, 161-2, 169, 173, 175, 181, 185, 186, 187

and the sick, 221-2
  size of, 46-7, 113, 119
  worshipping a., 17, 19-21, 28, 30-44, 84-5, 96, 105, 114, 136, 150, 151
  see also adults, church, community, modern world

baptism, 159-65, 168-76, 191, 263, 264, 265
  forms the people who celebrate, 15, 106-7
  rite of, for adults, 164-5
  rite of, for infants, 168-77
  see also initiation

baptismal 'promises', 164, 169, 182, 184, 185, 229

betrothal ceremony, 150, 238

bible, 258

bidding prayers, *see* prayers of the faithful

bishop, 165, 166, 178, 181, 182, 183, 185, 198, 209, 217, 269

blessings, Hebrew, 98-9
  of gifts, 97, 129
  of handicapped, 144
  of oil, 225
  of people, 131, 154, 163, 174, 249, 263

candles, 170, 171, 182

catechumenate, 161-3, 167-8, 174-5

celebrant, role of, 21, 87, 90, 94, 97-9, 117
  see also priest

celebration, evokes response of faith, 34, 171-2
  human need for 11-14, 21, 37-8, 131-2, 142-4
  meeting place of human and divine 11-14, 23, 32, 106, 192-4, 224
  of family occasions, 150, 154
  presence of Holy Spirit in, 15-29
  spirit of Christian c., 13-14, 15
  see also liturgy, modern world,

284

faith, 32, 40-1, 43, 160, 161, 171-5
family, 32, 108, 153-5, 161, 169,
  173-6, 177, 185, 210, 249, 253-5,
  261
  and handicapped, 141-4
fasting, 220
folk Mass, 114
funerals, new rite of, 275-82
  structure of, 277-81
gifts, presentation of, 95-7, 128-9
  see also procession
Gloria, 62, 88
godparents, 173, 177, 186
handicapped, 113, 140-4, 226
Holy Spirit, and marriage, 258, 263
  creates community, 28, 30
  in eucharistic celebration, 15-29,
    87, 99
  in initiation, 165, 178-9, 182, 183
  in John 19:30, 18
  in New Testament, 15, 28-9
  in old Roman liturgy, 16
  in penance, 207
  in sacrament of the sick, 223
  invocations, *see* epicleses
  in unitate Sancti Spiritus, 21-2
  with the Church in its ministry, 24
homily, 93-4, 110, 127, 138, 140,
  155, 162, 169, 229, 246
house Mass, 38-9, 113, 147-52, 155-6
hymns, 59, 85, 102, 125, 169, 170,
  278
  see also music
ICEL, 80n, 89
illness, 214
incense, 86, 92
initiation, a process, 159, 160, 178,
  180, 184
  communion final stage of, 33, 159
  rites of, 159-88
  see also baptism, confirmation
Kyrie, 62, 88, 89
laying-on of hands, 165, 181, 183,
  187, 227
lay ministers of communion, 131,
  148, 221
lectionary, for children, 110, 127
  Sunday, 91-2

Lent, preparation for baptism, 163-4
liturgy, and time, 42
  builds community, 151-2
  Christ's presence in, 31
  Holy Spirit in, 15-29
  is event, 40-1
  preparation for, 30-44
  should be joyful, 101, 144, 177
  verbalism in, 77, 121, 144
  worship of the whole Church, 44,
    105, 176
  see also celebration, modern world
liturgy and life, 31, 32, 40-1, 160,
  192-4, 207, 214-18, 230
marriage, 231-55, 256-64
  celebration of, 242-51
  family life is preparation for, 32
  new rite of, 246-7
  preparation for, 232-42
  special problems, 251-5, 256-64
  theology of, 231-2
  see also 'mixed marriage'
Mass, and anointing of sick, 227
  and baptism, 165, 166, 176, 187
  and confirmation, 165, 182
  and funerals, 279
  and marriage, 242-51, 258-9
  and religious profession, 267-8,
    269
  structure of, 83-102, 122, 134-5
  see also assembly, celebration,
    communion, liturgy, Roman
    Missal; for parts of the Mass,
    see individual entries
ministries, various, 20, 95, 104,
  176-7
mission, *see* Church, modern world
'mixed marriage', 256-64
  and upbringing of children, 256,
    264
modern world, Church's mission to,
  17f, 29, 30, 34-5, 151-2, 153, 167
  divorced from cultural roots, 74-
    80, 113
  needs celebration, 11-14, 37-8, 43
  see also celebration, liturgy and
    life
movement, 13, 66-72, 96-7, 105,